FREE $TUFF From AMERICA ONLINE

Luanne O'Loughlin

 CORIOLIS GROUP BOOKS

Publisher	Keith Weiskamp
Editor	Jenni Aloi
Proofreader	Diane Cook
Interior Design	Rob Mauhar
Cover Design	Keith Weiskamp and Bradley O. Grannis
Layout Production	Rob Mauhar and Anthony Stock
Publicist	Shannon Bounds

Library of Congress Cataloging-in-Publication Data

O'Loughlin, Luanne, 1960
    Free Stuff From America Online/Luanne O'Loughlin
       p. cm.
    Includes Index
    ISBN 1-883577-17-9 : $19.99

Printed in the United States of America

10 9 8 7 6 5 4 3 2 1

Acknowledgments

This project was inspired by a lunch and launched by a phone call. Along the way, I have collected thousands of E-mail messages and logged countless hundreds of hours on America Online. The good stuff I've downloaded occupies over 40 high-density disks and required the acquisition of a new hard drive. I'm sure I've learned more about America Online than the average user would ever want to know. In fact, before they log on, my friends now call to ask "Where on America Online can I find . . . ."

I've just completed my third year of telecommuting. Working from home is more than an 8:00 to 5:00 job—especially when you're telecommuting cross-country. That said, I must thank Tom and Carly for their patience with interrupted dinners and convoluted schedules. It was Carly who originally inspired me to find a way to work from home, and for that I hope we'll always be thankful. My husband Tom served as my number 1 PC beta tester. We regularly debated over the merits and challenges of PCs versus Macs (still ongoing) in making the selections for this book. He saved me innumerable hours and never tired of hearing me ask, "Does this download work?"

I am immensely thankful for the opportunity provided by Keith Weiskamp, Coriolis Group Books publisher. He knew I was enthralled by America Online and found a way to work me into the *Free $tuff* series. I think we're both pleased with the outcome.

No one deserves more credit than Ron Pronk, who served as the point man on this project. Ron ably directed, guided, and clarified the focus through each section of the book. His talent, patience, and sense of humor would lead me to recommend him to others. But I won't because I want to work with him again! Ron made Free $tuff *fun stuff.*

And although I can't list everybody involved in this book project, here are several more individuals whose assistance and/or direction was instrumental in getting this book finished:

- Jeff Duntemann, another driving force at Coriolis Group Books. I know that Jeff contributes the spice to all Coriolis Group projects and that he helped define the *Free $tuff* series.

- Jenni Aloi's concise, clever changes masterfully polished some muddy words and phrases. I am indebted to her dedication to the task.

- Shannon Bounds and Tom Mayer, who continue to diligently spread the good word on the *Free $tuff* books so we can jointly help the uninformed to see the light.

- Patrick Vincent, who surfed first with *Free $tuff from the Internet*. Pat used his immense book and online experience to clarify issues and ease my fears. Pat blazed the trail for the *Free $tuff* Series. One small step for Pat, one giant leap for the *Free $tuff* Series.

- Jennifer Watson, a true America Online goddess. Jennifer maintains the keyword list that we've used as the basis for the appendix in this book. You'll find it in the Mac Software files. Specific directions are in the appendix.

- Pam McGraw and Marshall Rens for being America Online's corporate pillars of support throughout this mission. Pam put up with my pesky questions, often peppered by E-mail, and saw to it that I received numerous beta copies for the multimedia user interface.

- Rob Mauhar and Anthony Stock for making this book look like a work of art—at least to me.

And, last, but certainly not least, I'd like to thank the thousands of individuals who actively contribute to the community known as America Online. The creators of hundreds of programs and files mentioned in this book will see that the lucid descriptions they provided serve as the basis for each featured topic.

In fact, I would appreciate feedback from readers, too. Please send me your comments, criticisms, and suggestions. Online, I'm LuanneO. So now you know where and how to find me on AOL!

Luanne O'Loughlin
Severna Park, Maryland

Contents

Business: A Fact-Finding Mission

Careers and Jobs   97

Computer Companions

Cooking and Gourmet Endeavors   *149*

Educational Ideas

Entertaining AOL

Fun and Games   225

Government 243

FREE $TUFF *from the Internet*

Health and Family   *265*

Kid $tuff 289

The Law 317

Military and Aviation 345

Personal Finance

Science and Space   *383*

Shopping   *405*

Sports and Recreation 419

Travel 435

List of Keywords   457

FREE $TUFF

One of the advantages of being disorderly is that one is constantly making exciting discoveries.

A.A. Milne

Life's Little Surprises and Other Free Things

Serendipity is the word that comes to mind each time I log on to America Online. As the modem groans and beeps, eye-catching icons entice me to enter the world of AOL and the magic of this dynamic online service. I love making wonderful discoveries, apparently by accident. Is there a contest? Shall I check today's news? How are my friends on the bulletin boards? Has anyone sent me E-mail? Some are thrilled by adventure in Las Vegas. I'm enthralled by the icons of AOL.

As the commercial online services and the Internet have grown by leaps and bounds, all the forecasters have been astounded by the compounded growth of America Online. In August 1994, AOL announced their subscriber count had surpassed the 1,000,000 member mark. And that was only eight months after they announced the achievement of 500,000 subscribers. There's something exciting going on at AOL. They've commendably sustained their popularity and customer service amidst astounding growth.

Each week brings new *partners* to the online community, and their entrances are heralded on the Welcome screen. NBC, Court TV, Lifetime, *Chicago Tribune*, *The New York Times*, *Atlantic Monthly*, *Time*, National Public Radio, DC Comics, and scores more often greet arrivals.

America Online is constantly changing and apparently amorphous. On any given day, new forums, files, and features will be available. Somewhat less often, files will disappear! We've made every effort to check and double-check the material in *FREE $TUFF from America Online*, but you may, some day, somewhere, encounter directions to a file that has been relocated or removed. We apologize for the inconvenience but accept that it's a fact of life on the electronic frontier. Should you wish to commiserate, you can always send me E-mail (LuanneO).

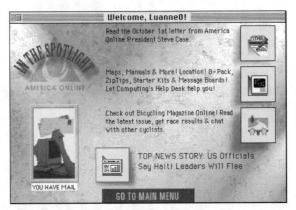

The Welcome Screen invites users to three featured forums, announces the leading news story, and proclaims the presence of E-mail.

It's easy to see why America Online is so popular. AOL brings the world community to each subscriber's home at an affordable and understandable price. There are no confusing fees for time of use, extended services, or modem speeds. For under $10, five hours of information and entertainment are yours—to maximize.

And the stories are true. Fabulous friendships, dating, and marriages have sprouted online. I have friends who've flown cross-country to meet their online dates. I've put faces to my online companions when we've met for lunch. Take a stroll through the bulletin boards and you will find sharing that hasn't been seen since it was routine for Moms to stay at home and for Dads to go to work. Online neighbors develop an intertwined community just like the small towns of yesteryear.

Imagine my surprise when I realized that three contributors on a publishing board also share concerns on a health board. Others share anxiety and joy about children, parents, spouses, health, life, death, and politics. The conversations at the backyard fence have come to life to be stored electronically and communicated among friends.

We build trust through open sharing on the various bulletin boards, many of us initiating conversations and postings under assumed names. The caution we've learned through the outside world is not forgotten in Cyberspace. Our friendships build gradually as we enter the fold. At some point we begin sending "private" E-mail and even exchanging phone numbers, good old U.S. Postal Service snail-mail addresses, and photographs. The truly bold and beautiful post photos in the Gallery.

So What Makes AOL Members Extraordinary?

AOL members are friends waiting to happen. You will quickly be welcomed and made to feel that you are a member of the club. When you take those first steps to reach out and send a message, rather than just lurking in the wings, it's like walking into a party and making fast friends. In the online world, you can be charming in your bathrobe!

AOL members are computer-comfortable and computer-literate. They know how to give a helping hand, and they remember what it was like to be the new kid online. You need never be afraid to ask a question. Your courteous manners will be rewarded with polite and detailed responses from other members or from the consumer-sensitive staff. On the other hand, should you make rude and aggressive questions or comments, called *flames*, you likely will incur the wrath of acerbic counterparts.

Certainly, hundreds of thousands have joined courtesy of the "free" disks bundled with magazines, books, and modems. But they have stayed online to be in the community and to access and share information.

There's also another really simple reason why many have chosen AOL over the "other" services. Most members are home users (read: not corporate sponsored) and they want to know what their bill will be each month. America Online makes it easy. For $9.95, you get five hours of online time. As of January 1, 1995, each additional hour is $2.95, and they prorate those additional hours to the minute. In most of the country, there are free access lines, so you're not incurring telephone company toll charges. For subscribers to the competition, there are membership charges, baud rate charges, extended services fees, ad infinitum. Just looking at the competitions' rate charts scares me. CompuServe and Prodigy may be the front-runners, but neither is growing at the sizzling and furious rate of AOL. Together, the online services are adding an average of 22,000 new customers per week—approximately 70 percent of whom are joining America Online.

Who Is This Book For?

America Online estimates that 98 million U.S. households have a home computer, and AOL has reached 1 million of them. Who are AOL's users? We're made up of people from all walks of life, including students, hobbyists, parents, sports fans, investors, news groupies, shoppers, travelers, and hundreds more.

These are people who have gathered together to learn, play games, share their programming prowess, commiserate, and communicate. Hat pin collectors and hockey fans, attorneys and actors, computer wizards and car collectors can all be found online. They possess dazzling demographics and their dedication to this new medium has spurred major corporate entities to create hypnotic forums for AOL users: Time-Warner, ABC, NBC, Knight-Ridder, Tribune, Hachette, IBM, Apple, National Geographic, MTV, The Smithsonian, Macworld, and Disney are counted among AOL's partners.

Why This Book?

AOL users like to have fun and they like to find new features and "freebies." I've prowled/trolled/lurked throughout as many areas as I could find to share some of the best, most fun, unique, and exciting "stuff" online. I hope you share my excitement for the fun and fortunes of information to be found within. With this book, I've created a treasure map that allows you to bypass the swamps and head straight to the gems. *FREE $TUFF from America Online* takes you to the best stuff—the most creative clip art, the funniest sound bites, the most useful business newsletters, and the facts behind serious news events. We've turned AOL inside out for a better view of the online universe. We'll help you get *more* out of AOL. (Refer to the *Getting Started* section to find out just how to access this hoard of goodies.)

What "Stuff"?

The variety of "stuff" is mind boggling. I've sifted through the chaff to find the wheat. I've cracked open the oysters to find the pearls. I've looked through the haystacks and found the needles. I've . . . oh, you get the idea!

But just to make sure I haven't lost you, I've selected some interesting tidbits to whet your appetite:

Jupiter from the Hubble Space Telescope: Turn to page 397 to get the real picture through the refined lens.

Jacqueline Kennedy Onassis signature GIF: You've heard that she had a whispery voice, but what did the former First Lady's signature look like? I've found it for you, and on page 340 you'll find the directions to her "John Hancock."

Photographs of the Supremes: No, not Diana Ross and the girls, the Justices of the Supreme Court of the United States. If you can't live another day without knowing what Judge Ginsberg, the new justice, looks like, see page 256.

Do you know how James Brown feels? I've got directions for you to hear the sound bite on page 281.

Lunch with your banker? You may be starting a new business and need a professional business plan. I'll direct you to the package on page 73.

College Bound? Take a peek at page 196 to find schedules for the SAT, ACT, PSAT, GMAT, MCAT, and others.

Are you a Neil Young fan? Or do you prefer Prince? Warner Reprise has the sound bites and concert schedules for their artists. Turn to page 205.

The O.J. Simpson scoop: Sneak over to page 341 to find the Grand Jury transcripts and his mug shot.

Moon Phaser: Will Halloween fall on a full moon this year? What phase will the moon be in for Saturday night's date? You can find the directions to this program on page 399.

In the next section, we'll introduce the tools you'll need to take advantage of this bounty. Those tools will help you to open the files, hear the sounds, and view the photos. Whether you have a Mac or a PC, we'll guide you to the tools you need.

What Does Free Really Mean?

The simplest definition is that all the "stuff" in this book is *free for you to try*. You can download photos and demos and tips and newsletters and sounds—and view and listen to them to your heart's content.

If you find shareware you like and intend to use, you are encouraged to re-member your ethics and pay the fee. Many of the photos may be used for your personal enjoyment, but require fees to be paid before they can be placed in commercial publications. Heed the copyright notices. The first issues of news-letters may be downloaded for free, but the snail-mail subscription will have an invoice. Clip-art samples may be free, but the complete collection is avail-able for a fee.

Try-before-you-buy is the pre-eminent motto. Try, sample, taste, test, appraise, experience, and enjoy the bounty that is AOL.

And then there's the cost of computer time. I've spent hundreds of hours cull-ing the best and checking and double-checking the keywords/shortcuts and directions. I've saved you lots of money—just call it a finder's fee! Yes, you still have to pay your membership and hourly charges, but only you can decide if it's worth $2.95 to sample a $300 software package. My philosophy: Save time and money—for time is money.

Perhaps you've been away (somewhere obscure where there are no phone lines) and at the end of your billing month, you have extra time remaining on your monthly allowance. Grab this book and find something fun and useful!

With *FREE $TUFF from America Online*, we've found the best and saved you hundreds of dollars in online time. Think of this as a mind-broadening experi-ence. We're going to help you find more "stuff" than you ever knew existed. You can have fun showing and telling your online friends and neighbors—and perhaps even your brother-in-law, Hugo.

FREE $TUFF

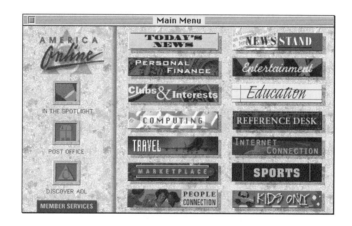

A place for everything,
everything in its place.

Benjamin Franklin

Getting Started

If you're not already familiar with America Online, run back to the bookstore or newsstand and grab (preferably, purchase) one of the many computer and trade magazines that include a bound-in disk. That way you can start today! Otherwise, call AOL at 1-800-827-6364. They'll send free software, a free trial membership, and 10 *free* hours to explore.

Shortcuts to $avings

I'm convinced that finding shortcuts to any task is a basic human instinct, and far be it from AOL to stand in the way of nature. AOL's primary shortcut to online savings is its use of *keywords*. Keywords are one- or two-word *jumps* to specific destinations. Rather than clicking and selecting window upon window, you simply use the keyword function and type the buzzword.

You could maneuver through layers of windows to get to *Today's News*—or type Ctrl+K then *news*. On a Mac, that's ⌘+K. You can also find keywords under the Go To menu. Windows users also have the option of selecting the keyword icon, which has the red, swooping arrow. Keywords can be used at any point in the system—and you can use them to jump from *news* to *health* to *Wired* to *weather*.

Throughout the book, I'll be providing keyword references, often mid-sentence (Keyword: *news*) so that you can travel from window to window without having to open and close each. Using keywords, you can zip from one area to another in a minimum of time—after all, time *is* what you pay for. *Zip, flash, click and you're there!*

Remember our mantra: *Save time and you save money!*

I've included the current keyword list at the end of this book, but you may want to check for the Ultimate Keyword list that you can download (Keyword: Mac Software).

Navigation Notes

Because I want you to get the most out of AOL in the least amount of time, I've also included a set of navigating tools—I'll call these directions Navigation Notes— at the end of each topic. The Navigation Notes begin with *Where*. The Navigation Notes tell you how to use menus (the Where information) to get to where you're going or which keyword to use (the Keyword information) to bypass menus and go directly to your desired location. Here's an example on how to get information on airfare deals.

Where

Travel

Travel Forum

Keyword

Travel Forum

Read/Save

Bargain Box

To read this week's Bargain Box, you could use the keyword *Travel Forum* to go straight to the screen you need. Then just select *Bargain Box*. Alternatively, you start from the Main Menu, and select the following in sequence: Travel, Travel Forum, and Bargain Box.

If the Bargain Box was a downloadable file, you would follow the download directions. (Read/Save would be omitted.)

Don't forget—keywords can be used from any point in the system. Keywords may seem like small savings, but they truly save online time as you become more familiar with the ins and outs of AOL.

After you select the library, you may need to use the *more* button on the screen until the desired program appears on the list. As additional programs are added to the archives, older files will appear further down the list. The *more* button will help you find the files noted. Call me silly, but I'm assuming that using the *more* button will be intuitive for you.

One final comment on Navigation Notes: Due to programming changes, some areas may not be accessible through the "Where" directions. If that seems to be the case, go ahead and try the keyword.

Cross-Platform Access

When you select File Search from the "Go To" menu, AOL guides you to the Main Download libraries that accommodate the files native to your system. Mac users get Mac files, and PC users get PC files.

To access the cross-platform files, Mac users should use the keyword *PC Software,* while PC users employ the keyword *Mac Software.* There are minor differences in the paths; one user may see an icon labeled *Software Search,* while another may see *Search the Libraries.* A little intuition goes a long way.

Text files, GIFs, fonts, clip art, and sounds are among the files that Windows, DOS, and Mac users can share. If you are looking for a specific item, check both places. When I searched for documents on copyrights, I found superior information in PC Software, while the particular sound made by a purple dinosaur could only be found in the Mac files.

FAQs

FAQ is the abbreviation for Frequently Asked Questions. FAQs are generally formatted as questions and answers and are available for a variety of topics, including the Internet and commercial software. FAQs are compiled by serious users who know their way around the software and the manual. Many users would rather have a FAQ than official documentation, as FAQ authors often compile a superior guide. Be sure to check the file search area (Keyword: File Search) for FAQs of interest.

Windows users will want to become familiar with WAOLHELP, and Mac users will find AOL FAQ invaluable!

Shareware

You'll find tens of thousands of shareware programs in AOL's libraries—perhaps in excess of 50,000 have been uploaded. The libraries also include macros for popular software, GIF (image) files, HyperCard stacks, utilities, financial programs, children's software, and hundreds of other categories. A file search on the Mac lists approximately 60,000 files available for you to download. The same request on a PC reveals over 61,000 files. Certainly, there are a number of files, such as text, TIFF, EPS, and others that are cross-referenced to appear on both lists. In any event, these are impressive numbers. The available files don't include the tremendous number of files found in the software libraries of sponsored forums, so the total available files on AOL is truly much larger. It has been said that AOL has the largest file collection of any of the commercial online services.

Try before you buy is the definitive premise of shareware. Distributed on an honor system, shareware is provided for evaluation for a defined period of time before purchase. Generally, the shareware package is complete, but more often users are given incentives (other than their integrity) for registering. Payment of the registration fee may entitle the user to upgrades and future editions, notices of "fixes," and even enhanced versions. Shareware is distributed with disclaimers and conditions that users must adhere to, and we encourage you to promptly pay the authors and developers so they can continue to provide valuable and useful software at a reasonable cost.

I've also included demo files among my recommendations. You'll find most demos in the Industry Connection (Keyword: industry connection). One very large software publisher has a demo of a financial management program available for download. I thought it was an exciting discovery until I tried the demo—it was a time-hogging slideshow that failed to allow any interaction by the user.

Suffice to say, the demos that you'll find in *FREE $TUFF from America Online* allow for interaction. They may be disabled in some way—perhaps allowing only 10 records in a database or not supporting printing—but you'll still be able to interact with the program to determine if it possesses the attributes you require. A number of shareware files are also called demos by their authors.

Uploading and Downloading

Uploading is the process of sending a file, while *downloading* is the process of receiving a file. Files uploaded to AOL are generally not immediately available for download by others. When AOL receives the files, they are tested for software compatibility and for viruses before they are posted as available downloads. There may be a five- to seven-day delay between uploading and downloading availability.

Choosy Mothers Choose GIF

Ask around and you'll find that some prefer the peanut butter pronunciation, while others opt for the one that sounds like a Christmas gif(t)—get it? Either way, GIF (Graphic Interchange Format) is a cross-platform graphics and compression format that combines high-quality images with small file sizes to minimize download time. While the GIF format is not computer dependent, special programs or conversion utilities (sometimes called viewers) are required to uncompress and display these image files on PC and Mac machines.

So what image files will you find? Photos of other AOL users (Gallery), Jerry Seinfeld (NBC), Bill, Hillary, Al, and Tipper (File Search), Weather Maps (Weather), Jupiter (Astronomy) and the Smithsonian Castle (Smithsonian).

The shareware programs that read and display GIFs have different attributes. They vary in file size and the speed at which they can display an image. Some can even display the GIF while the file itself is still being downloaded. Converters can change an image from GIF to PICT, which can be loaded into most desktop publishing or word-processing programs.

AOL's software treats GIF files as text, because the headers are removed from the GIF files to make them more compatible across Mac, Windows, and DOS platforms. Just use a GIF viewer and open the file from within the application.

GIF viewers are available throughout the America Online system, and some of the leading GIF viewers are listed in the "Tools of the Trade" table near the end of this section. You can use the file search function (Keyword: File Search, then GIF viewer) or search the download files in any of the following forums: Beginners Forum (Beginner), NBC Online (NBC), Popular Photography (photos), The Smithsonian (Smithsonian), and The Gallery (Gallery). Download the GIF viewer that is appropriate for your computer. Windows users can use both the Windows and DOS versions, of course. GIF viewers are shareware.

File Compression and Uncompression

File compression and uncompression are two more money saving tips. With archiving programs, you save both file space and transmission time. Many of the files you download must be opened by a specific compression/ uncompression program before the software can be used. These dual-function programs are often called archiving programs. The minor shareware fee paid for an archiving program will save money for you many times over as you compress your backups or when you send a file to a friend or associate.

New versions of AOL released in Fall 1994 have compression utilities built in. To look for these and other compression programs, use any of the following keywords: *file search*, *PC software*, and *Mac software*. The software libraries at keywords *Komando* and *Aladdin* contain selected utilities, as well.

If you need a specific archiving program in order to use a downloaded file, the file description will tell you. Files denoted ".sea" are self-extracting archives, which open upon delivery (that is, at the conclusion of the download).

The most popular archiving programs are listed in the "Tools of the Trade" table in this section.

Now Hear This

Sound applications will add genuine fun to your computing time. In the Entertainment Section—and throughout the book—we'll guide you to some of the best. But here's a sampler of online sound files:

- Al Haig in control at the White House
- James Earl Jones' "This is CNN" promo
- Forrest Gump's favorite phrases.

A sound application will let you listen to—and sometimes manipulate— these audio files. You'll find a selection of sound applications for DOS, Windows, and Mac systems in the "Tools of the Trade" table.

Tools of the Trade

	DOS	*Windows*	*Mac*
Frequently Asked Questions (FAQs)		WAOLHELP	AOL FAQ
GIF Viewers & Converters	CSHOW: 1.04a GIFDESK: 4.5 PC: CSHOW 8.6A QPEG: 1.4dDOS JPEG	3.0 VuePrint Viewer PaintShopPro: WIN WINGIF	GIFConverter 2.3.7 GIFwatcher 2.2.0 GraphicConverter 2.0 CyberGif 1.3
Compression/ Uncompression	PKZIP/PKUNZIP 2.04g	ZIPWHACK: 1.0 WIN WINZIP	StuffIt Lite 3.0.7 StuffIt Expander UnZip 2.0
Sound Applications	PCVOC: DOS Speaker VOC	PLAY: WAV File Player WPLANY: 0.9b	Sound App 1.2.2 SoundBuilder 2.0.2

These clever and useful utilities will help you to make the most of America Online.

Baud Rates and Downloads

Throughout the remaining sections of this book, I'll be introducing you to hundreds of files. You'll probably start by downloading many of these to your PC or Mac in unfettered excitement. But pace yourself: Give yourself time to experiment with each new program, otherwise you'll swamp your hard drive faster than you can say "America Online."

File Descriptions—More Clues

The file description can be thought of as a key to the goods. All downloadable files have file description screens for you to view before downloading.

Subj: Teachers Desktop Pub.Sampler sea
From: Charlie938

File: Teachers Desktop Pub.Sampler (134579 bytes)
DL time (9600 baud): < 3 minutes
Download count: 99
Uploaded on: America Online

AUTHOR: Charles Doe/SchoolHouse Mac
EQUIPMENT: Any Mac
NEEDS: HyperCard 2.x or player
LOCATION: MED:Miscellaneous

KEYWORDS: HC Stack Graphics Projects Ideas Articles

Contains samples of the graphics, projects, ideas and articles available in the nearly 1500k stack from SchoolHouse Mac. This particular sampler has a little less useful clipart than some of the samplers we've uploaded, but we wanted to give you an idea of topics, projects and tutorials, the larger stack contains.

Teachers Desktop Publishing with HyperCard came about because of HyperCard's power and flexibility. The combination of graphic and writing tools along with the capability of creating stacks of varying sizes and printing in different sizes make HyperCard an excellent, basic desktop publishing program for teachers.

Teachers Desktop Publishing with HyperCard stack is a departure from our other SuperClipArt stacks in that it combines about 400 pieces of clipart, borders, and backgrounds, with approximately 14 simple desktop publishing project ideas for personal use and use with elementary and middle school students.

The sampler contains complete information about the stack and ordering.

The keyword for Mac Education Forum is MED

This file has been checked for infection by Symantec Anti-Virus for Macintosh (SAM). LS

The File Description Screen provides download information.

This file was uploaded to AOL on May 12, 1994. It is a Macintosh Hypercard stack and it's stored in the Macintosh Education Forum: Miscellaneous Library. From the Macintosh File Search screen, you can use the keywords *HC, Stack, Graphics, Projects, Ideas,* and *Articles* to find the program. There have been 99 downloads since this program was uploaded to America Online. Notice that the download time is specified as:

DL time (9600 baud): < 3 minutes

From this line, we know that the user's modem signed on at 9600 baud. The programming at AOL Central customizes this line in the file description to your baud rate. At 9600 baud, the file transfer will take less than three minutes. It can take even less time if you set the Download Manager or Flashsessions to grab this file in AOL's lowest use periods.

Throughout this book, I've used 9600 baud as the standard—wherever download times are given. Of course download times will be greeater if you're using a slower modem.

AOL's heaviest use periods are in the evening, beginning when the folks in D.C. begin the commute home and lasting until the folks in Seattle are slipping off to sleep. That said, plan your downloads in the middle of the night or during morning hours. When you use this approach, you will receive files up to 30 percent faster than the "published" rate. If you only have one phone line, that will probably be the most convenient time for your household, too.

A Few Good Tips

If you didn't visit the Beginners Forum (Beginners) when you joined, it's not too late. Stop in occasionally to download an updated list of keywords or to obtain directions in learning a new online technique.

Members Helping Members (MHM) is crammed full of gems and advice. Three bulletin boards are particularly helpful: *Where on AOL do I find...*, *AOL Hints & Tips*, and *General AOL Questions*. I only have one "reservation" about this area: Mac, Windows, and DOS users see only those questions and responses that are "native" to their system. Actually, they are separate boards, so if a Windows user is asking where to find information on car prices, and you use a Mac, you'll never read the question nor the answer.

Cross Platform Navigation Guide

The steps you use to access software from computing vary depending on whether you are using a Mac or PC. Use the following guidelines to help navigate to the software described throughout this book.

Mac Computer/PC Files	PC Computer/Mac Files
Where	**Where**
Computing	Computing
Software Center	Apple Computing Forums
PC Software Center	Macintosh Software Center
File Search-Over 50,000 Files	File Search-Over60,000 files
Same screen Windows users see	*Quickfinder Search Phrase screen*

Keyword
⌘+K
>PC software

Select
File Search-Over 50,000 files

Same screen Windows users see

Keyword
Ctrl+K
>Mac Software

Select
File Search-Over 60,000 files
Search all files
Quickfinder Search Phrase screen

FREE $TUFF

Home is the place where,
when you have to go there,
they have to take you in.

Robert Frost

Around the House

House, home, apartment, central location—whatever you choose to call it, it is here that we seek refuge from the cold, cruel world. In and around this happy abode we eat, sleep, craft, plan, and maintain. In this section, I'll concentrate on other ways to keep the home fires burning.

In our little refuges, many of us craft, while others shape the outdoors through gardening. The most skilled may even maintain their cars. There's a fine line between crafts and hobbies, so if what you're looking for is not here, be sure to check the Sports, Recreation, and Hobbies section.

We've got a lot of ground to cover in this section, but you'll soon see that all topics come together under the roof and around the house.

Crafts

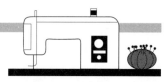

Sew, stitch, or knit? In this topic, I'll guide you to the best of the online crafts. If you don't know the difference between a bobbin and a needle, you'll find help on the Crafts/Sewing Center message boards (Keyword: Exchange). The message boards often carry notices of free catalogs and samples.

Stitch This!

Now you can try an interactive demo of Quilt-Pro, the drawing program for quilters. With Quilt-Pro, you can draw freehand blocks, create appliqué blocks and templates, print blocks any size, calculate yardage, copy blocks and quilts to the Clipboard, and so much more. This demo includes generous selections from the Quilt-Pro libraries. There are 50 blocks, 20 borders, and 50 fabric patterns to preview, as well as four quilts to play with.

Subj: Quilt Pro (WIN)
Date: June 10, 1994
From: Komando
File: QPDEMO.ZIP (587925 bytes)
DL Time: 17 minutes
Author: Quilt-Pro Systems
Needs: Windows 3.1, PKZIP 2.04g

Where

Marketplace
Komputer Clinic featuring Kim Komando

Keyword

Komando

Select

Komando Libraries

Demonstration Versions (WIN/DOS)

Other Programs

Download

Quilt Pro (WIN)

Amish Diamond Quilt

Look here for instructions, including yardage, for sewing a wall hanging or bed-size Amish Diamond quilt using three fabrics. This file includes precise directions, making it quite easy to craft your quilt.

Subj:	Amish Diamond Quilt
Date:	October 22, 1993
From:	BzMouse
File:	AmishDiamond text (6618 bytes)
DL time:	< 1 minute
Author:	Betsy Brazy
Needs:	Text reader

Where

The complete sequence of steps through Computing can be found on page 15. Of course, you can save time and money by using the Keyword shortcuts.

Keyword

Mac: File Search

PC: Mac Software

Select

>Quilt wall hanging

Download

Amish Diamond Quilt

Cross-Stitch for Windows

This is a fabulous cross-stitch program. I could sit for hours and design with this. Once cross stitchers find this, it's going to be a very popular download. Simply select DMC colors from the color palette and design away on the electronic graph paper. You can create an easy-to-use chart to help you with the design—the program allows you to design in color and then print with symbols. I can't say enough good things about this treasure!

Subj: Cross stitch
Date: May 18, 1994
From: Mikew12512
File: CROSS_ST.ZIP (97272 bytes)
DL time: < 2 minutes
Needs: Windows
Type: Shareware $30

Where

Clubs & Interests

SeniorNet

Keyword

Senior

Select

Showcase & Exchange

>cross stitch

Download

Cross stitch

Knitware Sweater Design

Knitware Sweater Design assists hand and machine knitters in custom design-ing sweaters and prints the pattern instructions to knit from. It allows for any yarn gauge, provides a variety of "mix-and match" sweater-style components, provides 28 standard sizes, and allows all measurements to be customized. I looked all over for a Mac version, but couldn't find one.

Subj: KWS: V1.10 KNITWARE Sweater Design
Date: January 23, 1993
From: Nick WT
File: KWS.ZIP (124494 bytes)
DL time: < 3 minutes
Author: Morningdew Consulting Services, Ltd.
Needs: PC, UnZIPing program
Type: Shareware $35

Where

The complete sequence of steps through Computing can be found on page 15. Of course, you can save time and money by using the Keyword shortcuts.

Keyword

File Search

Select

>sew knitting home

Download

KWS: V1.10 KNITWARE Sweater Design

Home Hints

Collections of hints fall into the category of news you can use. There's always a better way to clean the house, have sparkling pots and pans, change the oil in the car, and get stains out of hubby's shirt. If you don't find what you're looking for in this download collection, check the noted boards for top-notch hints.

Where

People Connection

Select

PC Studio

Advice & Tips

Tammy's Tips

Tammy's Favorite Tips

Where

Clubs & Interest

Select

Exchange

Home Health Careers

Health, Home, Family

In lieu of Heloise

Helpful Hints

This program contains hints for parents, homeowners, handypersons, gardeners, and pet owners. Tips on car care, cleaning, food, plants, and pets are all combined into a mini-Heloise type guide. You will find many useful and helpful tips for everyday activities. The information is provided in electronic book format using Another Company's Writer's Dream. It is very easy to read and offers search capabilities. If you'd like to design your own electronic books, Writer's Dream is available online. Helpful Hints can also be read as text files.

Subj: HINTS: Helpful Hints and Tips
Date: September 27, 1993

From: Frodo
File: HINTS.ZIP (47740 bytes)
DL time: < 1 minute
Author: Joy's Software
Needs: UnZIPing program
Type: Shareware $10-15

Where

The complete sequence of steps through Computing can be found on page 15. Of course, you can save time and money by using the Keyword shortcuts.

Keyword

PC: File Search

Mac: PC Software

Select

>helpful hints

Download

HINTS: Helpful Hints and Tips

Yard Sale Tips

Do you own a few expired neckties? Bell-bottom pants? Soleless shoes? Maybe it's time for a yard sale. This file will explain everything from how to get organized, through pricing and display, and of course, how much money to have in the till.

Subj: TXT Yard Sale Tips
Date: August 14, 1994
From: Fonecard
File: Rags to Riches (9216 bytes)
DL time: < 1 minute
Author: James Moz
Needs: Text reader

Where

Clubs & Interests

SeniorNet

Keyword

Senior

Select

Showcase & Exchange

Download

TXT Yard Sale Tips

Cheap $kate Newsletter

Issue #2 is a small but useful and informative personal and family finance newsletter from Northern California. This issue covers topics such as: how to determine the right allowance for your kids, homemade products, great thrifty recipes, tips on Social Security, and a section on home financial terms.

This newsletter was written in the DART Hypertext system (also available online).

Subj: CHEAP: V2.0 Cheap$kate Newsletter
Date: September 14, 1994
From: Bryce Lane
File: CHEAP994.ZIP (110459 bytes)
DL time: < 3 minutes
Author: The Maxsons
Needs: DART, UnZIPing program
Type: Shareware

Where

The complete sequence of steps through Computing can be found on page 15. Of course, you can save time and money by using the Keyword shortcuts.

Keyword

File Search

Select

>money tips bargains

Download

CHEAP: V2.0 Cheap$kate Newsletter

Saving Money

Shop&Sav is an efficient, easy to use program designed to guide you to more informed purchasing. By comparing pricing for common grocery items (taking into account both price and quantity), the program can help ensure that you always carry out your grocery shopping in the most economical manner possible. Shop&Sav includes a handy coupon tracking system and offers the ability to use abbreviated units of measure. You can estimate the price of your grocery run before you leave for the store. Definitely worth the $5 registration fee!

An icon (CART.ICO) is provided for Windows users.

Subj: SHOP&SAV: Shop and Save
Date: April 25, 1993
From: RTMWare
File: SHOP&SAV.ZIP (155471 bytes)
DL time: < 4 minutes
Author: Robert McCann (RTMware)
Needs: An UnZIPing program
Type: Shareware

Where

The complete sequence of steps through Computing can be found on page 15. Of course, you can save time and money by using the Keyword shortcuts.

Keyword

File Search

Select

>shopping grocery coupon

Download

SHOP&SAV: Shop and Save

Rebate Tracker

Will you ever see that rebate check? Rebase is a rebate tracking database for mail-in rebates, rebate coupons, or mail-order items. Simply enter information about rebate offers you send in, then check the rebate or offer off as it is received. You can print a list of all rebates in the database or list them to screen.

This is the full version of Rebase, which allows tracking 100 rebates and 100 mail-order items. A full report generator is included. Registration gets you version 3.0 when it's available.

Subj: REBASE: V2.2 Rebate Tracker
Date: December 16, 1993
From: PC Robin
File: REBASE22.ZIP (32990 bytes)
DL time: < 1 minute
Author: John L. Berger (Pennsylvania Software & Communications)
Needs: An UnZIPing program
Type: Shareware

Where

The complete sequence of steps through Computing can be found on page 15. Of course, you can save time and money by using the Keyword shortcuts.

Keyword

File Search

Select

>coupon refund home

Download

REBASE: V2.2 Rebate Tracker

Refunding

Refunding Explained, a short MS Works article, covers
what you need to know to start Re-FUN-ding. This is a unique
hobby, where well-known companies give you back money, gifts,
or free products for trying their products. Refunding Explained
includes a glossary of refunding terms, a brief description of refunding, and information on how you can start into this great hobby! You can
receive some really great stuff from refunding, including cash, VCRs, clothes,
and free groceries. With the same directions, you'll also find the corresponding text file to download.

Subj: WPS: Refunding Explained
Date: June 22, 1994
From: Writer 650
File: EXPLAIN.WPS (7894 bytes)
DL time: < 1 minute
Author: Tammy Jackson
Needs: MS Works or word processor that can read .WPS files
Type: Freely Distributed

Where

The complete sequence of steps through Computing can be found on page 15.
Of course, you can save time and money by using the Keyword shortcuts.

Keyword

PC: File Search
Mac: PC Software

Select

>refund rebate

Download

WPS: Refunding Explained
TEXT: Refunding Explained

What I Make, What I Spend, and What's Left

Around the House is a power-packed, user-friendly home and personal information manager. The application keeps track of names, addresses, and phone numbers and features an appointment calendar, an income and expense tracker, a household inventory module, a vehicle logbook, an easy-to-use word processor with mail-merge, plus much more. It also prints pre-defined labels and reports, and includes a report writer.

Subj: ATH: V2.0 Around the House
Date: June 23, 1994
From: MSW Dan
File: ATH20.ZIP (425223 bytes)
DL time: < 11 minutes
Author: Bill Strugell (BlueCollar Software)
Needs: UnZIPing program
Type: Shareware $29

Where

The complete sequence of steps through Computing can be found on page 15. Of course, you can save time and money by using the Keyword shortcuts.

Keyword

File Search

Select

>sturgell, bluecollar

Download

ATH: V2.0 Around the House

Parties, Gifts, and Holidays

Let's see. New Year's, Martin Luther King's Birthday, Inauguration Day, Valentine's Day, President's Day, St. Patrick's Day, Easter, Passover, Memorial Day, Graduations, June Weddings . . . There's a lot to celebrate (and those holidays are for just the first six months of the year).

I've found a few tidbits to help you prepare for special events, and with these you'll be the epitome of the perfect host, hostess, or guest.

Uncommon Scents

Who doesn't love a sweet-smelling, luxuriously hot bath? Check out this stack to get the details on how to make your own bath soaps and bath salts for Christmas or Valentine's Day gifts. These luxury items sell for big bucks in specialty stores so enjoy a splurge with this recipe. Makes a great crafts project for kids or fund raising.

Subj: Uncommon Scents
Date: September 11, 1993
From: PshbtnPres
File: Uncommon.sit (31257 bytes)
DL time: < 1 minute
Author: Pushbutton Press
Needs: HyperCard, any Mac

Where

The complete sequence of steps through Computing can be found on page 15. Of course, you can save time and money by using the Keyword shortcuts.

Keyword

File Search

Select

>gifts bath soap

Download

Uncommon Scents

It's My Party

Party.PUB is a party invitation card template. It's simple to follow: Just replace anything you don't like with your own choices or creations. *Now* if you can't get a party going, you *know* it's your cooking!

Subj: MSPUB2: Party Invitation Template
Date: August 9, 1994
From: SUNSHIN763
File: PARTY.ZIP (204654 bytes)
DL time: < 5 minutes
Author: Stephen Smith
Needs: UnZIPing program, Win 3.1, MS Publisher V2.0
Type: Freely Distributed

Where

The complete sequence of steps through Computing can be found on page 15. Of course, you can save time and money by using the Keyword shortcuts.

Keyword

File Search

Select

>template greeting card

Download

MSPUB2: Party Invitation Template

Birthday Greetings

Birthdays should be special and with this electronic birthday card, which allows you to personalize your message with the giver's and recipient's names, you're bound to make someone's day. You can even set the recorded sound to whatever you desire.

Subj: E Cards Happy Birthday 2.1
Date: June 14, 199)
File: ECards Happy Birthday 2.1.sea (99983 bytes)
DL time: < 2 minutes
Author: Charles G. Marlowe
Needs: Color Mac, System 7+

Where

Marketplace

Komputer Clinic featuring Kim Komando

Keyword

Komando

Select

Komando Libraries

Kool Shareware & Stuff (Mac)

Download

E Cards Happy Birthday 2.1

Holiday Organizer and Gift Planner

Having trouble getting your gift-buying list organized? Here's a unique gift-giving database organizer for the disorganized giver in you. Whether you buy gifts for lots of people or you start buying Christmas gifts in July, this little file will help keep you organized and on budget. Through planning ahead, GiftBox encourages thoughtful gifts, with time and money well spent. It's also fun, easy to use, and a free gift for yourself!

Subj: Organizer/Holiday/Gift Planner
Date: October 9, 1993
From: Lake Group
File: GIFTBOX v.1.0.sea (151190 bytes)
DL time: < 4 minutes
Author: Lake Group
Needs: Mac

Where

The complete sequence of steps through Computing can be found on page 15. Of course, you can save time and money by using the Keyword shortcuts.

Keyword

File Search

Select

>holiday organizer

Download

Organizer/Holiday/Gift Planner

Wedding and Party Organizer

This template will help you keep track of everything you could possibly imagine in preparation for a party. You'll be able to track invited guests, invitations sent and responses received, side of family, table assignments, gifts, and all ceremony and reception essentials, among other things. You can use this organizer for any event where invitations and thank-yous are required.

Subj: Wedding and Party Organizer FM TPLT
Date: October 23, 1993
From: Bruce5153
File: Wedding Organizer 2.2 (79062 bytes)
DL time: < 2 minutes
Author: Video Marketing
Needs: PC or Mac, Filemaker Pro v.1

There's a FileMaker Pro Demo online (Keyword: Claris).

Where

The complete sequence of steps through Computing can be found on page 15. Of course, you can save time and money by using the Keyword shortcuts.

Keyword

Mac: File Search

PC: Mac Software

Select

>bridal invitations

Download

Wedding and Party Organizer

Gift Wrapper

If you've ever cut your paper just a little too short or if you just can't wrap gifts, this stack is for you. Simply enter the dimensions of your box, and it tells you the required length and width dimensions of the wrapping paper. After that, there are detailed instructions, with illustrations, for wrapping your gift. You're bound to find this a great tool to learn how to wrap. The author asks for a $1 shareware fee as a token of your appreciation. Hint: Make sure you wrap gifts near your computer or you'll be running back and forth.

Subj: Gift Wraper v.1.0
Date: March 30, 1994
From: Tuilkap
File: Gift Wraper.sit (12594 bytes)
DL time: < 1 minute
Author: Tuilkap
Needs: HyperCard 2.1 or HyperCard Player

Where

The complete sequence of steps through Computing can be found on page 15. Of course, you can save time and money by using the Keyword shortcuts.

Keyword

File Search

Select

>gift wrap

Download

Gift Wraper v.1.0

Christmas Clip Art

If you want to make your Christmas greetings and packages more festive, try adding some Christmas ClipArt to your annual newsletter, cards, or gift tags.

If you enjoy these and the Christmas giving mood strikes you, please donate a toy or something to your local Toys for Tots or other charity, or just drop a note to the author, BenW5.

Subj: Christmas ClipArt PNTG
Date: December 14, 1990
From: BenW5
File: Christmas ClipArt.sit (12343 bytes)
DL time: < 1 minute
Author: BenW5
Needs: Mac Paint and StuffIt

Where

The complete sequence of steps through Computing can be found on page 15. Of course, you can save time and money by using the Keyword shortcuts.

Keyword

File Search

Select

>gift tags tree

Download

Christmas ClipArt PNTG

Gadget Guru

You may have seen him on television—maybe on NBC's Today Show on weekend mornings? The Gadget Guru has the inside line on all the new gadgets that can make your life easier. He knows where to find a gift for someone who has everything—from an automatic bread baker to an indestructible mailbox.

The Gadget Guru, known to his mother as Andy Pargh, travels around the country attending trade shows and the like, in search of the newest, latest, and greatest new products to keep readers informed of the newest and latest consumer products on the market.

Andy's subjects are always timely, fresh, and full of information, and are delivered in an entertaining format. A selection of the best from Andy includes the following articles:

- New Products for the Bath
- Painting Easier with New Gadgets
- Baby Gadgets are Plentiful

- Car Alarms in Demand
- New Sporting Goods

 The Gadget Guru has a free catalog. To get on the list, you'll need to enter through the Gadget Guru message board (Keyword: Gadget Guru).

Where

Clubs & Interests

Gadget Guru Electronics Area

Keyword

Gadget Guru

Select

Gadget Guru Archives

Download

New Products for the Bath

Painting Easier with New Gadgets

Baby Gadgets are Plentiful

Car Alarms in Demand

New Sporting Goods

Video Tape Library

So, which tape has "The Empire Strikes Back" recorded on it? Sometimes finding a particular movie or show from your enormous videotape library is like finding a needle in a haystack. Look aimlessly no more. VIDEO_1 is a complete database for keeping track of your videotape collection. It allows for two unique numeric fields to identify your tapes, and can sort by actors, directors, type of movie, and various other ways. VIDEO_1 also prints various reports, and in general allows your collection to be either strictly or informally organized, according to your preference.

Subj: VIDEO_1: V2.00 Video Tape Library
Date: December 28, 1992
From: BST254
File: VIDEO.ZIP (217216 bytes)
DL time: < 6 minutes
Author: Robert Burger
Needs: PC, UnZIPing program
Type: Shareware

Where

The complete sequence of steps through Computing can be found on page 15. Of course, you can save time and money by using the Keyword shortcuts.

Keyword

File Search

Select

>home movies film

Download

VIDEO_1: V2.00 Video Tape Library

Homeowners Forum

Is the toilet running again? Do your tomato plants need to be covered yet? When you need this type of advice, turn to the United Homeowners Association (UHA) for handyman tips and year 'round maintenance.

UHA provides AOL members with information on such matters as home improvement and remodeling, landscaping and safe gardening practices, dealing with contractors and service people, reviews of new household products and books for the home, reports of product recalls or hazards, insurance, refinancing, reverse mortgages, equity loans, energy conservation, home security, travel, food, and safety and health issues. UHA will advise you on just about anything you can imagine for your home.

If you need to know the differences between grout, mortar, concrete, and cement, you've come to the right section.

In this area, Ask the Expert is a terrific value and resource. Select Ask the Expert, and then type and send your question. You'll receive a direct E-mail response, and compiled responses are posted to the message board.

Where

Clubs & Interests

Homeowners Forum

Keyword

Home

Select

Ask the Expert

A life may depend on this tip: Product recalls are posted in the Homeowners forum. At last check, there were recalls on pacifiers and baby swings. This should be a regular check-in when you sign on to AOL (Keyword: Home).

Handyman Guide and Home Safety Tips

Check out these hot items and you'll find out how to measure heating or cooling needs for your home. Earthquake tips (don't jump!) and a little music round out this topic.

BTU Calculator

Specifically for the super handyman in your house, this program is designed to simplify the process of sizing heating and cooling units used in commercial and residential structures. If you've ever tried to calculate the heat loss or gain of a structure, you already probably know that it's difficult. This program asks for the parameters necessary for the calculations and then performs the calculations for you.

BTU will translate the cooling into tons as well as BTUs and will give the cubic foot per minute (cfm) necessary for proper cooling or heating of the area analyzed. The program is chock full of help screens and features that make it a pleasure to operate.

If you are in the heating and cooling business, this program may be of importance to you. In fact, it may even cut the time you spend on job estimates.

Subj: BTU: V3.10sw Heating & Cooling
Date: May 19, 1993
From: PC Robin
File: BTUSW310.ZIP (270848 bytes)
DL time: < 7 minutes
Author: David W. Ostler (Enchanted Tree Software)
Needs: UnZIPing program
Type: Shareware, $149.95 to $259.95 depending on options

Where

The complete sequence of steps through Computing can be found on page 15. Of course, you can save time and money by using the Keyword shortcuts.

Keyword

File Search

Select

>Air condition bid

Download

BTU: V3.10sw Heating & Cooling

Earthquake Preparedness

This text-based guide provides a practical approach
to individual and family earthquake preparedness. It
stresses what to do and know about to get ready for
an earthquake, how to survive during a quake, and
what to do afterwards. Topics include how to prepare your home structurally, what supplies to have
on hand, and what types of planning are needed
for children and other family members. Very down-
to-earth topics, such as dealing with injuries, avoiding panic, and finding sources of drinkable water
are covered. This guide was written with the
people of Southern California in mind, but would be appropriate for anyone
living in a quake prone area. Re-read this often and keep a copy with your
emergency supplies.

Subj: QUAKE: Earthquake Preparedness
Date: January 22, 1993
From: Nick WT
File: QUAKE.ZIP (9260 bytes)
DL time: < 1 minute
Author: John Cairns
Needs: UnZIPing program, text reader, or DOS "type" command
Type: Public domain

Where

The complete sequence of steps through Computing can be found on page 15.
Of course, you can save time and money by using the Keyword shortcuts.

Keyword

PC: File Search
Mac: PC Software

Select

>emergency home safety

Download

QUAKE: Earthquake Preparedness

Home WAV

FOUNDHM.WAV is a 7.48 second sound bite from a Jimmy Buffett song. Jimmy sings, "And I have found me a home."

Subj:　　WAV: Buffett: Found Me A Home
Date:　　May 8, 1994
From:　　JBParrotHd
File:　　FoundHm.wav (166475 bytes)
DL time: < 4 minutes
Author:　JBParrotHd
Needs:　　PC or Mac, Windows 3.1, or WAV file player
Type:　　Public domain

Where

Computing

PC Software

Keyword

PC:　File Search

Mac: PC Software

Select

>home sound music

Download

WAV: Buffett: Found Me A Home

In the Garden

Spring, Summer, Fall, and Winter, a true gardener always has a plan, whether it's growing seedlings indoors or spreading mulch outdoors. There are a number of gardening programs online, but let's just say some are modem hogs. Enjoy the few I've selected for you.

Gardening

Daisies, daffodils, or dandelions? The Garden Guide is an informational database program that contains vital information for the home gardener. It can help you determine the location and size of your garden, as well as how to improve the soil quality and use the correct tools for the job. It even tells you the proper methods for planting and tilling and how to prepare for winter.

Composting, herbs, flower bulbs, and cut flower gardens are all included. This program also has the ability to generate a worksheet to plan your garden on paper, and includes various garden recipes to take advantage of your bounty.

Subj: GARDEN: V1.0 Garden Guide
Date: April 1, 1993
From: Nick WT
File: GARDEN15.ZIP (64890 bytes)
DL time: < 1 minute
Author: Donna and John George (Ascend Software)
Needs: DOS 3.0 or higher
Type: Shareware $10

Where

The complete sequence of steps through Computing can be found on page 15. Of course, you can save time and money by using the Keyword shortcuts.

Keyword

File Search

Select

>gardening horticulture

Download

GARDEN: V1.0 Garden Guide

Garden Reference

A chirping bird lets you know you've opened the right program for managing your lawn and garden. The primary feature of the Garden Reference is a diary in which you record such important dates as when seeds were planted, date of harvesting, when sprayed for insects, and so on. The stack also provides a section for keeping records of the plants' watering needs, light requirements, location in the garden, or whatever you feel is useful to you. It also includes some basic information about soil and watering, and a place to make notes about pests in your garden. Give it a try and send the author a note with your comments to make future versions more useful.

Subj: Garden Reference
Date: August 5, 1992
From: Bobtravelr
File: Garden Reference.sit (185351 bytes)
DL time: < 5 minutes
Author: Bob Blea
Needs: HyperCard 2.0+, StuffIt

Where

The complete sequence of steps through Computing can be found on page 15. Of course, you can save time and money by using the Keyword shortcuts.

Keyword

File Search

Select

>Gardening

Download

Garden Reference

Garden Maze GIF

You've probably seen those 3-D images that are all the rage, probably at your local mall. As you stand in front of the dotted image, you suddenly see the hidden picture. Imagine my surprise when I found a garden maze GIF for your computer screen. This GIF file is a color, 3-D, stereo-noise image of a garden maze. The maze itself isn't that difficult but the fact that it is a stereo-noise image increases its difficulty. The object is to try to make your way from the left dot all the way to the dot on the right by going through the maze. Don't worry—I found the answer file, too!

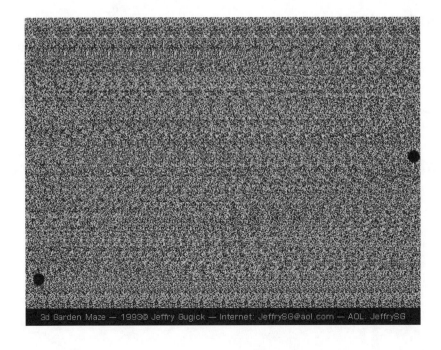

Subj: 3d Garden Maze GIF
Date: October 3, 1993
From: JeffrySG
File: 3d Garden Maze.GIF (128100 bytes)
DL time: < 3 minutes
Author: Jeffry Gugick
Needs: GIF viewer, 8-bit video board (at least)

Where

The complete sequence of steps through Computing can be found on page 15. Of course, you can save time and money by using the Keyword shortcuts.

Keyword

Mac: File Search

PC: Mac Software

Select

>garden maze GIF

Download

3d Garden Maze GIF

3d Garden Maze Answer GIF

Car Time

Your fabled car gets you where you're going in style or otherwise. Once you've owned a car, you'll never want to be without one again. To help you keep your car happy and healthy, you have to stay on top of the maintenance. This topic contains the best car maintenance programs and a couple of surprises.

PowerMac Car Crash

If we're going to talk about auto maintenance, let's make sure you have a car crash sound. More than once you've booted a Mac to see the frowning face and hear the "sad Mac" sound. Well, the new PowerPC Macs play a sound during startup when something isn't quite right.

Apple's engineers have inserted the sound of a screeching car slamming into a wall into their computer's ROM. What will they think of next?

Having a bad day? This is a good one to share with your co-workers!

Subj: PowerMac Crash Sound
Date: May 8, 1994
From: Darien M
File: PowerMac Crash (54519 bytes)
DL time: < 1 minute
Author: DarienM
Needs: System 7 or sound editor

Where

The complete sequence of steps through Computing can be found on page 15. Of course, you can save time and money by using the Keyword shortcuts.

Keyword

Mac: File Search

PC: Mac Software

Select

>Power Mac Crash Sound

Download

PowerMac Crash Sound

Auto Maintenance Stack

This great stack was created to help keep accurate records of all car repairs. The stack has fields for the date, mileage, parts used, repairs done, notes, and more. And the documents are included. It's comprehensive and easy to use. Sorry to all you Mac Plus, SE/20, and SE/30 users, this stack was created for a 13" monitor or larger.

Subj: Auto Maintenance Stack.sit
Date: June 25, 1992
From: CD Ritchie
File: Auto Maintenance.sit (26974 bytes)
DL time: < 1 minute
Author: CDRitchie
Needs: HyperCard 2.0+, 13" screen or larger

Where

The complete sequence of steps through Computing can be found on page 15. Of course, you can save time and money by using the Keyword shortcuts.

Keyword

File Search

Select

>Auto maintenance

Download

Auto Maintenance Stack.sit

Mopar Diagnostics

Mopar Diagnostics was crafted to help owners of Plymouths, Dodges, Chryslers, and other cars to save large sums of money on auto repairs. This file has helped the author's friends to save over $4,000 (several different mechanics' estimates minus actual cost with stack's advice). With illustrations, this file is easy to use. It simplifies repairs even for one who has never popped the hood.

Subj: Mopar Diagnostics Stack 1.2
Date: August 14, 1991
From: DavidZatz
File: Mopar.sit (83136 bytes)
DL time: < 2 minutes
Author: David A. Zatz
Needs: HyperCard 1.2+, StuffIt

Where

The complete sequence of steps through Computing can be found on page 15. Of course, you can save time and money by using the Keyword shortcuts.

Keyword

File Search

Select

>auto mopar diagnostics

Download

Mopar Diagnostics Stack 1.2

GM Car Repair

Get this before trouble strikes. Quickcode is a program that will give professional and backyard auto mechanics a quick reference of onboard computer trouble codes for GM passenger cars. It is easy to use and very useful to auto mechanics and do-it-yourselfers. No need to search through several books to find the code's definition. Just enter the code number and Quickcode gives you its definition.

Subj: CODEGM: V1.01 GM Car Repair
Date: March 6, 1994
From: PC Robin
File: CODEGM.ZIP (4348 bytes)
DL time: < 1 minute

Author: Max Robinson
Needs: DOS (not Windows), UnZIPing program
Type: Freely Distributed

Where

The complete sequence of steps through Computing can be found on page 15. Of course, you can save time and money by using the Keyword shortcuts.

Keyword

File Search

Select

>General Motors Repair

Download

CODEGM: V1.01 GM Car Repair

VIN Codes

The PCVIN Information System is an easy-to-use computerized system that translates a vehicle's VIN code into meaningful information about your car. This information can be useful when having your car serviced. This version covers U.S passenger cars, imports, and jeeps between 1981 and 1991. There are two parts to this file. When you download both files, it will take a total of 10 minutes at 9600 baud.

Subj: PCVIN: V1.0 VIN Auto Decoder 1/2
Date: September 28, 1993
From: Frodo
File: PCVIN1.ZIP (227072 bytes)
DL time: < 6 minutes
Author: Paul M. Allen (PMA Technology Group)
Needs: UnZIPing program, both parts of the program!
Type: Shareware

Where

The complete sequence of steps through Computing can be found on page 15. Of course, you can save time and money by using the Keyword shortcuts.

Keyword

File Search

Select

>automobile service

Download

PCVIN: V1.0 VIN Auto Decoder 1/2

PCVIN: V1.0 VIN Auto Decoder 2/2

Free Mercedes

Enough of all these repairs! Wouldn't you rather have a Mercedes? I found a grayscale GIF of the MB 500SL. Now that's a freebie!

Subj: Mercedes Benz 500SL.GIF
Date: March 2, 1991
From: TriStar500
File: Mercedes 500SL.GIF (22085 bytes)
DL time: < 1 minute
Needs: GIF viewer

Where

The complete sequence of steps through Computing can be found on page 15. Of course, you can save time and money by using the Keyword shortcuts.

Keyword

Mac: File Search

PC: Mac Software

Select

>German Car

Download

Mercedes Benz 500SL.GIF

Pet Care Forum

AOL's Pet Care forum will help you care for your animal friends. The hosts are veterinarians who bring their knowledge of animals right to your home. From dogs and cats to reptiles and birds, the Pet Care forum will provide you with helpful hints and up-to-date information on how to care for that special family member.

Where

Clubs & Interests

Pet Care Forum

Keyword

Pet Care

Preventive Health Care

This file is an electronic version of a brochure published by the American Veterinary Medical Association. The brochure is entitled *Preventive Health Care and Risk Factor Management: Keys to Helping Your Pet Live a Longer, Happier Life.*

Subjects covered include aging, obesity, kidney disease, heart disease, feline urologic syndrome, periodontal disease, the role of veterinarians in preventive medicine, the connection of diet and disease, and the role of the pet owner in maintenance of proper health care for his/her pet.

Subj: Preventive Health Care
Date: October 3, 1994
From: HOST VET
File: PreventiveMed.txt (8710 bytes)
DL time: < 1 minute
Author: American Vet. Medical Assoc.
Needs: Text reader

Where

Clubs & Interests

Pet Care Forum

Keyword

Pet Care

Select

Pet Care Library Center

Veterinary Library

Download

Preventive Health Care

Companies That Do Not Test on Animals

This file lists cosmetics and household product companies that *do not* conduct tests on animals. It also specifies companies that have moratoriums on testing, rather than bans. It also lists which products are cruelty-free (contain no animal by-products) and notes those companies that sell by mail order. The file was last updated in Spring 1994. These directions will also guide you to the corresponding list of companies that *do* test on animals.

Subj: Companies that DO NOT TEST/Animals
Date: August 11, 1994

From: DavidL164
File: NOTEST.TXT (25052 bytes)
DL time: < 1 minute
Author: CEP, NAVS, and PETA
Needs: Text reader

Where

Clubs & Interests

Pet Care Forum

Keyword

Pet Care

Select

Pet Care Library Center

Pet Care Library

Download

Companies that DO NOT TEST/Animals

Companies that DO TEST/Animals

Gordon Setter Puppies GIF

Charming gordon setter puppies—they are the epitome of cuteness. If you don't have a dog, you'll want one after viewing this GIF.

Subj: Gordon Setter Puppies
Date: October 2, 1994
From: MarleneZ
File: pups.GIF (53305 bytes)
DL time: < 1 minute
Author: MarleneZ
Needs: GIF converter

Where

Clubs & Interests

Pet Care Forum

Keyword

Pet Care

Select

Pet Care Library Center

Dogs

Download

Gordon Setter Puppies

CatPause Screensaver

CatPause is a screensaver module that uses photos of cats and some amusing special effects to keep you smiling all day long. The enclosed Read Me file tells you how you can customize the module with photos of your own cats.

Subj: CatPause
Date: October 1, 1994
From: Bfelt
File: CatPause.sit (87223 bytes)
DL time: < 2 minutes
Author: Ultimate Software
Needs: Mac, System 7, AOL 2.x or StuffIt, After Dark or DarkSide of the Mac
Type: Freeware

Where

Clubs & Interests

Pet Care Forum

Keyword

Pet Care

Select

Pet Care Library Center
Cats

Download

CatPause

Where to Find More Goodies

You'll find related goodies in several sections of *FREE $TUFF from America Online*: In Personal and Home Finance, you'll discover a household register and programs to help you buy your next house. It should come as no surprise that you'll find recipes and organizers, along with gift ideas, in Cooking. Hobbyists will find their preferred programs and freebies in Sports, Recreation, and Hobbies.

In addition to scanning these sections, you might also want to try the File Search, PC Software, and Mac Software Keywords, and look in the main libraries for holiday art and greetings.

FREE $TUFF

Some books leave us free and
some books make us free.

Ralph Waldo Emerson

Books,
Magazines,
and Literature

There must be a strong association between America Online members and book lovers. Perhaps it's the association between personal computers and the written word. The more time we spend at the computer, the more we write and the more we consider ourselves to be writers—and writers are readers. So there.

Throughout AOL's message boards, in virtually every topic and forum, members often recommend books to each other. In this chapter, I'll guide you to some of my favorite places to read reviews, gather opinions, and shop for books and magazines.

THE NEW YORK TIMES BOOK REVIEW

The New York Times Book Review is probably the most famous and well regarded critique of literary works in the world. AOL users are most fortunate to have selected portions of this resource at their disposal.

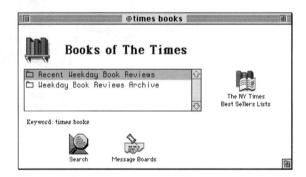

Hundreds of reviews are archived and the current week's lists are online. Hard-cover works include:

• Fiction

• Non-Fiction

• Advice

• How-To

• Miscellaneous

You can find these same categories in paperback, with the addition of New And Noteworthy Paperbacks.

The Recent Weekday Book Reviews and Weekday Book Review Archive are the primary focus for book lovers online. You'll still want to purchase your

Sunday Times for the complete Sunday reviews, but I know you'll be impressed with this literary treasury.

Where

Newsstand

The New York Times

Times Arts

Books

Keyword

Times Books

Select

The NY Times Bestseller Lists

or Recent Weekday Book Reviews

or Weekday Book Reviews Archive

Mercury Center

The Mercury Center's book reviews are not as well assembled as those in the New York Times Online area, but if you're looking for something special, the Text Search option here will help you with your search. Regular readers will want to check this area often. These reviews are somewhat harder to find because they are listed by the name of the article or column—rather than by the name of the reviewed book.

Where

Newsstand

San Jose Mercury News

Keyword

Mercury

Select

Entertainment

Books

Bumper Stickers

Drive home your support for Mercury Center! Colorful Mercury Center bumper stickers proclaim: "Meet Me in Mercury Center." Bumper stickers are free, so order one for your bike, too.

Where

Newsstand

Mercury Center Online

Keyword

Mercury

Select

Advertising

Mercury Mall

Catalog

Bumper Sticker

 Order Form

Make sure to provide your address to receive the bumper sticker.

Chicago Online

Chicago Online's reviews are also a bit difficult to locate. If you're looking for a specific review, your best bet is to use Search Chicago Online from the main Chicago Online screen. You can locate some of 1994's political books with the following Keywords: Richard Nixon, Dan Quayle, Barbara Bush, James Carville, and Mary Matalin. You might also want to try Book Review.

Where

Newsstand

Chicago Online

Keyword

Chicago

Select

Entertainment

Search Chicago Online

AOL Computing Resource Center

The AOL Computing Resource Center is made up of three areas: Resources, Databases, and Publications.

Within the Databases area you will find New Product Information, which will guide you to book reviews on computer books—a must for all AOL users. This publication includes the computer-related periodicals and books also found in AOL's Newsstand—and more.

The access is different for PC and Mac users. Those with Macs toggle between Resources, Databases, and Publications. PC users will see all content options.

You'll find the cross-platform titles here. If you're looking at the computer titles in the Newsstand, you'll see a limited selection of titles, depending on your system and the platforms covered by the content of each magazine.

Where (PC)

Computing

Keyword

Computing

Select

Technology News

[magazine title]

Where (Mac)

Computing

Resource Center

Keyword

CRC

Select

Publications

[magazine title]

New Product Information/New Books

What's new in IDG's *For Dummies* series? What's *The Mosaic Handbook* about? Are you considering the purchase of *Microsoft Word 6 for the Macintosh Step by Step*? Highlights, cover prices, ISBNs, and pertinent facts abound. In the New Product Information area, you'll find the latest information on PC software, hardware, books, and general industry news. This information is gathered primarily from manufacturer press releases received directly from the companies and authors. All press releases are generally reprinted in full—exactly as they're received—with little or no editing!

Where (PC)

Computing

Keyword

Computing

Select

Technology News

New Product Info

Books, Videos . . . .

Where (Mac)

Computing

Resource Center

Keyword

CRC

Select

Databases

New Product Information

Books, Videos . . . .

Read/Save

New IDG. . . . For Dummies

Read/Save

New IDG. . . . For Dummies

Bestseller Lists

In the Entertainment department, you'll find the only center for pre-release book news. The book reviews are compiled by Kirkus Reviews of New York from new releases approximately two months before the books are available at book stores and libraries. It's a great way to stay abreast of all of the hot new books. The reviews and comments are written by contract reviewers who receive new books from the major publishers. Each report concentrates on the most notable releases for the period, and the online report is updated twice each month. If it's August, there must be a new Tom Clancy book . . . .

Where

Entertainment

Book Bestsellers

Keyword

Books

Read/Select

Coming Soon in Fiction

Coming Soon in Non-Fiction

Book Bestsellers

Entertainment's Book Bestsellers list is compiled by *The Wall Street Journal*. *The Journal's* list reflects nationwide sales of hardcover books for the week ended two Saturdays prior at more than 2,500 B. Dalton, Barnes & Noble, Bookland, Books-a-Million, Bookstar, Bookstop, Borders Books & Music, Brentano's, Crown Books, Doubleday, Scribners, Super Crown, and Waldenbooks stores. Bestseller lists are updated weekly. It's fun to compare the lists found here with those in *The New York Times'* feature.

Where

Entertainment

Book Bestsellers

Keyword

Books

Read/Select

Hardcover Fiction Bestsellers

Hardcover Non-Fiction Bestsellers

Critics' Choice

Critics' Choice is a multimedia syndicate, specializing in reviewing entertainment. Their features are syndicated to newspapers, as well as audiotext systems. Critics' Choice provides an intelligent guidebook to pleasures and products to rescue you from the exhausting clutter of entertainment choices and to help you choose the best, while avoiding the worst, before committing money and time. In this topic, I'll direct you to the Critics' Choice book reviews. Later, in the *Entertainment* section, we'll take a look at the other entertainment reviews.

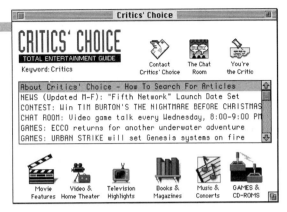

Where

Entertainment
Critics' Choice

Keyword

Critics

Select

Books & Magazines

Book Reviews

The folks at Critics' Choice have done a great job of organizing hundreds of book reviews so that you can access them quickly. By checking Current Reviews, you can read about the new children's books released in December or the cookbooks released in October. The index is grouped by month, with the current month appearing at the top of the list. Within each month, articles are categorized by topic such as health, cookbooks, computers, and fiction. When you don't know the month of release, Search Critics' Choice is your best bet.

Where

Entertainment

Critics' Choice

Keyword

Critics

Select

Books & Magazines

Current Reviews

The complete selection of each month's Current Reviews can be downloaded from the Book Archives option on the Books & Magazines screen.

Top 10

Is Nancy Drew still in the top 10 choices for young girls? Find out with Critics' Choice Top 10 Lists, which are updated weekly and are provided by Ingram Books, one of the nation's largest book distributors. You'll find Top 10 Fiction, Non-Fiction, Mass Paperbacks, Trade Paperbacks, Juvenile Hardcover, and Juvenile Trade Paperbacks.

Where

Entertainment

Critics' Choice

Keyword

Critics

Select

Books & Magazines

Top 10

Read/Save

[Date and List]

E-mail List

To become a member of the Critics' Choice E-mail list, just send a request by clicking on the Contact Critics' Choice icon. CC E-Mail list members receive advance information about contests, articles, and reviews by private E-mail. This is a totally free service, designed to save you online time by letting you know what you can find in Critics' Choice quickly and conveniently. Your membership implies no obligation whatsoever, and can be canceled at any time.

Where

Entertainment

Critics' Choice

Keyword

Critics

Select

Contact Critics' Choice

E-Mail

Please put me on the CC E-Mail List.

Signed, [screen name]

The 1991 Pulitzer Prizes

I haven't yet found the other years, but the 1991 Pulitzer Prize list is available for literary types and trivia buffs. The categories include: Public Service, Beat Reporting, International Reporting, Spot News Reporting, Investigative Reporting, Explanatory Journalism, National Reporting, Feature Writing, Documentary, Criticism, Editorial Writing, Editorial Cartooning, Sport News Photography, Feature Photography, Fiction, Drama, History, Biography, Poetry, General Non-Fiction, Music, and a Special Award. Drumroll, please . . . and the winners were . . . .

Subj: The Pulitzer Prizes '91
Date: December 30, 1993
From: ArisC
File: PULITZER (2603 bytes)
DL time: < 1 minute
Author: None
Needs: PC or Mac, reader

Where

Entertainment

Critics' Choice

Keyword

Critics

Select

Books & Magazines

Book Archives

Download

The Pulitzer Prizes '91

Industry Scoop

For the news behind the new releases, stop in at the Cowles/SIMBA Media Information Network and Inside Media for all the information on book and magazine publishing (Keyword: Simba).

Writer's Corner

The Writer's Club brings together the fraternity of aspiring writers who share their creations, tips on form, and style, as well as their excitement and love for writing with others who enjoy writing.

Founded by writers for writers, the Writer's Club encompasses message boards for fiction, non-fiction, romance, poetry, screenwriting, editing/indexing, and the National Writers Union, as well as the Club News and Updates message board. You'll find information, conversation, and motivation for any type of writing!

Looking for a short story to read? Would you like a critique of your work? Check out the Writer's Club Fiction and Nonfiction libraries.

Weekly chat sessions offer free advice and support for: Travel, News, Magazine, Children's, Novel, Dark Fiction/Horror, SciFi, Mystery, Poetry, Technical, and Business writers. This is not the definitive list, so be sure to look for your favorite topic.

Where

Clubs & Interests

Writers

Keyword

Writers

On the Newsstand

Dozens of magazines and newspapers are available at AOL's Newsstand icon. They cover current and political events, sports, computing, automobiles, science, and money. Columnists and Me-

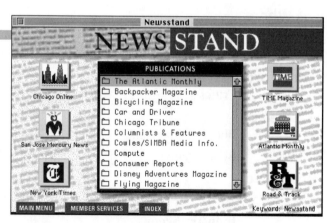

dia Information can also be accessed from this screen. Here is a partial list of just the current offerings on the Newsstand!

The Atlantic Monthly
Backpacker Magazine
Bicycling Magazine
Boating
Car and Driver
Chicago Tribune
Christianity Online
Columnists & Features
Compute
Connect
Cowles/SIMBA Media Info.
Consumer Reports
Cycle World
Disney Adventures Magazine
FamilyPC Online
Flying Magazine
Home Magazine
Home Office Computing
HomePC
Longevity Online
MacHome Journal
MacTech Magazine

Macworld
Military City Newsroom
Mobile Office
National Geographic
The New Republic
Omni Magazine
PC World
PC Novice/PC Today
Popular Photography
Road & Track
San Jose Mercury News
Saturday Review Online
Scientific American
Smithsonian Publications
Stereo Review
TIME Magazine
@times/The New York Times
Windows Magazine
Wired Magazine
Woman's Day
Worth Magazine

THE ATLANTIC MONTHLY ONLINE

At *The Atlantic Monthly Online* you can read current articles from the magazine, check out special features available only online, send letters to the editor, participate in live conferences with *Atlantic* editors and contributors, download transcripts of past conferences, and engage other readers and the editors in lively and thoughtful message-board discussions.

Articles appear online on the day the magazine hits the newsstand—usually between the 22nd and 27th of the month. The only articles from the magazine that you will not find online are those for which *The Atlantic Monthly* does not have the author's permission to post (typically one or two articles per issue). No article is ever abridged for online consumption. Because of technical constraints, longer articles are split into multiple parts.

The Atlantic Monthly brings to this endeavor more than a century's worth of experience in publishing a general-interest magazine—and next to no experience in producing an online room. So consider this a work in progress; they welcome your feedback.

An *Atlantic Monthly* Tidbit
How many submissions does the magazine receive each year?
75,000 poems
12,000 short stories
60,000 non-fiction manuscripts and queries

Where

Newsstand

Atlantic Monthly

Keyword

Atlantic

SATURDAY REVIEW ONLINE

Saturday Review returned to publication as an online magazine in the same great tradition of the former print version. Art and culture are among the central themes. To expand the boundaries of online publications, and encourage interaction and participation, *Saturday Review* provides areas for users to submit listings of events in their own region, to comment on recent books and movies, to offer topics for debate or discussion, and more.

As a budding or fully blossomed author, you are encouraged to submit a review of your favorite book. *Saturday Review* will consider publishing it here. Although no payment is offered, you'll get a byline. Send a message to *SatRev* E-mail if you are interested.

Where

Newsstand

Saturday Review

Keyword

Saturday

TIME ONLINE

TIME Online, the electronic, interactive version of *TIME* magazine, is an experiment in which the world's oldest and largest newsmagazine plugs into the world's newest and fastest-growing medium.

The text of the current issue appears online each Sunday by 4 p.m., Eastern time. The text of the stories that appear in *TIME*'s international editions (but are not available in the U.S.) appear each Wednesday.

It is inevitable that something newsworthy happens after *TIME* goes to press, and the stories detailing these events cannot be included. As a bonus to *TIME Online* readers, some of these stories appear every week here at the end of the current issue, but only in *TIME Online*.

Daily news is provided through TIME Daily, an exclusive new service of *TIME Online*. The Daily goes online every weekday (except holidays) at 8:00 p.m. Eastern time.

You can also find domestic covers and other artwork in the *TIME* archives.

Where

Newsstand

TIME Online

Keyword

Time

Expand Your Magazine Search on the Internet

Hundreds of magazines on the Electronic Newsstand can easily be accessed through America Online's Internet Connect.

Mini-Navigation Notes:

   Keyword: Gopher

   Select: Literature

The Online Bookstore

No time to get to the bookstore? If you've got time to go online, you can have books on your doorstep within five business days.

The Online Bookstore, run by Read USA, Inc., offers current computer and general interest books, at discount prices. Computer books are discounted 18 to 20 percent off list prices, and general interest books are discounted 15 percent off list prices. Books that are specially requested are sold at a 10 percent discount. As an added bonus, America Online members get an additional 5 percent off the discounted prices.

The books and categories are easy to review, and the Search for Books option can help you search for specific titles, topics, authors, or publishers.

Orders are shipped within two business days, usually arriving to you within five business days. If the order cannot be filled for whatever reason, you will be notified immediately. Shipping is through UPS or the U.S. Postal Service.

Where

Marketplace

Online Bookstore

Keyword

Bookstore

Save Money on All Your Favorite Titles

All of the chain bookstores are offering special discounts to their preferred customers who purchase a preferred buyer card. Well, Stacey's does them one better. Their preferred buyer program, Literary License, is free. Use of your Literary License registration number not only saves you the usual 25 percent off the cover price of *San Francisco Chronicle* hardcover fiction and non-fiction bestsellers, but it also takes 10 percent off all your other purchases (except where noted). In addition, registered Literary License holders receive a newsletter and special interests updates. To request a Literary License, simply send your name and address through the Orders/Inquiries screen.

Where

Newsstand

San Jose Mercury News

Keyword

Mercury

Select

Advertising

Mercury Mall

Stacey's Bookstores

Orders/Inquiries

Register and complete the order screen

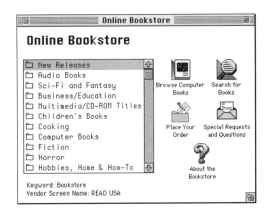

Classic School Project?

If you're looking for a classic, say something by Hemingway, Dickens, or Steinbeck, use the message screens within Stacey's and the Online Bookstore to see if the title you need is available. Stacey's screen is noted as Order/Inquiries, while the Online Bookstore screen is Special Requests and Questions. Then, use Barrons Booknotes (Keyword: Barrons) for the booknotes on the classic. There's more than one way to get your homework done online.

Literary Resources

Are you searching for just the right quotation for your next report? Perhaps you need a thought of the day to inspire your best work. I've found a selection of quote programs that fit the bill.

Quotable Quotes 3.0

This upgraded stack has 1,200 hand-picked quotes—a significant undertaking by the author. The quotes are divided into seven parts, each with its own design, font, and clip art. Features include a Quotes menu, access fields to see quotations within a part, and a more user-friendly AuthorIndex. Topics include: art, books, computing, cooking, definitions, eating, film, humor, love, music, philosophy, women, and writing. It's an interesting and amusing collection. Of course, I've tried it.

Subj:	Quotable Quotes 3.0
Date:	November 25, 1992
From:	RobinSeer
File:	Quotable Quotes 3.0.sea (288205 bytes)
DL time:	< 7 minutes
Author:	RobinSeer
Needs:	Mac, HyperCard 2.x

Where

Bypass Computing and get to the Free Stuff faster with Keywords.

Keyword

File Search

Select

>Quotes or Quotations

Download

Quotable Quotes 3.0

Meaningful Quotations

A cup of coffee, a bagel, and how about a quote to start your day? In 1980, Leroy Syrop, a chemist, businessman, and philospher, published *Meaningful to Me*, a composite of his favorite quotations. These quotations, by authors, philosophers, and others, are included in this program. Follow the author's directions to have a randomly chosen quote appear on your screen upon startup.

Subj: MEANING: Meaningful Quotations
Date: June 30, 1994
From: Jump Shoes
File: MEANING.ZIP (58359 bytes)
DL time: < 1 minute
Author: Jump Shoes
Needs: PC, UnZIPing program
Type: Freely Distributed

Where

Computing

Keyword

File Search

Select

>Meaningful quotes

Download

MEANING: Meaningful Quotations

Daily Quotes

Quote for the Day is great if you like to introduce a piece of writing with a quote, or if you simply enjoy spending an hour leafing through a book of quotes—to see who said what on a subject. Using this program, you can pop up a quote for 10 seconds when you start Windows, display it on the screen during your entire session, or run it minimized for instant inspiration. The program has hundreds of quotes, and lets you search for a quote based on author and/or subject.

Subj: QUOTE.ZIP: Daily Quotes
Date: April 18, 1993
From: Susan G
File: quote.zip (62246 bytes)
DL time: < 1 minute
Author: Thomas Tuerke
Needs: Windows
Price: $8

Where

The complete sequence of steps through Computing can be found on page 15. Of course, you can save time and money by using the Keyword shortcuts.

Keyword

File Search

Select

>Daily quotes

Download

QUOTE.ZIP: Daily Quotes

Shakespeare Glossary

Here's the complete ASCII text file of a glossary of terms having to do with Shakespeare. This will help students and teachers alike in understanding the vocabulary in the works of William Shakespeare. This glossary was originally posted on the Internet at archive site oes.orst.edu.

File: Shakespeare Glossary.sea (42581 bytes)
Date: March 23, 1993
DL time: < 1 minute
Author: Moby Lexical Tools
Needs: Mac, text reader

Where

The complete sequence of steps through Computing can be found on page 15. Of course, you can save time and money by using the Keyword shortcuts.

Keyword

Mac: File Search

PC: Mac Software

Select

Shakespeare Glossary

Download

Shakespeare Glossary.sea

Magazine Tracker

Voracious readers tend to be messy filers. If this description fits you, then read on. This magazine tracker is a menu-driven program that allows you to set up a specialized database to catalog journals or magazines. You can set up to 15 different classifications of magazines and up to 15 magazines in each category. You can then enter the month of publication, page number, and a statement about the article that you want to reference. Later, you can search the database for specific articles. The program is easy to use, and with a little experimentation you can set up the best database for your interests.

Subj: Keep Track of Magazine Articles
Date: August 19, 1990
From: PC BobL
File: MAGAZINE.ZIP (41582 bytes)
DL time: < 1 minute
Author: Mike Keeney
Needs: PKUNZIP
Type: Shareware

Where

The complete sequence of steps through Computing can be found on page 15. Of course, you can save time and money by using the Keyword shortcuts.

Keyword

File Search

Select

magazines and articles

Download

Keep Track of Magazine Articles

Dictionary and Thesaurus

Quicker than a hop, skip, and a jump—look here to find a dictionary and the-saurus that are available through the Internet Gateway. The *American English Dictionary* and *Roget's Thesaurus* are just waiting for you to arrive with a query.

Where

Internet Connection

Gopher & WAIS Databases

Keyword

Gopher

Select

Reference

American English Dictionary

Roget's Thesaurus

Type a word and wait for the definition and pronunciation.

You can also find the Webster's *Dictionary of Computer Terms* in the Reference department.

Where to Find More Goodies

Press the Keyword function (Ctrl+K or ⌘+K on a Mac), type *magazine*, and click on Search. Over 70 magazine references will pop up before your eyes. You can also try the Search function on the Keywords Books or Book Reviews.

Stop in at Members Helping Members (MHM) and leave a message in the Where on AOL Do I Find... icon. Mention what you are looking for and check back in a couple of days for a response. MHM is free (Keyword: MHM).

FREE $TUFF

Work is the greatest thing in the world, so we should always save some of it for tomorrow.

Don Herold

Business: A Fact-Finding Mission

The line between work and play blurs on America Online. You may log on to leave a message in the parenting area to ask a question about how to make play dough, and before you know it, you've jumped to Hoover's Company Profiles and searched the database for the trademarked modeling compound, Play-Doh. Suddenly, Hasbro, Inc. pops up on the screen and you find yourself counting the number of execs making in excess of $500,000 per year. Let's just say *s-e-v-e-r-a-l.* Apparently Hasbro is doing something right—your flour, water, and oil recipe is unlikely to do them great harm. Back to Hoover's to consider more great business opportunities . . . .

Hoover's Company Profiles

The Hoover's Company Profiles database was created and is maintained by The Reference Press, Inc., of Austin, Texas. The Reference Press is the leading provider of high-quality, reasonably priced company information to the mass market. This database was designed to provide accessible, lively, and interesting-to-read information about the companies that affect our daily lives. The Hoover's Company Profiles database includes profiles of approximately 1,100 of the largest, most influential, and fastest growing public and private companies in the U.S. and the world. An average rate of 150 companies are added per quarter. Additional companies will continue to be added to the Hoover's Company Profiles database on an ongoing basis. All company profiles are updated annually and, in a few cases, more frequently.

You can extract competitive information, new business opportunities, and personal investment stock selections from Hoover's Company Profiles. For example, as an investor or potential investor, you can use these profiles for your portfolio. Small businesses can also use the profiles to research their larger competitors. Perhaps your company is considering developing a product to

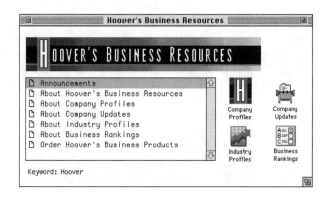

sell to a major retailer—these profiles can be the place you begin your research on whether the product will be profitable.

Where

Personal Finance

Hoover's Company Profiles

Keyword

Hoover

Select

Company Profiles

Industry Profiles

Search

Company Name

Industry

The International Corporate Forum

Each corporation participating in The International Corporate Forum Online Conference has submitted prepared corporate remarks and background information. Read these remarks by double-clicking on the The Prepared Remarks button. Once you have read through the presentations and would like to ask some questions, select Submit Questions.

Participants include The Money Store, SPSS, Inc., Horizon Healthcare Corp., QMS, Inc., US West, Inc., Pacific Telesis Group, Reinsurance Group of America, and Human Genome Sciences, Inc.

For each conference there is a two-week period (once the prepared remarks are online) in which you can ask questions. At the end of the two weeks, the Forum staff screens the questions and chooses a list consisting of 15 questions for each participating company. The screening process will ensure that there are no duplications, that all questions are investment related, and that they are of interest to a large number of investors. Due to time constraints, not every question submitted will be answered. However, the chosen questions and answers will be published for everyone's viewing during the weeks (dates are available in either the Annual Conference folder or by clicking on the Conference Schedule button) of the physical presentations made by the corporations.

Where

Personal Finance

International Corporate Forum

Keyword

ICF

Select

Submit Questions

Receive Answers

Commerce Business Daily

The United States federal government purchases over $450 million worth of products and services each year. Wouldn't you like to know what this money buys? The United States Department of Commerce and the United States Government Printing Office are responsible for publishing the *Commerce Business Daily* (CBD), a daily list of U.S. Government synopses of proposed contract actions that exceed $25,000 in value.

The CBD lists notices of proposed government procurement actions, contract awards, sales of government property, and other procurement information. Each edition contains approximately 500-1000 notices and each notice appears only once. A new edition of the CBD is issued by the Government Printing Office every business day. Federal Information News & Dispatch, Inc., provides the CBD in electronic format, the day before publication is printed and mailed by the Government Printing Office.

This is a terrific resource for anyone with a product or service to sell to the federal government. The CBD online is packed with timely and concise facts to act on.

Where

Personal Finance

Microsoft Small Business Center

Commerce Business Daily

Keyword

CBD

Select

Readers Guide to C.B.D

C.B.D. Services Listing

C.B.D. Supplies Listing

Microsoft Small Business Center

Microsoft and America Online, working together with more than 20 companies and associations serving the small business market, have created the Microsoft Small Business Center. The Small Business Center was created as a place where small business owners, or people considering starting a small business, can find information and help on a wide variety of subjects:

- Articles on subjects like exporting, finance, and marketing from organizations like the U.S. Small Business Administration, the U.S. Chamber of Commerce, the National Federation of Independent Business (NFIB), Dun & Bradstreet, *Inc. Magazine*, and many others

- Small business seminars offered by the American Management Association and others

- Downloadable software templates and programs that you can use in your business

- Real-time, personalized help for your small business from the Service Corps of Retired Executives (SCORE); SCORE counselors are online and ready to help you with questions and issues every Wednesday night from 7-11 PM (EST), or leave messages for them in the message board area

Where

Personal Finance

Microsoft Small Business Center

Keyword

MSBC

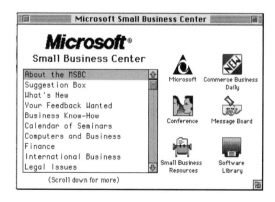

Small Business Resources

The Microsoft Small Business Center's Small Business Resources Directory includes fact sheets and contact information on over two dozen sources, including American Institute for Small Business, *Nation's Business*, National Federation of Independent Business, and the Small Business Administration.

Where

Personal Finance

Microsoft Small Business Center

Keyword

MSBC

Select

Small Business Resources

Guerrilla Marketing

Jay Conrad Levinson presents a system for creating a guerrilla marketing strategy for any business, along with an example of such a strategy. This strategy paper is based upon the best-selling marketing book in the world, *Guerrilla Marketing*, and oriented to the small business owner. Especially created for readers of online business strategy columns, Mr. Levinson regularly uploads files for AOL members.

Subj: Guerrilla Marketing Strategy
Date: September 9, 1994
From: JAYVIEW
File: GM Online Column 5 (5019 bytes)
DL time: < 1 minute
Author: Jay Conrad Levinson
Needs: Any computer, Text reader

Where

Personal Finance

Microsoft Small Business Center

Keyword

MSBC

Select

Software Library

Strategies for Business

Download

Guerrilla Marketing Strategy

Creating a Business Plan

Have a great business idea, but don't know how to implement your idea in writing? This document tells how to write a business plan that will form a strong foundation for your small business. It contains examples and simple how-to instructions for writing your business plan. When you meet with bankers or potential investors, you had better have a well-thought-out business plan in your briefcase. What briefcase?

Date: June 25, 1994
File: 3503.TXT (21516 bytes)
DL time: < 1 minute
Author: Jim Sitton
Needs: Text reader

Where

Personal Finance

Microsoft Small Business Center

Keyword

MSBC

Select

Software Library

Strategies for Business

Download

Creating a Business Plan

 For more business plans and software use Keywords: File Search, PC Software, and Mac Software to search the available files. Enter *business plan* in the word search line.

Advertising Tips to Use Today

Children and sex appeal sell everything, right? To find the real deal in advertising, check out this report, which contains the five secrets to writing great ads and sales letters. Although simple, these concepts are very powerful. Start using these ideas in your advertising and you will see your ad responses increase by up to 500 percent or more. Ensure success—follow these guidelines with every ad campaign.

Date: June 15, 1994
File: ADSECRET.TXT (6898 bytes)
DL time: < 1 minute

Author: Ron Ruiz
Needs: Text reader

Where

Personal Finance

Microsoft Small Business Center

Keyword

MSBC

Select

Software Library

Strategies for Business

Download

5 Secrets to Writing Great Ads

SIC Codes

Do you need an at-your-fingers collection of SIC codes? You can count on finding one online in the Microsoft Small Business Center! This file has listings for most, if not all, the four, six, and eight numbered SIC and Dun codes. You will find this area a great tool for searching categories of businesses to make decisions on buying mailing lists, search census data, and other business uses.

Date: April 28, 1994
File: SICcodes.sit (58393 bytes)
DL time: < 1 minute
Author: Scott Chandler
Needs: Any computer, StuffIt, a database that can import tab fields

Where

Personal Finance

Microsoft Small Business Center

Keyword

MSBC

Select

Software Library

Mac Business Library

Download

SIC codes

Take Me to Your Leader

Take a peek at these files to find directories of executives in eight different categories, including telecommunications and computer companies, and marketing and sales executives. These directories are free when you download them from AOL. These directions will also lead you to a fax directory.

Where

Personal Finance

Microsoft Small Business Center

Keyword

MSBC

Select

Software Library

>Strategies for Business (or)

>Mac Business Library (or)

>PC Business Library

Download

Telecommunications Companies

Computer Companies Directory

Marketing & Sales Executives Dir.

and more!

Writing with Power

Review this article from *The Entrepreneur's Notebook, Ideas That Work*, edited by Mark S.A. Smith to discover the powerful world of written communication. Success begins with words.

Subj:	How To Write With Power
Date:	August 20 ,1994
From:	FKangas
File:	ArtWrite (5045 bytes)
DL time:	< 1 minute
Author:	Mark S.A. Smith
Needs:	Any computer

Where

Newsstand

San Jose Mercury News

Keyword

Mercury

Select

Business

Small Business

Software Library

Download

How ToWrite With Power

WordPerfect Macintosh FAQs

AOL's Industry Connection enables AOL users to connect with dozens of software publishers and computer suppliers to stay on the cutting edge of this technology. The companies involved in the Industry Connection use their online presences to provide customer support and service. WordPerfect offers several support options and perhaps the best are the collections FAQs. WordPerfect has compiled collections of questions and answers most often addressed by WordPerfect's Macintosh support personnel. Templates, file conversions, recommended books, import filters, installation, defaults, and many more concerns are involved. Don't be puzzled, don't pull your hair out—check the FAQ!

Subj: WordPerfect FAQ [date]
From: WP Chuck
File: FAQ 5-24-94.sit (5236 bytes)
DL time: < 1 minute
Author: WordPerfect Corporation
Needs: Mac, WordPerfect, Text reader

Where

Computing

Industry Connection

Business

WordPerfect Corporation

Keyword
>WordPerfect

Select
>WordPerfect Technical Support
>
>Software Libraries
>
>WordPerfect Help & Info Files

Download
>WordPerfect FAQ [date]

Microsoft Knowledge Base

The Microsoft Knowledge Base search system allows you to search all the documents on Microsoft products for a title, word, or set of words that you specify. This little gem gives you the ability to quickly locate specific articles from over 18,000 articles now available. You'll find information on the full range of Microsoft products here, at your fingertips. Updated documentation, specific compatibility issues, and the features of upgrades are easily accessible.

Where
>Computing
>
>Industry Connection
>
>Listed Companies
>
>I-M
>
>Microsoft

Keyword
>Microsoft

Select
>Knowledge Base
>
>Search the Knowledge Base

Microsoft and WordPerfect are both recognized as leaders in software publishing. They provide solid support through their online forums. But, they aren't the only firms online. Check the Industry Connection whenever you need software support. It's a terrific, easily accessible resource—and you'll save dozens of productive hours thanks to the dynamic firms online.

Toner Tuner Demo

Toner Tuner, one of the Working Software Printing Utilities, allows you to save toner or ink when making draft
prints by printing drafts in light gray. This utility works with
QuickDraw and PostScript printers, ink jet or laser printers, and it works with
both System 6 and System 7.

This demo works just like the actual utility, but it prints less-than-desirable
information in the center of each "Toner-Tuned" page. This only happens when
you turn Toner Tuner on in the Print dialog box—it won't affect your regular
printouts. Test Toner Tuner on your next draft.

Subj: Toner Tuner demo
Date: January 17, 1994
From: WORKINGSW
File: Toner Tuner Demo 1.0.5.sit (48542 bytes)
DL time: < 1 minute
Author: Working Software, Inc.
Needs: Mac, ability to unStuffIt

Where

Computing

Industry Connection

Business

Working Software

Keyword

Working

Select

Software Library

Download

Toner Tuner Demo

Marketing Morphs

Marketing and desktop publishing have merged, especially in small businesses.
The same person who leads the sales meetings also designs brochures. This
same marketing writer creates the Yellow Pages and the company's marketing
materials. I've collected a few small tools especially for the small business-
based marketing managers out there. (Been there, done that!)

Let Your Fingers Do the Walking

Here's the Clip Art of the famous Yellow Pages walking fingers!

File: YP Logo.cpt (20483 bytes)
DL time: < 1 minute
Author: Bruce Gruen & AT&T
Needs: Postscript-compatible printer

Where

Personal Finance

Microsoft Small Business Center

Keyword

MSBC

Select

Software Library

Mac Business Library

Download

Yellow Pages Clip Art

Desktop Publishing Corner

Do you need a trifold brochure, but you don't have the time to make your own template? Use this handy template that's based on blocks of various styles. The cover is composed of various gray tones with gradated blocks for header and footer emphasis. The interior follows the motif. You'll like the look. Several users have printed (litho) in PMS colors, and now use them as "blanks" in their laser printer. If you're printing sufficient quantity, you can get the price way below those charged by the "canned" paper mail-order houses.

File: DW 3Fold.01.sea (41992 bytes)
Date: September 13, 1994
DL time: < 1 minute
Author: Fred Showker
Needs: Any computer, EPS and/or DTP software

Where

Personal Finance

Microsoft Small Business Center

Keyword

MSBC

Select

Software Library

Mac Business Library

Download

DW 3-Fold Brochure Template

Business Card Power

Get the most out of your business cards. Here's a discussion by designer/publisher Fred Showker on your business card as a marketing agent and an identity builder. Included are tips and tricks on how to plan, design, print, and use your powerful business partner, the business card! Read the *Electronic Journal for Design, Type & Graphics* (discussed later in this section) for more ideas, and actual award-winning business card templates.

Subj: Business Card Power
Date: August 21, 1994
From: AFA Shwkr
File: BizCard.tx (9232 bytes)
DL time: < 1 minute
Author: Fred Showker DesignWorks
Needs: Text reader

Where

Personal Finance

Microsoft Small Business Center

Keyword

MSBC

Select

Software Library

Strategies for Business

Download

Business Card Power

PR Kit

PR Kit is a shareware program designed to help the small and home-based business strengthen its marketing efforts through the use of do-it-yourself, free and low-cost public-relations activities. PR Kit gives ideas and advice and includes sample materials that can be modified and used. The program files come in both text and Windows Write 3.1 format.

Subj: DOS: PR Kit (for WIN users too)
Date: March 12, 1994
From: GPlummer
File: PRKIT.ZIP (34129 bytes)
DL time: < 1 minute
Author: Gary Plummer
Needs: PKUNZIP, Windows or DOS text reader

With an UnZIP program, Mac users can read this as well.

Where

Personal Finance

Microsoft Small Business Center

Keyword

MSBC

Select

Software Library

Sales & Marketing

Download

DOS: PR Kit (for WIN users too)

Cowles/SIMBA Media Information Network

The Cowles/SIMBA Media Information Network is here to serve the media and information industries with several informative services. You will find the latest industry news in the *Cowles/SIMBA Media Daily* newsletter, back issues of newsletters, user contributions, and a message board that covers virtually every area of media and information. Each daily issue of *Cowles/SIMBA Media*

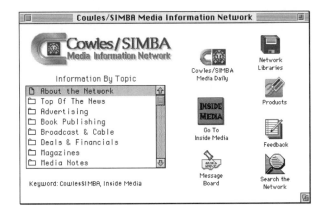

Daily covers the top media and publishing news including TV, cable, and online services, as well as books, magazine, and newspaper publishing. Takeovers, executive moves, rumors, earnings, successes, and losses are also vibrantly covered in *Cowles/SIMBA Media Daily*.

Subj: Cowles/SIMBA Daily [date]
Date: September 15, 1994
From: SIMBA05
File: CSM0915.TXT (14851 bytes)
DL time: < 1 minute
Author: SIMBA
Needs: Text reader

Where

Newsstand

Cowles/SIMBA Information Network

Keyword

SIMBA

Select

Network Libraries

Cowles/SIMBA Media Daily

Download

[selected date]

 The Cowles/SIMBA Network Libraries offer several newsletters including the *Electronic Education Report* and the *Multimedia Business Report*.

Maximum PR Media List

A substantial list of media E-mail addresses has been compiled by Adam Gaffin (adamg@world.std.com) and it's available in the Cowles/SIMBA Information Network Libraries on AOL. Every few months the Media List is completely updated.

With this list, you'll have access to newspapers, magazines, radio and TV networks, and publishing houses. *Anchorage Daily News*, *USA Today*, *International Herald Tribune*, *Cornell Daily*, *The Tech* (MIT), *Forbes*, *Glamour*, *Playboy*, C-SPAN, NBC, National Public Radio, Radio Havana, *UnixWorld*, and *The Small Business Gazette*, all can be reached with this definitive listing!

Subj: Media List [date]
From: Simba02

File: MLIST814.TXT (35723 bytes)
DL time: < 1 minute
Author: Adam Gaffin
Needs: Text reader

Where

Newsstand

Cowles/SIMBA Information Network

Keyword

SIMBA

Select

Network Libraries

User Library

Download

Media List

Newsletter Library

The best central depository for online newsletters is your hard drive. Select some favorites, as I have, and check monthly for updates. Newsletters are a terrific way to stay current and learn new methods to perform your job even more successfully. The newsletters I've selected are both creative and packed with powerful ideas.

Digital Artists Newsletter

DAETA, a free, full-color newsletter published by Summerhouse Consulting for digital artists and desktop-publishing professionals is here! This is a very attractive package and desktop publishers will want the facts behind the newsletter production as soon as they see it. DAETA provides tips and tricks for color separation, printing, and computerese to digital artists and designers who don't have time to become systems analysts. Please reply by E-mail to Summerhouse if you are interested in a direct subscription to your AOL mailbox.

Subj: Digital Artists Newsletter APPL
Date: August 15, 1994
From: Summerhouse
File: DAETA.sit (429668 bytes)
DL time: < 11 minutes
Author: Summerhouse Consulting
Needs: Mac, System 7.x, 256 color monitor

Where
> Computing

Keyword
> Mac Software

Select
> Graphics Forum
>
> Software Search
>
> >Printing

Download
> Digital Artists Newsletter APPL

ELECTRONIC JOURNAL OF DESIGN, TYPE & GRAPHICS

> *DT&G, The Electronic Journal of Design, Type & Graphics*, is a DocMaker stand-alone file that's been formatted into a very readable newsletter. The tips are terrific reminders and lessons for desktop publishers and graphic designers. Paper, press releases, publicity, and other promotions are featured. Don't miss the valuable coupons in each issue.

> You can locate other *DT&G* issues by using the Keywords QuickFind or Mac Software, and then searching for DT&G. Paper & Press Releases edition includes over $100 in coupons.

> *Subj:*   DT&G: Paper & Press Releases
> *Date:*   August 26, 1994
> *From:*   AFA Shwkr
> *File:*   DT&G2.7.sit (134481 bytes)
> *DL time:* < 3 minutes
> *Author:*   Fred Showker, DesignWorks
> *Needs:*   Mac, Color, ATM, Helvetica, and Times Helpful

Where
> Personal Finance
>
> Microsoft Small Business Center

Keyword
> MSBC

Select
> Software Library
>
> Mac Business Library

Download
> DT&G: Paper & Press Releases

HomeBiz Newsletter

The HomeBiz Network provides you with weekly newsletters that are jam-packed with scores of valuable and useful tips for small business owners. For instance, take a look at issue #32, which highlights the guests and topics from NET's *Home Business* TV show for the week of September 5-9, 1994. You'll also find such helpful information as "Do's and Don'ts of Trade Show Booths," "$mart Marketing Research," and "Marketing your Crafts."

Subj: HomeBiz Newsletter #32
Date: September 12, 1994
From: HomeBizNET
File: NEWS#32.WPS (8083 bytes)
DL time: < 1 minute
Author: Merlyn Reineke
Needs: Text reader

Where

Personal Finance

Microsoft Small Business Center

Keyword

MSBC

Select

Software Library

Strategies for Business

Download

HomeBiz Newsletter #32

The Newsletter Business—Mac or ASCII

This is a self-standing, color, electronic newsletter published by members of the America Online newsletter community. Here you will find tips, ideas, and advice about the tricky industry known as the newsletter business. After you read it, why not join the groups in The Microsoft Small Business Center area for Newsletter publishers. This is a quick download full of hard to find information, including association addresses and book reviews. There are two versions available to accommodate both PC and Mac users.

Subj: The Newsletter Business
Date: April 19, 1994
From: Holden7831
File: Chronicle #1_.sit (36843 bytes)

DL time: < 1 minute
Author: Holden7831
Needs: Any computer, text reader

Where

Newsstand

Cowles/SIMBA Media Information Network

Keyword

SIMBA

Select

Network Libraries

User Library

Download

The Newsletter Business

ONLINE MARKETING LETTER

This download is the complete text of Issue # 4 of *The Online Marketing Letter* published by Jonathan Mizel, entitled: "How To Create Direct-Mail Pieces So Powerful, You'll Almost Be Afraid To Use Them." Basically, the subject discusses how to fine tune your direct-mail campaigns with online testing techniques, as well as provides information on proper forum posting (to generate the maximum possible publicity). Get the most from your online marketing. *The Online Marketing Letter* is published eight times a year.

Subj: Online Marketing Newsletter #4
Date: September 9, 1994
From: JMizel
File: INTERNT4.TXT (14000 bytes)
DL time: < 1 minute
Author: Jonathan G. Mizel
Needs: Any computer

Where

Personal Finance

Microsoft Small Business Center

Keyword

MSBC

Select

Software Library

Strategies for Business

Download

Online Marketing Newsletter

Printing Guide

If you haven't discovered it yet, printers and graphic designers speak their own language. Unfortunately, if you want to communicate effectively with these professionals, you will have to learn their language. As a business person who deals with printing purchases, failure to learn this language will eventually cost you time and money. The file's author has assembled a dictionary of commonly used printing terms. Terms like blue line, color separation, dot gain, emulsion, halftones, match prints, PMS, service bureau, and many more are well explained. Learn them. Use them. Pay for the printing that you wanted, not whatever gets handed to you.

Subj: Guide to printing
Date: September 1, 1994
From: LDMedia
File: Guide to printing.sit (3892 bytes)
DL time: < 1 minute
Author: LDMedia
Needs: Text reader

Where

Personal Finance

Microsoft Small Business Center

Keyword

MSBC

Select

Software Library

Strategies for Business

Download

Guide to printing

Print Shop Graphics Galore

Look here to find dozens of business graphics for Print Shop, including: Graph, Stamp, U.S. MailboxVisa Card, MasterCard, Gold Bars, Oil Well, Commodities, Stock, Pie Chart, Contract, Diploma, 1040 Form, Urgent, Stamp Pad, Computer, Microscope, Judge, Rush, Presentation, Podium, Board Meeting,

Business Man and Woman, OutBasket, Broken Pencil, Hand Truck, Delivery Boy, Inaugural, Dollar, Checkbook, and American Express. Perhaps the gold bars, stocks, and commodities clip art could add a special something to the annoucement that the company president was indicted last evening on stock fraud charges?

Subj: NPS: 60... Business Clip Art
Date: May 8, 1991
From: MikeO10
File: PSBIZNEZ.ZIP (17193 bytes)
DL time: < 1 minute
Author: Unknown
Needs: UnZIPing program, New PrintShop or a PS Converter

Where

The complete sequence of steps through Computing can be found on page 15. Of course, you can save time and money by using the Keyword shortcuts.

Keyword

PC: File Search
Mac: PC Software

Select

File Search

>Print Shop Business

Download

NPS: 60... Business Clip Art

ClickArt MacPaint

ClickArt MacPaint files allow you to sample the art selections found in T/Maker's eight portfolios: Business Cartoons, Business Images, Christian Images, Events & Holiday Cartoons, Holidays, Newsletter Cartoons, Personal Graphics, and Publications. The downloadable file contains two to four images from each of T/Maker's award-winning series of ClickArt electronic image portfolios.

Subj: ClickArt Samples (MacPaint format)
Date: October 13, 1991
From: TMaker
File: ClickArt(MacPaint).sit (83730 bytes)
DL time: < 2 minutes
Author: T/Maker Company
Needs: Mac, MacPaint-compatible application or DA

Where

Computing

Industry Connection

Keyword

Industry Connection

Select

Listed Companies

S-Z

T/Maker

Software Libraries

ClickArt Library

Download

ClickArt Samples (MacPaint format)

Music Soothes the Savage Executive

All work and no play makes for a very tedious day. With music you can put it all in perspective. These sounds might not say "business" to you, but at least they've got a pseudo-business theme.

Taking Care of Business

Do you need celebration music? Something to announce successes? A sound bite from Bachman-Turner Overdrive's song "Taking Care of Business" can be found in the PC software library. I think it would be fun to play it each day when you return from lunch—to get charged up for the afternoon's work.

Subj: WAV: BTO: Business
Date: August 28, 1994
From: SR Razor
File: BUSINESS.WAV (226050 bytes)
DL time: < 6 minutes
Author: SR Razor
Needs Any computer, Windows 3.1 or WAV file player

Where

The complete sequence of steps through Computing can be found on page 15. Of course, you can save time and money by using the Keyword shortcuts.

89

Keyword

PC: File Search

Mac: PC Software

Select

> business

Download

WAV: BTO: Business

Money Can't Buy Me Love

When you're considering that stock option plan, employee benefits package, or appraising your employee review, The Beatles' "Money Can't Buy Me Love" could be a good tune—especially for start up and shut down—and *definitely* on Friday afternoons.

Subj: Money Can't Buy Me Love.FSSD
Date: April 4, 1992
From: LiliMrlene
File: MoneyCan'tBuyMeLove.sit (23146 bytes)
DL time: < 1 minute
Author: LiliMrlene
Needs: Mac, Sound Utility or System 7, StuffIt

Where

The complete sequence of steps through Computing can be found on page 15. Of course, you can save time and money by using the Keyword shortcuts.

Keyword

Mac: File Search

PC: Mac Software

Select

[x] Music & Sound

> money music

Download

Money Cant Buy Me Love.FSSD

Great Business Software in the Classifieds!

I don't know why they put it there, but in the Classifieds section, AOL has stashed away some great business and home office shareware. Zip Code Finders,

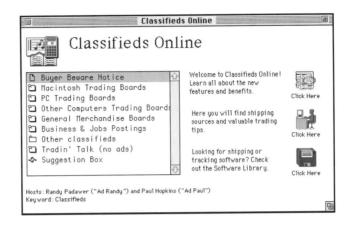

Address Books, Shipping Label Templates, Mailing Lists, and UPS Manifests are among the great and incredibly useful tools to be found here.

Where

Marketplace

Classifieds

Keyword

Classifieds

Select

Software Library

General (or)

Mac/Apple II (or)

Windows/DOS Software Library

Snail-Mail at Its Finest

If you can't send your business correspondence and other materials online, at least you can try some of the following ideas. Each of these is designed to help *you* help the post office or U.P.S. get your mail to its destination just a bit faster—or at least work with your snail-mail carrier a litle more efficiently.

Pony Express Rides Again

Pony Express solves all your mailing questions and automatically calculates mailing prices for all areas of country. Using point of origin and destination ZIP codes, Pony Express will give you a listing of rates for various methods of

mailing your letter or package, including approximate number of days to destination. It allows for COD and insurance costs to be factored as well.

The U.S. Postal Service Rates and Options section includes:

- Express Mail-Post Office to Addressee
- First Class
- Priority Mail
- Third Class
- Fourth Class
- Insurance to $600.00 (registry to $25,000.00)
- COD Fees,
- Intra-BMC Discounts
- Oversize Package Fees
- Return Receipt
- Special Delivery
- Special Handling
- Certified Mail
- Registered Mail

The UPS Rates and Options section includes:

- Next Day Air Letter
- Next Day Air
- 2nd Day Air (except to Alaska)
- Ground Service (commercial and residential)
- Insurance to $25,000.00
- COD Fees
- Oversize Package Fees
- Acknowledgment of Delivery

Obviously, it's packed with what you need for small business shipping.

Subj: DOS: Postal & UPS Rate Calc
Date: February 2, 1994
From: Ad Randy
File: PE150.ZIP (173020 bytes)
DL time: < 4 minutes
Author: Melisco Marketing, Inc.
Needs: PC, MS-DOS, any unZIPing program

Where
Marketplace

Classifieds

Keyword
Classifieds

Select
Software Library

Windows/DOS Software Library

Download
DOS: Postal & UPS Rate Calc

UPS Shipping Costs

Never worry about taking the right amount of cash to the UPS station again. With this handy-dandy program find out the cost to mail your package anywhere in the world. It doesn't include all of the cost comparisons as the program above, but it's worth a look.

Subj:	MAC: UPS Shipping Costs
Date:	February 6, 1994
From:	Ad Paul
File:	UPS Cost! (226660 bytes)
DL time:	< 6 minutes
Needs:	Mac

Where
Marketplace

Classifieds

Keyword
Classifieds

Select
Software Library

Macintosh Library

Download
MAC: UPS Shipping Costs

UPS Zone Finder

This formula in FileMaker Pro was created to automatically give you the UPS Zone once you enter the ZIP code. It was created with a ZIP code of 28405 as the shipping point so you will have to revise the formula according to your shipping point. The ZIP codes, their ranges, and the equation are all here. Simply removing the author's zone and replacing it with yours for each range of ZIP codes will get you the proper code.

Subj: MAC: UPS Zone Finder
Date: February 6, 1994
From: Ad Paul
File: UPS Zip Code Zone (15422 bytes)
DL time: < 1 minute
Author: Jeff Curry
Needs: Mac, FileMaker Pro

If you don't have FileMaker Pro, try the demo in the Claris Library (Keyword: Claris).

Where

Marketplace

Classifieds

Keyword

Classifieds

Select

Software Library

Macintosh Library

Download

MAC: UPS Zone Finder

Zip Your Priority Mail

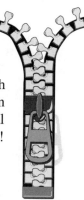

Now you can produce professional-looking priority mail. You get the Priority Mail forms free at your local U.S. Post Office, and with this convenient program you simply run them through a laser printer. The template is all set and you need only type in your return address and the recipient's address for a professional look. At least your postmaster will appreciate the time you spent!

Subj: MAC: Priority Mail Label Template
Date: February 5, 1994
From: Ad Paul
File: USPS Priority Label (3034 bytes)
DL time: < 1 minute
Author: oida
Needs: Mac, PageMaker 4.2+

Where

Marketplace

Classifieds

Keyword

Classifieds

Select

Software Library

Macintosh Library

Download

MAC: Priority Mail Label Template

1994 Area Code Finder

You know the number, but you're not sure of the area code. What are the new area codes for 1994 in Michigan, North Carolina, and Pennsylvania? Do you need a map of area codes or a list of time zones and postal codes?

Subj: AreaCodeFinder 3.1
Date: February 22, 1994
File: AreaCodeFinder 3.1.sea (104099 bytes)
DL time: < 2 minutes
Author: John J. Calande III
Needs: Mac, System 6.07 or better, System 7 compatible

Where

Marketplace

Kim Komando's Komputer Clinic

Keyword

Komando

Select

Komando Libraries

Kool Shareware & Stuff (MAC)

Download

AreaCodeFinder 3.1

Best Address and Phone Demo for Windows

This is a terrific Windows address/phone book. It will even automatically dial your phone using your modem.

This file (phone.exe) is self-extracting and contains a self-displaying graphic of the main screen of the phone book. The actual program costs $15 and will be shipped to you on three high density diskettes.

Subj: WIN: Best Addr/Phone demo
Date: June 20, 1994
From: Charbonn1
File: PHONE.EXE (30145 bytes)
DL time: < 1 minute
Author: Charbonn1
Needs: PC (386+), 4Mb RAM, Windows 3.1

Where

Marketplace

Classifieds

Keyword

Classifieds

Select

Software Library

Windows/DOS Software Library

Download

WIN: Best Addr/Phone demo

Where to Find More Goodies

You will find business information in the most unusual places online. (See the following chart.) Consider the great software that's in the classifieds. Medical offices might check the Better Health and Medical Forum (Keyword: Health), travel agencies may find items of interest in the Travel Department (Keyword: Travel), and each of the major newspapers online has extensive business coverage and archives (Keywords: @times, Chicago, and Mercury).

Area:	Keyword:
Capital Connection	Capital
Massachusetts Forum	Mass
Michigan Forum	Michigan
Utah Forum	Utah
Virginia Forum	Virginia
White House Forum	White House

In *Free $tuff from America Online*, you'll also want to look in *The Law* and the *Personal Finance* sections.

FREE $TUFF

The employer generally gets
the employees he deserves.

Walter Gilbey

Careers
and Jobs

At some point, you may begin wondering if the grass is greener on the other side of the factory. If so, your next career move just might be made online. Career counselors, employment statistics, resumes, and job search databases can all be found on AOL. Read on for potentially lucrative discoveries.

The Career Center

AOL's Career Center is America's premiere electronic career and employment guidance agency. It's the only professional agency you can access from your home or office via your personal computer. The Career Center represents leading-edge technology in the delivery of professional guidance and information 24 hours per day, 7 days per week, straight to your personal computer.

Through the Career Center, you can:

- Access career articles on issues important to your career development
- Display the Appointment Book to schedule a private counseling session with a professional counselor to receive assistance in dealing with your career needs
- Browse the Resume Templates to help you create your own resume
- Access the Cover Letter Library to download a variety of employment letters that you can edit and use in your own job search
- Utilize the Career Guidance Services to complete a series of career guidance exercises or access a database of 13,500+ career options to determine a career direction that's right for you
- Access the Occupational profiles database to obtain information on over 245 occupations, such as duties, entrance qualifications, salary, future employment need, working conditions, and more

Where

Education
Career Center

Keyword

Career

The Talent Bank

The Talent Bank is a searchable database service of the Career Center designed to help AOL members quickly and easily locate other AOL members who possess certain knowledge, skills, or credentials. The Talent Bank has been designed to:

- Provide you with a convenient means of advertising or marketing your knowledge, skills, interests, and credentials to the entire AOL membership
- Help you quickly and easily identify AOL members who have certain interests, expertise, and credentials that you are interested in finding.

The Talent Bank can be helpful if you are interested in securing employment for yourself, or if you are in a position to offer full-time, part-time, temporary, or seasonal employment, a consulting position, a volunteer position, an advisory board member position, or an informational interview opportunity.

Where

Education

Career Center

Keyword

Career

Select

Join the Talent Bank

Search the Talent Bank

What Color Is Your Resume?

The Resume Database is comprised of the resumes of job seekers, but it's a great place for ideas when you're creating your own resume. You'll find general template files for letters and resumes, as well as the resumes of others, for specific positions. It's easy to find resumes that relate to your skills and career path.

Where

Education

Career Center

Keyword

Career

Select

Resume Templates

Chronological-Style Resumes

Functional-Style Resumes

Targeted-Style Resumes

Alternative Resumes

Select the Resume Library to download actual resumes.

Uncle Sam Wants You

Careers with the federal government are no
longer a mystery. Now you can find out what
jobs match your skills and whether Uncle Sam pays
more than Bob's Bike Shop. Using the search function,
you can type a career category or job title and the first list
will show all government agencies that possess those types of positions.

When you select an agency from that list, you'll then review a list of all of the
positions (not openings) within that agency. There's a detailed description of
the mission of the agency followed by the position names, academic degree(s)
required, and Government Service pay step (where appropriate). The report
concludes with the addresses for applicants to contact.

Where

Education

Career Center

Keyword

Career

Select

Federal Employment Service

Search the FES Database

Employer Contacts Database

Finding the names and addresses of employers to contact is a major task re-
quiring hours and hours of research time. But sweat no more. By using the
Employer Contacts database, a collection of profiles of 5,000+ American employers, you can quickly and easily identify companies that match your occupational interests and goals. Employer Contacts is the painless way of finding
potential employers that you can contact.

Research has indicated that the most successful means of finding employment
is by contacting employers directly. So get online and get a job.

Where

Education

Career Center

Keyword

Career

Select
Employer Contacts Database

Search Demand Research

>position and location

Career Counseling

Perhaps the best career value online is the direct contact with career counselors. You can meet privately with an experienced, professional career counselor online (in real time) to discuss your career needs and problems. Counseling is available on an appointment basis—you can sign up for a session by referring to the Appointment Book in the Career Counseling section of the Career Center. If you are experiencing difficulty in selecting a career direction, career counseling is usually recommended after you have completed the *free* Career Focus 2000 program or the non-free Career Analysis Service.

As a freebie seeker, I strongly recommend the Career Focus 2000 program. This service consists of a series of four "workbook" exercises that you can download and complete at your leisure. Career Focus 2000 is designed to guide you in selecting a career direction in line with your personality style, and in developing a plan for reaching your career goal.

Downloading the complete set of four booklets (eight files) will take less than eight minutes with a 9600 baud connection.

Where
Education

Career Center

Keyword
Career

Select
Career Guidance Services

Career Focus 2000

Booklets 1-4

Download
[booklet name]

Career Counseling One-on-One

The Career Center's career counselors can help if you're in need of information or assistance with such issues as: job hunting, career change or selection, substance abuse, self-employment, educational planning, financial aid, career development, and co-worker and/or employer relationships.

Through this area you can receive guidance and counseling from either of two experienced, professional counselors who have counseled thousands of adults and students. James Gonyea or James Meath are available to assist you online via real-time private counseling sessions, by E-mail, or by the bulletin board service.

To speak with either counselor on a private basis, please see the Monthly Schedule and Appointment Book menu items on the Career Counseling menu. If you prefer, you can leave a question for the counselors on the Ask the Counselor bulletin board. They usually respond within 48 hours.

Where

Education

Career Center

Keyword

Career

Select

Career Counseling services

Appointment Book

Select counselor and time—complete message

Occupational Profiles Database

The Occupational Profiles database contains profiles of hundreds of today's most popular occupations. The Occupational Profiles database has been created from information derived from the federal government's *Occupational Outlook Handbook* (OOH). The OOH is an extensive directory of occupational literature developed by a team of occupational statisticians and analysts employed by the U.S. Department of Labor—Bureau of Labor Statistics.

The OOH is published every two years by the federal government, and is considered by many occupational analysts, employment and career counselors, and other professionals who use occupational literature to be one of the most comprehensive, up-to-date, and accurate sources of information about occupations.

You will find detailed profiles on hundreds of the most popular occupations currently found in the American society. The latest edition of the OOH describes about 250 occupations in detail—covering about 107 million jobs, or 87 percent of all jobs in the nation.

Of course I had to look up the Writers and Editors Profile and I am more than happy to share those directions with you. (Psst . . . . You can go straight to the salary information.)

Where

Education

Career Center

Keyword

Career

Select

Occupational Profiles Handbook

Search the Occupational Database

>editor

Read/Save

Writers and Editors

Job Listing Database

The Job Listing database is the central screen for accessing three services designed to help you find employment opportunities and/or new employees for your company. These services include Help Wanted-USA, the E-Span employment database, and a jump to the Classifieds bulletin board.

Where

Education

Career Center

Keyword

Career

Select

Job Listings Database

Help Wanted-USA

Take a look at this database, which contains information on thousands of employment opportunities (help wanted ads) nationwide. On average, you can

expect to find 4,000+ job openings each week! Occupations are professional in nature, cover most career fields, and represent companies nationwide. Employment listings are collected by private consultants in cities nationwide and electronically uploaded to the Career Center. This database is updated weekly, usually late on Tuesday or early Wednesday morning.

Where

Education

Career Center

Keyword

Career

Select

Help Wanted USA

>[position and location]

E-Span Employment Database

This database contains information about employment openings in various career fields from companies nationwide. These business, engineering, health care, and service industry openings are carried by the E-Span service employment services, which advertises positions on behalf of employers. The majority of these listings are unique to E-Span and are not available to the general public. This database is updated every week, usually on Monday.

Where

Education

Career Center

Keyword

Career

Select

Job Listings Database

Search E-Span Database

>[position and location]

Classifieds Online

If you wish to view help wanted ads that other America Online members have posted, or if you wish to post your own help wanted ad, take a peek at the Classifieds bulletin board area in the Marketplace.

Where

Marketplace

Classifieds

Keyword

Classifieds

Select

Business & Job Postings

Professional Salaried Jobs Message Board

Princeton Review/Student Access Online

I can't quote the numbers, but I do know it's becoming more common to change jobs and careers throughout one's lifetime. The first true career job step—the post-college job search—may be the most critical. *Princeton Review* and *Student Access Online* have created a file of articles specifically related to the career planning and job search for college students.

Where

Education

Princeton Review/Student Access Online

Keyword

Student

Select

Internships & Jobs

Read/Save

How to find a Job with the College Job Center

Surviving While You're Looking For a Job

America's Top Internships

Action Verbs for Resumes

When your resume is telling your story, it's your only chance to get it right. Make sure that your resume contains the powerful business-action words that convey your skills and experiences with flair. The AOL participant who has provided this list uses it daily when creating resumes for clients. This file is shareware and contains one list of verbs, but is in seven formats:

- MS Word 5.x
- MS Word 3.x

- RTF interchange format
- Stationery
- Macwrite
- Text
- Text only with line breaks

Subj: AWR Action Verbs for Resumes
Date: July 21, 1994
From: WM HARTZER
File: AWR Action verbs.sea (33398 bytes)
DL time: < 1 minute
Author: Wm Hartzer
Needs: Any text reader or formats noted above
Type: Shareware

Where

Education

Princeton Review/Student Access Online

Keyword

Student

Select

Students' Software

PC Exchange

Download

AWR Action Verbs for Resumes

Kaplan Online

Admission tests are the first step on the road to grad school and a professional degree. Kaplan Online gives you up-to-the-minute information about how to raise your test scores and get into the school of your choice. To explore Kaplan Online, click on the icon that expresses your area of interest.

Where

Education

Kaplan Online

Keyword

Kaplan

Select

GMAT - Business School

GRE - Graduate School

LSAT - Law School

MCAT - Medical School

NCLEX - Nursing

Download

[diagnostic test]

 You'll find more information on *Kaplan Online* and the *Princeton Review* in the *Education* section of this book.

Mercury Resources

The Mercury Center is truly one of AOL's best resources. Section by section throughout this book, I've gravitated to Mercury and made another serendipitous discovery. Job seekers and career changers need up-to-date information and they'll find it in the Mercury Center.

In the Career Articles and Employment folders you'll find statistics on employment trends, tips for success, book reviews, and articles on the changing face of business.

Where

Newsstand

San Jose Mercury News

Keyword

Mercury

Select

Advertising

Employment

Browse Mercury News Employment Articles

You can also browse or search the Employment Classifieds from the Employment screen.

Calling All Pilots, Doctors, Lawyers, and Publishers

Throughout AOL users gather together to share job tips and contacts. In virtually every location you'll find a folder related to a career activity. In the knitting folder, there may be shared stories of contract knitting or starting a shop. In the Better Health and Medical forum, students consider medical career paths and professionals share their knowledge. In the Aviation forum, there are extensive career folders where pilots, mechanics, and support personnel share tips on job openings and the best companies to work for. So find a board that meets your interests and ask away.

- Aviators will want to search the Commercial Aviation Message Board for the Careers folder (Keyword: Aviation).
- Health Professionals will find the Jobs and Relocation Opportunities folder in the Health Professionals Network on the Better Health & Medical forum's Health Message Center (Keyword: Health).
- Lawyers and Paralegals can create a folder on the Legal SIG message board (Keyword: Legal).
- Publishing and media job seekers can access the Jobs Offered and Jobs Wanted folders in the Cowles/SIMBA Media Information Network (Keyword: Cowles).

Careers in Advertising

Here's a brief description of the positions available in an advertising agency and what each person does in that position. *Careers in Advertising* is good for persons thinking of going into the advertising field. If you need additional information, feel free to contact Writer1 by E-Mail.

Subj: Careers in Advertising
Date: February 24, 1990
From: Writer1
File: Careers in Advertising (4241 bytes)
DL time: < 1 minute
Author: Anthony S. Policastro
Needs: Text reader

Where

The complete sequence of steps through Computing can be found on page 15. Of course, you can save time and money by using the Keyword shortcuts.

Keyword

Mac: File Search

PC: Mac Software

Select

> career advertising

Download

Careers in Advertising

Job Hunting for Medical Professionals

A former Army officer is now the president of Horizon Medical Search located in Nashua, New Hampshire. They specialize in the placement of physicians, physician assistants, physical and occupational therapists, and nurse practitioners. Services are provided at no charge to applicants; all fees are paid by the employer. Send E-mail to *HorizonMed* for further information.

E-Mail

HorizonMed

Aviation Resume Address Database

An aviation address database has been uploaded for use by maintenance technicians and pilots. The following files form an address database for mail merge using Word for Windows 6.0. All that is required of you is to create a mail merge cover letter and you're in business. Also included are files for international airlines and international repair stations. Although this database was initially created for maintenance technicians, it can be modified for pilots.

Subj: Aviation Resume Address Database
Date: September 29, 1994
From: JamesC1055
File: AVIALST4.DAT (36352 bytes)
DL time: < 1 minute
Author: James P. Coghill
Needs: Winword 6.0

Where

Clubs & Interests

Aviation Forum

Keyword

Aviation

Select

Software Libraries

DOS/Windows Software

Download

Aviation Resume Address Database

Postal Service Career Test

This is the partial, electronic form of a book that the author wrote in 1991, entitled *Preparation for a $25,000 U.S. Postal Job*. He scored a 100 on the exam using the methods developed and discussed in the book. He then tried to self-publish the guide, but was unsuccessful. Here it is presented as "Prayerware." It's self-extracting and you really do need MS Word to be able to view the tables properly.

Subj:	Post Office Career Tests sea
Date:	September 25, 1993
From:	Kendrake
File:	P.O.Career.Txt (140104 bytes)
DL time:	< 3 minutes
Author:	Ken Cross
Needs:	MS Word

Where

The complete sequence of steps through Computing can be found on page 15. Of course, you can save time and money by using the Keyword shortcuts.

Keyword

Mac: File Search

PC: Mac Software

Select

>postal job

Download

Post Office Career Tests sea

Job Hunt Network

Looking for a job? You will find this very helpful and detailed program a godsend in keeping track of potential openings. Brief instructions are provided. Future updates are a $10 shareware fee, or free to those who provide the feedback requested.

Subj:	Job Hunt Network 1.1
Date:	May 18, 1991

From: Porcari
File: Intro. Job Hunt Network 1.1 (16384 bytes)
DL time: < 1 minute
Author: Pete Gerardini Jr.
Needs: Mac, HyperCard 2.0

Where

The complete sequence of steps through Computing can be found on page 15. Of course, you can save time and money by using the Keyword shortcuts.

Keyword

Mac: File Search

Select

>Job hunt

Download

Job Hunt Network 1.1

Job Search Tracker

For those who'd rather track on paper, this job search form has been designed to keep track of resume mailings, interviews, positions, thank-yous, follow-ups, rejections, and acceptances.

Subj: Job Search Form
Date: May 24, 1992
From: Maura II
File: Job Search Record (40640 bytes)
DL time: < 1 minute
Author: Maura II
Needs: PageMaker 4.0

Where

The complete sequence of steps through Computing can be found on page 15. Of course, you can save time and money by using the Keyword shortcuts.

Keyword

Mac: File Search

PC: Mac Software

Select

>job tracking

Download

Job Search Form

Resume Templates

This StuffIt archive contains twelve professionally-designed resume templates. The templates are for use with PageMaker 5.0 for the Macintosh.

The current headings are Objective, Education, Work Experience, Special Skills, and References. Of course, you may personalize these with such headings as Personal Data, Hobbies and Interests, and Awards and Honors. Also included in this archive is an envelope template. Instructions are included on the template.

These templates are "Employment-ware." If you use one of the enclosed templates *and* get a job with it, please send payment of $15. The author's address is included on the File Description screen along with his Internet address.

Subj: Twelve PM Resume Templates
Date: September 9, 1994
From: AFA Chuck
File: Twelve Resumes.sit (99332 bytes)
DL time: < 2 minutes
Author: LiuDTP
Needs: PageMaker 5.0, AOL 2.x or StuffItExpander

Where

The complete sequence of steps through Computing can be found on page 15. Of course, you can save time and money by using the Keyword shortcuts.

Keyword

Computing

Mac Software

Select

>resume template

Download

Twelve PM Resume Templates

Job Tracking Database

This handy database will help you keep track of the resumes you have sent and when follow-up letters are due. You will also find valuable information on the preparation of a resume, cover letter, and follow-up letter. Still having problems? Simply get some online help.

An envelope printing utility is included as well, but a laser printer (HP compatible) is required for envelope printing.

Subj: JOBTRAK: Job tracking
Date: March 28, 1992
From: DennisB17
File: jobtrak.zip (224972 bytes)
DL time: < 6 minutes
Author: Dennis Betts
Needs: An UnZIPing Program, HP compatible for envelope printing
Type: Shareware

Where

The complete sequence of steps through Computing can be found on page 15. Of course, you can save time and money by using the Keyword shortcuts.

Keyword

File Search

Select

>resume work address

Download

JOBTRAK: Job tracking

Job Search Organizer

JOBS is a program and a group of databases that help you to organize the information necessary to successfully find a job. This system will help you organize and keep track of network contacts, target companies, executive search firms, temporary placement firms, direct mail, telephone logs, and job hunting expenses. Reports are included so you can print the data. JOBS currently runs in dBase III Plus or Foxpro 2.0 or later.

Subj: JOBS: V 2.0 Job Search database
Date: September 9, 1993
From: BobJoeK
File: JOBS.ZIP (88318 bytes)
DL time: < 2 minutes
Author: R.J. Kovach & Assoc.
Needs: An UnZIPing Program, dBase III or FoxPro
Type: Shareware

Where

The complete sequence of steps through Computing can be found on page 15. Of course, you can save time and money by using the Keyword shortcuts.

Keyword

PC: File Search

Mac: PC Software

Select

>Jobs Career Dbase

Download

JOBS: V 2.0 Job Search database

Business Man

Shall we perpetuate a stereotype? If so, you may want to add this seated businessman reading a newspaper to your PostScript or EPS art collection. Depending on your mood, he might be good for your dart board!

Subj: BusinessMan.sit (EPSF)
Date: April 15, 1990
From: Steward
File: BusinessMan.sit (35699 bytes)
DL time: < 1 minute
Author: Bruce Witcher, Jr.
Needs: Any application that uses PostScript

Where

The complete sequence of steps through Computing can be found on page 15. Of course, you can save time and money by using the Keyword shortcuts.

Keyword

Mac: File Search

PC: Mac Software

Select

>businessman

Download

BusinessMan.sit (EPSF)

Take This Job and Shove It

Have some fun on April Fool's Day or use this when you just can't stand your job any longer! Resign your position with this great quit notice. If you have an image-editing program, like PhotoShop, you can put in your own name and reason why you're quitting. This message is a modified Mac dialog box: "The application "X" has unexpectedly quit, because an error of type "Y" has occurred." Put your name in the "X" slot, your reason in the "Y" slot (noises emanating from coworker's cubicle, for instance), and give it to your boss!

Subj: Quit Notice! PICT
Date: September 27, 1994
From: P Ashley
File: quit notice.sit (3986 bytes)
DL time: < 1 minute
Author: Pat Ashley
Needs: PICT viewer and image editing program

Where

The complete sequence of steps through Computing can be found on page 15. Of course, you can save time and money by using the Keyword shortcuts.

Keyword

Mac: File Search

PC: Mac Software

Select

>job quit

Download

Quit Notice! PICT

Where to Find More Goodies

You'll find more goodies that help you to further your position in Corporate America in the *Business* section of this book.

On AOL, within Clubs & Interests, you'll see an icon for Professions & Organizations. Don't miss this opportunity for insider information.

Last, if you're testing the waters for a job hunt, you'll find classified ads in the *San Jose Mercury News*' and the *Chicago Tribune*'s forums.

FREE $TUFF

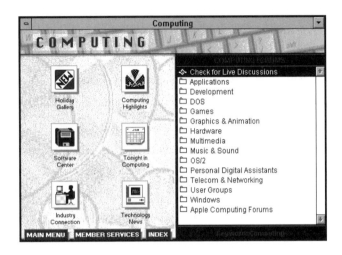

If it keeps up, man will atrophy all his limbs but the push-button finger.

Frank Lloyd Wright

Computer Companions

Filling the computer section of a computer book is a bit of a puzzle. Exactly which pieces should be put together so the result is a cohesive picture?

I've attempted to fill this section with handy and unusual utilities and various programs to show you the variety of shareware available. I've also provided information on many up-to-the-minute newsletters that will keep you abreast of the frequent changes in this fast-paced arena. Since many of us are on our second, third, or fourth computers, I've also included two sources for setting prices on computers for sale.

Virtually every forum has a download library. And, many of the selected programs can be found in several libraries throughout AOL. I've presented the programs that are based in my favorite forums. Some download libraries have tremendous selections of tested programs for your perusal. Not surprisingly, the computer magazines' online libraries top the list. Few can beat the selections found in the forums of *PC World*, *Macworld*, and *Windows Magazine*. However, there is one other forum that possesses a mother lode of great shareware and commercial demos: Kim Komando's Komputer Klinic.

We'll take some side roads through the Industry Connection, but for the most part, that's yours to explore on your own.

Unlike the other sections of this book, which provide directions for cross-platform access to programs, this section provides directions for only one computer platform. There are, however, a few text files that are readable by both Macs and PCs and do not require cross-platform direction.

NACOMEX Used Computer Prices

Time to trade in your Quadra for a Power Mac? Or jumping from a 386 to a Pentium? One of the first things you'll want to do is determine the street price for used Quadras and 386s. The National Computer Exchange, Inc. supplies price reports for the prior week. That's pretty current as used computer prices go. The listing also includes the 800 number for the National Computer Exchange so you can contact them directly for more information.

Where

Marketplace

Kim Komando's Komputer Klinic

Keyword

Komando

Select

Interesting Bits

NACOMEX Used Computer Market/Prices

Read/Save

NACOMEX Used Computer Prices NOTEBOOKS [date]

NACOMEX Used Computer Prices PRINTERS [date]

NACOMEX Used Computer Prices MONITORS [date]

NACOMEX Used Computer Prices MIDRANGE [date]

NACOMEX Used Computer Prices MICROS [date]

AmCoEx Used Prices Index

Need a second opinion? Then check out the American Computer Exchange in AOL's Classifieds forum.

Their publication (upload) schedule is somewhat sporadic, but you'll be able to make valid comparisons. Each price index includes an article on the state of change in the computer industry and average prices on used computer sales. These prices should be regarded only as a guide for your comparisons. You'll find AxExCo's 800 number included in the listings.

Where

Marketplace

Classifieds

Keyword

Classifieds

Select

Shipping Sources & Trading Tips

Read/Save

AmCoEx Used Prices Index [date]

AOL Savings

There's always a better way, right? You already know that AOL's users are an inventive bunch. Your fellow members have developed a number of programs to monitor online time and tools to use that time efficiently.

Take into account that AOL did not sponsor the development of these programs nor do they warrant, support, or endorse these programs. You may still

want to give these fee-savers a try since many of your fellow members have found them helpful.

AOL Time Log

AOL Time Log is a HyperCard stack that enables users to accurately keep track of the time spent on America Online, as well as calculate each month's bill automatically (an extremely useful function if you are accustomed to writing these things down). As the stack is opened, it checks your current billing date and compares it with that on AOL's computers. It then creates a new entry on expiration of this date, or informs you of the current billing date. It also remembers exactly when the log was created, as well as what time each individual entry was placed.

Subj: MAC: AOL Time Log
Date: February 12, 1994
From: Ad Randy
File: AOL Time Log-(Self Extracting) (72390 bytes)
DL time: < 2 minutes
Author: Andrew Taylor (Ataylor69)
Needs: Mac, HyperCard, America Online
Type: Shareware, $10

Where

Marketplace

Keyword

Classified

Select

Software Library

Mac Software Library

Download

MAC: AOL Time Log

TypeIt4Me

Any time you can enter text in your Mac via the keyboard, TypeIt4Me can do it for you—faster and more accurately. You simple enter abbreviated codes, which are then expanded to the words and phrases you've previously set. With the well regarded TypeIt4Me, you can save time online by speeding your writing, including your Chat Room conversations.

Subj: TypeIt4Me 4.2.1
Date: July 5, 1994
From: Komando3
File: TypeIt4Me 4.2.1.sea (105861 bytes)
DL time: < 2 minutes
Author: Riccardo Ettore
Needs: Mac, System 6.07 or better, System 7 compatible

Where

Marketplace

Kim Komando's Komputer Klinic

Keyword

Komando

Select

Komando Libraries

Kool Shareware & Stuff (Mac)

Download

TypeIt4Me 4.2.1

LogSpace

LogSpace is a WAOL add-on that formats session logs so that they are easier to read. Each message is separated, and has a clean, three-line header (Subj: Date: From:). LogSpace supports drag-and-drop from Windows or OS/2 (to start up), or you can run it from a command-line prompt.

Logging saves online time, but often leaves us puzzled by the results. With LogSpace, you'll no longer be puzzled by your log files.

Subj: LOGSPACE: v1.0 WAOL Log Formatter
Date: September 12, 1994
From: Chett1
File: LOGSPACE.ZIP (11978 bytes)
DL time: < 1 minute
Author: Charles Breiling
Needs: WAOL, UnZIPing program
Type: Freely distributed

Where

Computing

PC Software

Keyword

File Search

Select

>WAOL

Download

LOGSPACE: v1.0 WAOL Log Formatter

QuoteClip

QuoteClip is a utility designed to be used primarily by AOL Internet Newsgroup users. It eliminates the nuisance of manually "quoting" (in the Internet sense) original text when you are responding to a newsgroup post. To use this handy utility, select the text to quote from the Newsgroup's read window and then copy it to the Windows Clipboard. Then click on QuoteClip, which runs minimized, select Quote the Clipboard, and paste into the reply window. Your text will appear with each line preceded by a quoting character with the ">" as the default choice. You can remove these characters. Very small, simple, and easy to use...and free! It makes your responses more lucid.

Subj: QUOTECLIP: V1.0 WAOL Usenet Utility
Date: August 13, 1994
From: RussChinoy
File: QCLIP.ZIP (60019 bytes)
DL time: < 1 minute
Author: Russ Chinoy
Needs: PC, UnZIPing program, AOL for Windows
Type: Freely distributed

Where

Computing

PC Software

Keyword

File Search

Select

>WAOL

Download

QUOTECLIP: V1.0 WAOL Usenet Utility

Way To Go!

Way To Go! 2.0 (WTG) is the premier add-on navigator for America Online for Windows. Take a look at the options offered here:

- Contains an offline reader and retriever for E-mail, message boards, and newsgroups
- Provides cumulative time tracking and AOL billing management
  - Track time and money spent online for the current session
  - View logs of session activities, totals, and graphs throughout billing periods
- Provides macro/script language to automate routine tasks
- Manages lists of people (Address Book), online areas, and terms (Dictionary)
- Quickly inserts text into messages, chat rooms, and other areas for signatures or commonly used phrases
- Sends sound commands to AOL chat rooms
- Rapidly locates multiple members online at one time (as fast as 1 per second at 9600 baud)
- Captures and saves to disk selected messages, articles, or other screens on AOL
- Responds to instant messages while spending minimum time in the pay areas
- Enables you to "GoTo" your favorite keywords and areas on AOL
- Allows you to easily quote messages online with >> and << characters
- Turns Instant Messages on or off
- Minimize AOL during a file transfer
- Exits AOL when it doesn't respond to your commands

Subj: WTG 2.0: Navigator,Offline,Macro
Date: October 7, 1994
From: PrismElite
File: WTG20.ZIP (376288 bytes)
DL time: < 10 minutes
Author: Prism Elite Software
Needs: PC, VBRUN300.DLL, WAOL 1.5 or higher

Where

Newsstand

PC World

Keyword

PC World

Select

Software Library

General Utilities

Download

WTG 2.0: Navigator,Offline,Macro

Claris Demos

The Claris FileMaker Pro demos are particularly useful because most features are activated. This is far better than a "demo" that's merely a slide show. Since FileMaker Pro is available for both PC and Mac platforms, we can all try the programs.

FileMaker Pro Fact Sheet/Windows and Macintosh

FileMaker Pro 2.1 is a database system offering power without programming. This fact sheet details target users for the program, key features and benefits, report generation and file-sharing capabilities, system requirements and compatibility, and available customer support.

Where

Computing

Industry Connection
[Choose Claris]

Keyword

Claris

Select

Product Information

Macintosh Products

Windows Products

Read/Save

FileMaker Pro 2.1

FileMaker Pro

Power, sophistication, simplicity. These are the words that describe this package. Whether you're a first-time database buyer or an advanced user, FileMaker Pro makes sure you're productive in minutes.

This FileMaker demo is extremely popular—it's often referenced online—because it's handy to evaluate shareware files with FileMaker. But remember, this is a demo, not the full-blown app. Recipe files are just one example of the FileMaker shareware programs you can sample. Most download files that were created with FileMaker can be tested with this demo.

Subj: TRIAL (FileMaker Pro 2.1v3 Mac)
Date: September 19, 1994
From: Claris Lib

File: FMP 2.1v3 Trial.sea (606507 bytes)
DL time: < 16 minutes
Author: Claris
Needs: Mac, 1 Mb RAM, System 6.0+, 2 Mb for System 7, hard drive

Where

Computing

Industry Connection
[Choose Claris]

Keyword

Claris

Select

Software Libraries

Trail & Demo Software

Download

TRIAL (FileMaker Pro 2.1v3 Mac)

The Windows version is available by using the same directions.

Magazine Library

AOL's Newsstand is a good central location from which to start a search for shareware. In the Newsstand, you'll find a selection of computer titles mixed in with news magazines and other special interest titles. Because of their significant resources and spirit of competition, the magazines have put together top-notch software libraries. I'll introduce a few of the best. After that, the list is yours to explore.

- *Home Office Computing*
- *HomePC*
- *MacHome Journal*
- *MacTech Magazine*
- *Macworld*
- *Mobile Office*
- *PC World*
- *PC Novice/PC Today*
- *Windows Magazine*
- *Wired Magazine*

Within the Resource Center (more on that in a few pages), you'll find additional computer newsletters, book excerpts, and magazines. This list includes magazines found on the Newsstand, plus:

- *Boardwatch*
- Inside Technology
- *Macintosh Bible*
- *Mac Shareware 500*
- Newsbytes
- *Windows Shareware 500*

MACWORLD ONLINE

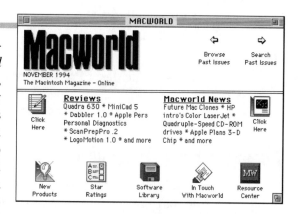

Macworld Online, the electronic source for *Macworld* magazine, includes reviews, news, and columns, but they don't yet put feature articles online. (Hint: They do tell you how to reach the honchos to encourage them to expand the service). *Macworld* is a great place to get answers to all of your hardware and software related questions. And the search function makes it very easy to find the specific information you need to purchase, upgrade, or install.

Many of *Macworld*'s writers and editors visit this area every day and respond to hundreds of messages and inquiries posted by readers. So make sure to post your own thoughts.

Where

Newsstand

Macworld

Keyword

Macworld

PC World Online

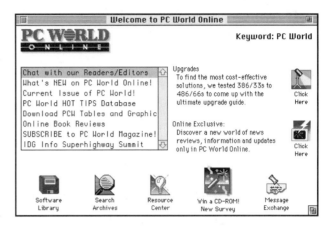

PC World Online, the electronic arm of *PC World* magazine, is designed to give PC users all the benefits of *PC World* magazine, combined with the advantages of electronic communication: speed, ease-of-use, and efficiency. *PC World Online* goes several steps beyond the magazine with features and benefits that can be found only in the online service. For example, you can communicate directly with the editors and post questions about hardware or software that usually receive an immediate response.

You can easily search through back issues for any topic or combination of topics, by simply entering a query such as "modem and fax" into a query box.

Where

Newsstand

Keyword

PC World

Windows Magazine

Windows Magazine's Superior Shareware files correspond to those covered in each printed issue. These programs are the cream of the crop, the finest, most useful, and ingenious Windows shareware currently available.

Each month, a few days before the magazine is distributed, new files are uploaded and initially installed in the New Uploads section of the library. After being showcased for a few days, the files are moved to their permanent home.

You are encouraged to use and enjoy these programs, but don't forget to pay the author his or her requested shareware registration fee if you decide to keep the program.

Where

Newsstand

Windows Magazine

Keyword

WinMag

PC Catalog

Tired of shopping endlessly for the best PC values? Shop no more. PC Catalog features more than 2,000 product listings, spanning networking, microcomputers, and new technology. All of these products are available for purchase directly from 175 manufacturers, distributors, and dealers nationwide. PC Catalog is your number one source for the latest technology and hard-to-find items. Order now by telephone from any of these vendors and save time and money.

You can shop from the online catalog or request that a copy of the printed catalog be mailed to you.

Where

Marketplace

PC Catalog

Keyword

Marketplace

Select

PC Catalog

Free PC Catalog Magazine

>[complete & send]

Microsoft WinNews Electronic Newsletter

New for Windows fans is *WinNews*, Microsoft's electronic newsletter. Perhaps you're curious about the features of the new version of Windows 95 or how it was assigned its original code name Chicago. Look here for such tidbits and for hard-hitting facts.

If you're not a Windows user and you're curious about the newsletter, don't fret. It can be read by any word processor.

Subj: TXT:Vol 1, #2 WinNews Newsletter
Date: September 23, 1994
From: ASaunders
File: V1N2.TXT (16380 bytes)
DL time: < 1 minute
Author: Microsoft Corporation

Needs: Text reader
Type: Freely distributed

Where

Computing

Industry Connection

[Choose Microsoft]

Windows News

Keyword

WinNews

Select

Win News Library

Download

TXT:Vol 1, #2 WinNews Newsletter

Computing Resource Center

The new Resource Center is made up of three Mac-related areas—Resources, Databases, and Publications—each of which includes a variety of services. For example, you can find information on virtual reality, look up computer terms, and read any of a number of online publications. PC users will find

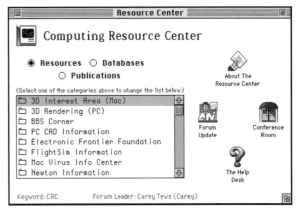

most of the same areas under Technology News on the Computing screen. If you have difficulty, just bypass the Where direction and use the Keywords.

Where (Mac)

Computing

Resource Center

Keyword

CRC

Where (PC)

Computing

Technology News

Keyword

Computing

The Boardwatch Forum

Boardwatch Magazine, published since March 1987, monitors activity among the online databases, commercial online services, and some 92,000 electronic bulletin board systems and online information services operating worldwide, including the Internet.

Each issue of *Boardwatch*, which you can access from any platform, provides various topical bulletin board lists covering specific types of bulletin boards or listings of bulletin boards from a particular geographic area.

Boardwatch also tracks developments in shareware, reviewing utilities and communications software of interest from the 70,000 titles currently in circulation.

Subj: Boardwatch Mag. [date]
Date: October 12, 1994
From: AFC Sarah
File: BW9409.ZIP (225075 bytes)
DL time: < 6 minutes
Editor: Jack Rickard
Needs: AOL software/UnZIP, text reader

Where

Computing

Resource Center

Keyword

Boardwatch

Select

Boardwatch Files & Archives

Download

Boardwatch Magazine [date]

Newsbytes

Newsbytes is a daily, international online newswire, providing independent computer and telecommunications news to an estimated 4.5 million readers on major online networks, magazines, newspapers, and newsletters, worldwide.

Like other major wire services, Newsbytes accepts no advertising. Reports are compiled by professional, staff journalists who adhere to the highest editorial standards. Editorial content is based solely on its news value—Newsbytes does not publish press releases.

Subj: NEWSBYTES [date]
Date: October 13, 1994

From: NewsBytes
File: NB101394 (87767 bytes)
DL time: < 2 minutes
Author: NEWSBYTES

Where

Computing

Resource Center

Publications

Newsbytes

Keyword

Newsbytes

Select

Download Newsbytes

Download

NEWSBYTES [date]

PC Vendors Database

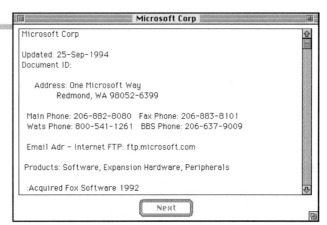

Do you need information straight from the manufacturer? Can't get verifiable information from the guys in the red shirts at the computer superstore? Do you need an address, fax number, 800 number, or Internet address? Do not pass go—go straight to the PC Vendors Database.

Let's pretend you're looking for Microsoft's information . . . .

Where

Computing

Resource Center

Keyword

CRC

Select

Databases

New Product Information

PC Vendors Database

PC Vendors Database (again)

>Microsoft

THE WEIGAND REPORT

The Weigand Report is an international subscription newsletter for Macintosh users. If you use your Macintosh in business, for communications, or for desktop publishing, you need *The Weigand Report*. This newsletter gives you a wealth of hard-hitting, decision-making insights, tightly focused product reviews, valuable industry insights, and time-saving tips and techniques. In the changing world of AOL, as this book is written, you can only get to *The Weigand Report* via the keyword.

Keyword

Weigand

Select

TWR Message Board

List Topics

Sample Issue/Info Requests

[follow E-mail directions]

PC Software

To simplify your search for fun and free software, we'll begin with the PC—Windows- and DOS-based—software and then cover the Mac software.

Atomic Time

This program uses your modem to dial the NIST atomic clock in Boulder, Colorado, and sets your PC's clock to within a second or so of the time signal sent by that clock. This program was mentioned in the October 1994 issue of *PC World* magazine.

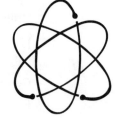

Subj: SetTime v1.1 for Windows
Date: September 19, 1994

From: PCW Dennis
File: SETTM1.ZIP (62976 bytes)
DL time: < 1 minute
Author: PC World Online
Needs: PC, Windows, PKUNZIP

Where

Newsstand

PC World

Keyword

PC World

Select

Software Library

Featured in 1994

Download

SetTime v1.1 for Windows

Andrews Loan Information Manager

For a limited time, Andrews Software Design is giving away 100,000 *free* copies of its Andrews Loan Information Manager 2.0 program (plus a mild $4.95 shipping fee). Use the truly intuitive graphical interface to see how interest and payment frequency affect your loan. Then use the spreadsheet-like amortization table to delve further into the loan figures. You can even write your loan notes and miscellaneous information right on the screen.

If you're not sure it's worth the $4.95, there is a demo in the Komando Libraries, Demonstration Software, Finance. It's a four-minute download at 9600 baud. To get your free copy, send your address to ASoftware on America Online.

Where

Marketplace

Kim Komando's Komputer Klinic

Keyword

Komando

Select

Komando Libraries

Demonstration Software

Finance

Download

Andrews Loan Manager (WIN)

Bill Clinton—with a Hillary Bonus!

This screen saver will display a small cartoon of Bill driving a bulldozer that is "destroying" your Windows screen. If you have a sound card, you can set up the screen saver to play actual audio clips of Bill. A contribution of $5 will register your copy of this program and you will receive a Hillary Clinton screen saver absolutely *free*!

Subj: Clinton Screen Saver (WIN)
Date: August 9, 1994
From: Komando
File: BILTAX.ZIP (83920 bytes)
DL time: < 2 minutes
Author: Jim Runkel
Needs: Windows 3.x, PKZIP 2.04G

Where

Marketplace

Kim Komando's Komputer Klinic

Keyword

Komando

Select

Komando Libraries

Kool Shareware & Stuff (WIN)

Download

Clinton Screen Saver (WIN)

Font Management

Windows 3.1 lets you use fonts quickly and easily. Using Windows 3.1's TrueType engine or Adobe Type Manager (ATM), you can have access to thousands of typefaces, all of which will work in any Windows program.

But there's a problem. It's often difficult to choose just the right font for the job. That's where Fonter comes in. It lets you view any ATM or TrueType font on the screen, in several ways. Even better, Fonter lets you create printed lists of all your fonts, with a text sample of each font. You can also print sample sheets or character set charts that will show you just what characters are in every font.

This one's a shareware best-seller, reviewed in *PC Computing*, *PC World*, and other publications.

Subj: Font Management (WIN)
Date: February 17, 1994
From: ZNasir
File: FONTER.ZIP (61112 bytes)
DL time: < 1 minute
Author: Ososoft
Needs: 386, 2 Mb RAM, 6 Mb HD space, VBRUN200.DLL, PKZip 2.04G

Where

Computing

PC Software

Keyword

File Search

Select

>fonter

Download

Font Management (WIN)

Lock'M Up 2.5

This shareware program, featured in John Hedtke's shareware column in the November 1994 issue of *Mobile Office*, was designed to password-protect your personal computer.

The ease of use and colorful screens are what separates Lock'M Up from other password security programs. Lock'M Up will stop the casual user from gaining access to your computer, but is not designed to thwart the most sophisticated hacker.

Subj: Lock'M Up V2.5 (DOS)
Date: October 10, 1994
From: CBMChris
File: LKMUP25.ZIP (55186 bytes)
DL time: < 1 minute
Author: Bill Travis
Needs: DOS 3.1+, 128K RAM, hard drive, unZIPing program
Type: Shareware, $15

Where

Newsstand

Keyword
Mobile

Select
Mobile Office Library

Download
Lock'M Up V2.5 (DOS)

MacAfee's ViruScan

ViruScan is designed to check floppy, hard, CD-ROM, and compressed (SuperStor, Stacker, Doublespace, etc.) disks for pre-existing infection of known and unknown viruses. This program works on both standalone and networked PCs, as well as on network file servers.

Subj: MacAfee's ViruScan v1.17
Date: September 28, 1994
From: BillF1030
File: SCANV117.ZIP (257433 bytes)
DL time: < 7 minutes
Author: MacAfee Associates
Needs: PC, PKUNZIP v2.04g or later

Where
Newsstand

PC World

Keyword
PC World

Select
Software Library

Virus!

Download
MacAfee's ViruScan v1.17

Mac Header Remover

A enormous number of files available on many BBSs and online services have been uploaded by members using a Macintosh computer. Sometimes when a file is uploaded with a Mac, extra information useful only to other Macs and prohibitive to PCs is included.

This famous Mac header remover strips out that information and allows the PC user to open many of these Mac files, including .GIF, .SND, and many popular application-specific file types.

Subj: AOMAC2PC: Mac Header Remover
Date: August 8, 1993
From: PC RobO
File: AOMAC2PC.EXE (8703 bytes)
DL time: < 1 minute
Author: Bill Pytlovany
Needs: PC
Type: Public domain

Where

The complete sequence of steps through Computing can be found on page 15. Of course, you can save time and money by using the Keyword shortcuts.

Keyword

File Search

Select

>AOMAC2PC

Download

AOMAC2PC: Mac Header Remover

PC Doctor

Having trouble with your system's interrupts and IRQs? Want to take a look at memory? Need to see a memory map to help you find the unused areas above video memory? Want to take a peek at loaded device drivers? You can do all of this and more with this super PC utility. Due to its pull-down menu interface, you'll find this program extremely intuitive and quite easy to use.

Subj: PCDOC: V3.1 PC Doctor
Date: September 7, 1992
From: PCC Lou
File: PCDOC.ZIP (46369 bytes)
DL time: < 1 minute
Author: Richard C. Leinecker
Needs: UnZIPing program
Type: Shareware

Where

The complete sequence of steps through Computing can be found on page 15. Of course, you can save time and money by using the Keyword shortcuts.

Keyword

File Search

Select

>PC Doctor

Download

The PC Doctor

PC-Shop

PC-Shop helps you design the computer of your choice, step by step, allowing you to see how much computer power your money can buy. You can compare or negotiate until you buy for the recommended price, or optionally get the list of vendors right from the authors. PC Shop is a real money saver for anyone planning to purchase *any* computer or peripheral.

Subj: PCSHOP: V3.2 Computer Shopping System
Date: May 14, 1994
From: RMozEntprs
File: PCS_0594.ZIP (47827 bytes)
DL time: < 1 minute
Author: Carlos R. Garcia (RMoz Enterprises)
Needs: PC, UnZIPing program, printer, mouse optional
Type: Shareware

Where

The complete sequence of steps through Computing can be found on page 15. Of course, you can save time and money by using the Keyword shortcuts.

Keyword

File Search

Select

>Garcia hardware

Download

PCSHOP: V3.2 Computer Shopping System

PrintEnvelope

Featured in the "Superior Shareware" section of the June, 1994 *Windows Magazine*, PrintEnvelope 3.00 for Windows prints any size envelopes and any size labels, on any printer! This program is packed with features like BMP graphic return address, address import from address book, Cardfile, dBASE, or ASCII mail list, automatic city/state entry, and auto-select orientation and paper bins.

Subj: PrintEnvelope v3.0
Date: October 3, 1994
From: SMaurer
File: ENVEL3.ZIP (225392 bytes)
DL time: < 6 minutes
Author: Maurer Associates
Needs: PC, VBRUN300.DLL
Type: Shareware, $29

Where

Newsstand

Windows Magazine

Keyword

WinMag

Select

Software Libraries

Superior Shareware

Download

PrintEnvelope v3.0

SOX: Sound Exchanger

SOX is a PC port of a UNIX program that converts digitized sound samples between various file formats. It also includes a few simple sound effects. SOX supports most of the standard PC, Mac, and workstation formats, including Windows 3.1 RIFF/WAV, Turtle Beach SMP, Sound Blaster VOC files, IRCAM SoundFile files, SUN Sparcstation AU files, mutant DEC AU files, Apple/SGI AIFF files, CD-R (music CD format), Macintosh HCOM files, Sounder files, NeXT SND files, SUN ADPCM (compressed) .AU files, and Soundtool (DOS) files.

Subj: SOX: V1.0 Sound Exchanger
Date: July 28, 1994
From: PCW Nancy
File: SOX10DOS.ZIP (63188 bytes)
DL time: < 1 minute
Author: Lance Norskog
Needs: UnZIPing program, sound card
Type: Freely distributed

Where

Newsstand

Multimedia World

Keyword

MMW

Select

Library

Download

SOX: V1.0 Sound Exchanger

How Do You Spell Relief?

Finally, a complete spell-checking utility to help you create error-free messages on America Online! Spell Check 3.0 supports WinCIM, CSNav, GoCIS, Notepad, DeskEdit, America OnLine, WinFax, and the Clipboard.

Numerous new features have been added to this version, including auto update, context-sensitive help, user-defined closings, a floating misspelled word dialog box, and much more.

Subj: WCSpell v3.0a E-Mail Spell Checker
Date: September 11, 1994
From: WinMag1
File: WCSPEL.ZIP (302054 bytes)
DL time: < 8 minutes
Author: Next Generation Software
Needs: VBRUN300.DLL
Type: Shareware, $11.95-$14.95

Where

Newsstand

Windows Magazine

Keyword

WinMag

Select

Software Libraries

Superior Shareware

Download

WCSpell v3.0a E-Mail Spell Checker

WinClock

WinClock 2.0 monitors system resources and warns you if you drop below the 25-percent mark. At no cost, WinClock tells you the time, saves screen space, and keeps Windows crashes to a minimum.

Subj: WinClock 2.0
Date: September 16, 1994
From: PCW Licia
File: WINCLOCK.ZIP (8965 bytes)
DL time: < 1 minute
Author: PC World
Needs: PC, Windows, PKUNZIP

Where

Newsstand

PC World

Keyword

PC World

Select

Software Library

Featured in 1994

Download

WinClock 2.0

WinGif

WinGif is the original GIF viewer for Windows. With it, you can view and manipulate .GIF, .PCX, .RLE, and .BMP files. You can also crop images and adjust brightness, contrast, gamma, dither, grayscale, change to monochrome, and much more. WinGif is small, fast, and great fun to use.

Subj: WinGif
Date: July 14, 1994
From: PCW Licia
File: WINGIF.ZIP (71919 bytes)
DL time: < 2 minutes
Author: PC World
Needs: PC

Where

Newsstand

PC World

Keyword

PC World

Select

Software Library

Featured in 1994

Download

WinGif

WinZip

WinZip is the best compressed file manager for Windows. You can create and uncompress PKZIP, LZH, ARJ, and other file types. You can view files in archives, check them for viruses, and extract all, or just a few files. Options galore. If you work with compressed files, you need WinZip.

Subj: WinZIP v5.5 ZIP & ARC Utility
Date: September 25, 1994
From: JulesBL
File: WINZIP55.EXE (275324 bytes)
DL time: < 7 minutes
Author: Nico Mak
Needs: Windows 3.1

Where

Newsstand

Windows Magazine

Keyword

WinMag

Select

Software Libraries

Superior Shareware

Download

WinZIP v5.5 ZIP & ARC Utility

Mac Software

All the bases have been covered for PC software, but Mac users shouldn't be left behind, especially since some of the best software on AOL is designed specifically for Mac users.

Easy Excel Calendar Template

I've seen a lot of templates in my AOL travels, but this calendar maker stands out. This Excel 4.0 spreadsheet allows you to create a calendar template for any month from January 1990 through December 2078. To use it, simply enter the month into cell D1 (at least the first three letters of the month) and the year (all four digits) into cell D2. This is very handy and totally free.

Subj: Calendar Template XL
Date: January 23, 1993
From: Gene Komar
File: Calendar.sea (15347 bytes)
DL time: < 1 minute
Author: Gene Komar
Needs: Any Mac, Microsoft Excel 3.0

Where

The complete sequence of steps through Computing can be found on page 15. Of course, you can save time and money by using the Keyword shortcuts.

Keyword

File Search

Select

>Excel calendar

Download

Calendar Template XL

Disinfectant

This is the latest version of the free Mac anti-viral program developed by John Norstad of Northwestern University. This version now handles the new "B" variant of the INIT 29 virus.

Be sure to read the complete File Description for more details on Disinfectant.

Subj: Disinfectant 3.5 - AntiVirus Software
Date: July 5, 1994
From: Komando3
File: Disinfectant 3.5.sea (176711 bytes)
DL time: < 4 minutes
Author: John Norstad
Needs: Any Macintosh

Where

Marketplace

Kim Komando's Komputer Klinic

Keyword

Komando

Select
Komando Libraries

Kool Shareware & Stuff (Mac)

Download
Disinfectant 3.5 - AntiVirus Software

Free RAM

This software was created for those who don't have a lot of RAM and want to know how much is available before trying to open the next program. It uses some toolbox calls that were not in use until System 7, so it won't run on earlier versions. To run the program most efficiently, put it in the Startup folder in the System Folder. It will show the current amount of free RAM up to 99,999K. If you have more than that, you don't need this application! Free RAM runs in the background and is automatically updated every second.

Subj: Free RAM 1.1
Date: July 30, 1994
From: Komando3
File: FreeRam 1.1.sea (45123 bytes)
DL time: < 1 minute
Author: Charles G. Marlowe
Needs: Mac, System 7

Keyword
Komando

Where
Marketplace

Kim Komando's Komputer Klinic

Select
Komando Libraries

Kool Shareware & Stuff (MAC)

Download
Free RAM 1.1

Kim's Quartet . . . . Kwartet?

All these "K"words get me confused, but this shareware combo should help me get my (computer) life back in order. Kim Komando, the Komputer Komando, has put together this little collection of small but powerful utilities to help make life with Mac a little easier.

- *MacErrors*. This is a small (49K) 3-D color-interfaced application that shows you the result code and description for all of the Macintosh system errors. Just type in a valid error ID and press Return or Enter. The result code and description will be displayed to you. If you enter an invalid ID, MacErrors will beep at you.

- *PopChar 2.6.2*. PopChar is a control panel that simplifies "typing" of unusual characters. Click the PopChar icon in the menu bar, select the character you want, and PopChar automatically inserts it in the current document as if you had typed the proper key combination on the keyboard.

- *SCSIProbe 3.5*. This is the latest version of SCSI Probe plus the SyQuest *User's Guide*. SCSIProbe identifies and mounts any SCSI device connected to your Mac. It shows the device's SCSI ID, type, vendor, name, and version. Install SCSIProbe's INIT on removable cartridges and the cartridges mount automatically. SCSIProbe makes Mac SCSI a blessing instead of a curse.

- *SuperClock! 4.0.4*. This is the latest release of SuperClock!, a control panel that displays the time on the right end of the menu bar. This version fixes two problems: no longer will your Mac Plus crash when you run this utility and the chime feature now works in all cases.

Subj:	4 Utilities to Make Life Easy
Date:	July 30, 1994
From:	Komando
File:	4 Great Utilities.sea (138652 bytes)
DL time:	< 3 minutes
Authors:	Marty Wachter, Guenther Blaschek, Robert Polc, Steve Christensen
Needs:	Mac, System 6.07 or better, System 7 compatible

Where

Marketplace

Kim Komando's Komputer Klinic

Keyword

Komando

Select

Komando Libraries

Kool Shareware & Stuff (Mac)

Download

4 Utilities to Make Life Easy

MacDOS Facilitates Inbreeding

Did I get your attention? MacDOS provides a DOS-like interface to the Macintosh operating system. Among other things, this enables you to list, delete, copy, and rename files and to work with folders on hard disks and floppies.

One of the most important features missing in the Mac is what users of *all* other systems call "wildcarding" and "filtering"—that is, the possibility of selecting and performing operations on all files within one or more folders that have similar names or have some characteristics in common.

When you open a folder on the Mac, you can have the filenames displayed in order of size, date, or name, but you see them all. Wouldn't it be nice to see only the text files, the Word documents, or the aliases? And what about selecting them and copying them in a single operation?

Registration entitles you to a 180-page User's Guide (in binary form as a series of MS-Word documents), access to full functionality, and support via E-mail.

Subj: MacDos 1.0.1
Date: July 30, 1994
From: Komando3
File: MacDOS 1.0.1.sea (233150 bytes)
DL time: < 6 minutes
Author: Giulio Zambian
Needs: Mac, System 6.07+, System 7 compatible

Where

Marketplace

Kim Komando's Komputer Klinic

Keyword

Komando

Select

Komando Libraries

Kool Shareware & Stuff (MAC)

Download

MacDos 1.0.1

Macintosh Drag and Drop

Tekkies—your search is over. This file contains the source code for the following *MacTech* magazine article "New Apple Technology: Macintosh Drag and Drop." You've wanted it for years, they finally delivered it, but they hardly told anyone!

Subj: 10.6 Drag and Drop
Date: May 25, 1994
From: MacTechMag
File: Drag and Drop.sit (4222 bytes)
DL time: < 1 minute
Author: Steve Kiene, MindVision
Needs: Mac, MacTech Magazine, Volume 10 Number 6

Where

Newsstand

MacTech Magazine

Keyword

MacTech

Select

MacTech Magazine Software Library

Download

10.6 Drag and Drop

Mac Mating Game

Macworld editors are frequently asked about transferring files from one Mac to another. We all know that using a floppy disk is way too time-consuming. There is, fortunately, a better way. This document describes the networking process so you can connect Macs to copy programs and and transfer files.

The nine-page Word document contains step-by-step instructions for connecting Macs.

Subj: How to Connect 2 Macs
Date: August 22, 1994
From: Pogue
File: How to Network Macs.sit (38023 bytes)
DL time: < 1 minute
Author: David Pogue
Needs: Microsoft Word

Where

Newsstand

Macworld

Keyword

Macworld

Select

Software Library

Download

How to Connect 2 Macs

Where to Find More Goodies

Take a look at the *Books, Magazines, and Literature* section to locate some purchasing sources with discounts on computer books.

Speaking of purchasing, don't miss the *Shopping* section of this book, nor the Marketplace on AOL. You'll find great online sources for purchasing computers and supplies (Keyword: Marketplace).

Another one of your best bets is to become familiar with the Industry Connection on AOL. There you'll find answers to a myriad of software, hardware, and compatibility questions—straight from the manufacturers. It's also a good idea to check for product information before making that next purchase (Keyword: Industry Connection).

For demos, check first in the Industry Connection, followed by Kim Komando's Komputer Klinic (Keyword: Komando). Of course, check the ever-popular magazines, and as another option, don't forget the magic Keyword: File Search.

FREE $TUFF

Tell me what you eat, and I will
tell you what you are.

Anthelme Brillat-Savarin

Cooking and Gourmet Endeavors

Scrumptious delights abound in the delicious opportunities cooked up by AOL and its members. If you love cookbooks, as I do, you'll rapidly discover that the recipes on AOL will appeal to your love of food in a distinctly different way from your current cookbook collection. The online recipes may not delight the senses in the same way as a well loved cookbook. Certainly, the download count indicates the popularity of a recipe or cooking style, but you can't see where the ingredients have been spilled on the pages. There are no glossy photos to show you how the finished dish should look.

Still, it's a treasure—the Fort Knox of cooking, and you've been given a pass key. You'll soon discover thousands of recipes and several good software programs to help you manage those recipes. Imagine you've been put in charge of the caviar warehouse. Or, you're a buyer for a gourmet food chain and you get to sample their offerings all day long.

There are so many cooking opportunities on AOL. There are far too many recipes to list them all for your consideration; a complete 500-page book could be written with the recipes online. Let's just say there are hundreds of files, containing thousands of recipes. There will always be spice in your cooking— just download a new recipe file each week.

I'll also point you to a few message boards where you can ask other members and experienced cooks about the differences between Devon Cream and Creme Fraiche, for recipes for home-brewed beer, and much more. My favorite is the recipe search—does anyone know where I can obtain the recipe for the original Caesar's Salad?

Cooking Club

When I was six, my mother was too sick to prepare dinner one evening, so Dad took over. I will remember that corned beef hash forever—and it is not a fond memory. From that day on, Legionnaire's disease wouldn't be enough to stop Mom from cooking. Too bad the AOL Cooking Club was not around at that time—it could have helped such culinary-handicapped individuals as my father.

In the Cooking Club, you can learn how to prepare food for yourself and your family. You'll discover a great deal of fun as you share nutritional tips and exchange recipes with the other members of the Cooking Club. One of AOL's all time best download libraries is located in this forum. You may even become a gourmet cook. Unfortunately, I think it's too late for my dad.

Where

Clubs & Interests

Cooking Club

Keyword

Cooking

Select

The Cupboard Message Board

List Categories

Tips and Techniques

Recipe Boxes and File Managers

As soon as electronic databases were created, cooks jumped at the benefits of electronic cookbooks. With the click of a button, dinner for four can be converted to dinner for 40. Demos, templates, text files, and relational databases await your inspection in these online files. Many recipes are quite sophisticated and unfortunately can be quite costly to create. I will focus only on those recipes that are unique *and* economical. You won't be banished from the kitchen anymore.

Recipe Box Deluxe

Recipe Box Deluxe is a darn good recipe template for FileMaker Pro. It's easy to use and does everything you could possibly imagine—and a few things you can't! It prints grocery lists and 3 x 5 cards or full-page recipes, it can do quick and easy searches, it's button driven, it lets you categorize, and it looks sharp!

Subj: Filemaker Pro Recipe Box Deluxe
Date: February 11, 1994
From: EBWATERS
File: Recipe Box Deluxe.sea (186399 bytes)
DL time: < 5 minutes
Author: Dave Triplett
Needs: Filemaker Pro
Type: Shareware, $10

Where

Clubs & Interests

Cooking Club

Keyword

Cooking

Select

Cooking Library Center

Mac Cooking Library

Download

Filemaker Pro Recipe Box Deluxe

Dave's Cookbook

Cookbook 1.10 is a new recipe/cookbook manager that runs under any version of MS-DOS greater than 2.10, and touts a great user interface for speeding the entry of recipes. It also possesses a wide assortment of functions that operate on the recipes (for example, searching for recipes based on keywords, authors, titles, and even ingredients; making shopping lists; scaling and printing recipes, and so on).

Dave calls this shareware, but he is giving it away *free*. Just send him an E-mail to let him know how you like the program.

Subj: Dave's Cookbook
Date: August 27, 1994
From: SirRedhawk
File: COOKBOOK.ZIP (44434 bytes)
DL time: < 1 minute
Author: Dave Woodall
Needs: PC, Microsoft mouse, MS-DOS ver 2.10 or later

Where

Clubs & Interests

Cooking Club

Keyword

Cooking

Select

Cooking Library Center

ASCII Cooking Library

Download

Dave's Cookbook

The Ingredients

You are about to enter the world of recipes. These are just a very few of the 1,000+ you'll find online. Many files have dozens of recipes—and every day (well, almost) more are added. If I've failed to include your favorite dessert or the best pasta salad, I just know it's somewhere online.

The CookBook

The CookBook is Scott Steinbrink's creation in ASCII text format for all computers. Scott's enormous undertaking includes: Stuffed Mushrooms, Herbed Cheese Pastry, Homemade Granola, No-Blunder Blender Breakfasts, Breads, Cookies, *Crepes Aux Fruits De Mer*, Non-Alcoholic Blender Drinks, Pitcher Drinks, Hot Drinks, Complete Dinner Menus, Meat Loaf, Crab Cakes, and Soufflés, plus dozens of sandwich suggestions and a selection of Impossible Pies. There are hundreds of recipes packed into a substantial file.

Subj: CookBook (in ASCII text format)
Date: March 1, 1990
From: EBWATERS
File: TEXTCOOKBOOK (104532 bytes)
DL time: < 2 minutes
Author: Scott Steinbrink
Needs: Text reader

Where

Clubs & Interests

Cooking Club

Keyword

Cooking

Select

Cooking Library Center

ASCII Cooking Library

Download

CookBook (in ASCII text format)

Temptations

Junior League Cookbooks are a well-regarded genre among cooking aficionados and I was thrilled to find selections in AOL's download libraries. Temptations include a selection of recipes from the highly renowned *Temptations Cookbook* published by the Junior League of Lansing, Michigan.

In this file, readers will encounter Chicken Wingdings, Lentil and Tomato Soup, Vegetable Stock, Beef Broccoli Strudel, Chicken and Shrimp in Champagne Sauce, Chicken and Ham Lasagna, Blueberry Flummery, Blueberry Sauce, and Plum Crumble.

I'll be back to finish this section after I try these!

Subj: Temptations Junior League Ckbk
Date: August 16, 1994
From: EBWATERS
File: Temptations (7451 bytes)
DL time: < 1 minute
Needs: Text reader

Where

Clubs & Interests

Cooking Club

Keyword

Cooking

Select

Cooking Library Center

ASCII Cooking Library

Download

Temptations Junior League Ckbk

Back Home Again

Not to be outdone by their friends in Lansing, the Indianapolis Junior League has provided a sampling of recipes from *Back Home Again*. A beautiful collection of truly special recipes.

The cookbook is divided into these nine sections:

- *A Warm Welcome:* Appetizers, Beverages, and Soups
- *Rise and Shine:* Muffins, Breads, Breakfast, and Brunch
- *Staples and Standbys:* Pasta, Pasta Sauces, Rice, Grains, and Beans
- *A Garden's Yield:* Salads, Salad Dressings, and Vegetables
- *The Butcher Shop:* Beef, Veal, Lamb, Pork, Poultry and Game, Marinades, and Chutney
- *Fresh Catch:* Fish, Shellfish, and Fish Marinades
- *Grande Finale:* Cakes and Cheesecakes, Special Desserts, Sauces, Pies and

Pastries, and Cookies and Candies

- *Gatherings:* Monthly Entertaining Menus
- *Cook's Notes:* Special Cook's Notes, Substitutions, Yields, and Cooking Terms

The file includes six appealing recipes: Savory Gruyere Cheesecake; Sour Cream Applesauce Bran Muffins; Pasta with Red Peppers and Ham; Spinach, Basil, and Pine Nut Salad; Turkey Breast with Orange and Rosemary; and Pears Poached in Cabernet.

Subj: Back Home Again
Date: August 7, 1994
From: EBWATERS
File: Back Home Again (7678 bytes)
DL time: < 1 minute
Author: Indianapolis Junior League
Needs: Text reader

Where

Clubs & Interests

Cooking Club

Keyword

Cooking

Select

Cooking Library Center

ASCII Cooking Library

Download

Back Home Again

HotChiliPepper.eps

On a color monitor, or with a color printer, this chili pepper is a bright and colorful design for a logo or insignia. The artist designed this as part of a Mexico-theme T-shirt. You may use it if you like. However, the artist demands payment of $15.00 if it is used in any publication or printed in any manner.

Subj: Hot Chili Pepper/Shareware EPSF
Date: September 8, 1994
From: MAJORWERKS
File: Hot Chili Pepper.sit (35645 bytes)
DL time: < 1 minute

Author: MAJOR WeRKS!

Needs: Color, eps capabilities, taste for salsa!

Where

The complete sequence of steps through Computing can be found on page 15. Of course, you can save time and money by using the Keyword shortcuts.

Keyword

Mac: File Search

PC: Mac Software

Select

>food hot

Download

Hot Chili Pepper/Shareware EPSF

Hot Salsa

In 1993, salsa outsold ketchup as the leading condiment. This is a collection of salsas—from the very mild to the wild. Avocado Salsa Cruda, Chicken Fajitas with Tomato-Coriander Salsa, Classic Cream Cheese-Salsa Spread, Corn Salsa, Curried Oysters with Banana Salsa, and Five-Alarm Salsa are just six of the many salsa-based recipes.

Subj: Salsa

Date: September 23, 1994

From: SirRedhawk

File: SALSA.TXT (67705 bytes)

DL time: < 1 minute

Author: Various

Needs: Text reader

Where

Clubs & Interests

Cooking Club

Keyword

Cooking

Select

Cooking Library Center

ASCII Cooking Library

Download

Salsa

Sweet Vidalia Onions

Vidalia Onions—A Recipe Collection from America Online. This luscious file features Marinated Sweet Onions, Stuffed Onion Bake, Sautéed Vidalias, Vidalia-Rice Casserole, Southern Style Baked Stuffed Onions, Memphis Onion Rings, Bean and Onion Salad, Cheddar Onion Pie, Grilled Vidalia Onions, Charcoal Roasted Onions, and Middle Eastern Grilled Onion Salad. You haven't had an onion if you haven't had a Vidalia.

Subj: Vidalia Onion Collection
Date: June 19, 1993
From: EBWATERS
File: ONION (7681 bytes)
DL time: < 1 minute
Author: Liz Waters
Needs: Text reader

Where

Clubs & Interests

Cooking Club

Keyword

Cooking

Select

Cooking Library Center

ASCII Cooking Library

Download

Vidalia Onion Collection

SPAM, SPAM, SPAM

Remember when steak was out and SPAM was in? This GIF ought to jog your memory— a picture of a blue can containing this all-time favorite food (whose, I don't know!). I'm still searching for SPAM-based recipes, so please consider this a call for SPAM uploads.

To view Mac GIFs on a PC, you need AOMAC2PC.EXE (available online). Type in: AOMAC2PC.EXE [old filename] [new filename]. Make sure the GIF name is a legal DOS file name (for example, change Lili'sLilies.GIF to Lilies.GIF).

Subj: Can of SPAM GIF
Date: January 30, 1993
From: LiliMrlene
File: Spam.GIF (38799 bytes)
DL time: < 1 minute
Author: LiliMrlene
Needs: Mac or PC, GIF viewer (and AOMAC2PC.EXE if you have a PC)

Where

The complete sequence of steps through Computing can be found on page 15. Of course, you can save time and money by using the Keyword shortcuts.

Keyword

Mac: File Search

PC: Mac Software

Select

>spam

Download

Can of SPAM GIF

Sourdough

Here's a recipe for both sourdough bread and sourdough starter. Well written and formatted in WordPerfect, it should read and print nicely using any version of WordPerfect 5.x or later for DOS or Windows.

Subj: WP51: Sourdough Recipe
Date: June 3, 1994
From: Bobcornet
File: SOURDOUG.RCP (5899 bytes)
DL time: < 1 minute
Author: Bobcornet
Needs: WordPerfect 5.x/6.x for DOS or Windows
Type: Freely distributed

Where

The complete sequence of steps through Computing can be found on page 15. Of course, you can save time and money by using the Keyword shortcuts.

Keyword

PC: File Search

Mac: PC Software

Select

>sourdough

Download

WP51: Sourdough Recipe

> **Message Board Screen**
> *Subj:* re: sourdough 94-06-06 19:31:33 EDT
> *From:* JGracey
>
> True sourdough is made using two things: water and unbleached white flour. The other ingredient is in the air around you, the wild yeasts that invade the starter. Mix one cup of flour to two cups water in a bowl, cover with a cotton kitchen towel, wait 3 days, and smell it. If it has a clean, yeasty aroma, you are in business. If it stinks, you throw it away & try again. Lest someone from the left coast howl in protest, I should add that the San Francisco type sourdoughs have been around for so long that they have become very strong and sour, but my home-cooked version has an incredible flavor and consistency that I have never found anyplace else. If anybody is interested in this, I'll be glad to post the full recipe for the bread you make from this fantastic starter.-JG

Coca-Cola Recipes

A collection of eleven international recipes that have a common ingredient—Coca-Cola. Recipes include: Italian Minestrone Sour, French Onion Soup, Chinese Pepper Steak, German Sauerbraten, Indian Chicken Curry, Hungarian Goulash, Russian Beef Stroganoff, Japanese Pickled Cauliflower, Grecian Green Beans, Banana Cake with Sea Foam Frosting, Scottish Oaten Bread, and Brazilian Iced Chocolate. All recipes are in ASCII file format and can be read with any text editor or word processor.

Subj: COLA: Coca-Cola Recipes
Date: January 22, 1993
From: Nick WT
File: C_COLA.ZIP (44741 bytes)
DL time: < 1 minute
Author: The Recipe Works
Needs: UnZIPing program, text reader
Type: Freely distributed

Where

The complete sequence of steps through Computing can be found on page 15. Of course, you can save time and money by using the Keyword shortcuts.

Keyword

PC: File Search
Mac: PC Software

Select

>coke

Download

COLA: Coca-Cola Recipes

Mission Impossibles

Over 80 famous Bisquick recipes collected from a variety of sources. These are main dish, all-in-one meals for breakfast, lunch, brunch, and dinner. They're excerpted from Master Cook II, but easily readable with a word processor. File 1 includes fruit, vegetable, and meat recipes. File 2 includes pizza, tacos, vegetables, tuna, and shrimp.

Subj: RECIPE "Impossibles" -1
Date: August 14, 1994
From: Martha2
File: IMPOSS1.MXP (56711 bytes)
DL time: < 1 minute
Author: Various
Needs: Any computer, text reader

Where

Clubs & Interests

SeniorNet

Keyword

SeniorNet

Select

Showcase & Exchange

Download

RECIPE "Impossibles" -1

RECIPE "Impossibles" -2

The SeniorNet Showcase & Exchange Library also has compilations of recipes from *Country Living Magazine*.

Olive Garden Recipes

Get eight Olive Garden recipes including breadsticks, salad dressing, spaghetti sauce, seafood chowder, and Fettucine Alfredo.

Subj: RECIPES Olive Garden
Date: September 14, 1994
From: Martha2
File: OLIVGRDN.TXT (12443 bytes)
DL time: < 1 minute
Author: Olive Garden/Others
Needs: Any computer, text reader

Where

Clubs & Interests

SeniorNet

Keyword

SeniorNet

Select

Showcase & Exchange

Download

RECIPES Olive Garden

Mrs. Fields' Chocolate Chip

This just may be the real Mrs. Fields' Chocolate Chip Cookie recipe. It's up to you to find out. Give this recipe a try and let me know what you think— I'm a tried and true chocoholic.

Subj: COOKIE: Mrs. Fields Cookies
Date: April 9, 1991
From: MikeO10
File: COOKIES.ZIP (957 bytes)
DL time: < 1 minute
Needs: UnZIPer, text reader

Where

The complete sequence of steps through Computing can be found on page 15. Of course, you can save time and money by using the Keyword shortcuts.

Keyword

File Search

Select

>cookie

Download

COOKIE: Mrs. Fields Cookies

Recipe Search

Are you seeking famous restaurant recipes? There's a message board devoted to your quest. If you're looking for Houlihan's Potato Soup or the original Caesar's Salad, this is the information center.

Where

Clubs & Interests

Cooking Club

Keyword

Cooking

Select

The Cupboard

List Categories

General Information

Restaurant Recipes

Bed and Breakfast Recipes

Bed & Breakfast U.S.A. has included a selection of favorite bread and breakfast recipes in their online area. The recipes are the bread and breakfast host's originals. They've been chosen because of the raves they've received from satisfied guests. Alaska Rhubarb Pie, Bittersweet Inn Coffee Cake, Cranberry Butter, Ham and Potato Bake Supreme, Sausage-Apple Bake, and Windyledge Honey 'n' Spice Blueberry Pancakes comprise just a small selection of the mouthwatering temptations.

You can read them online, but to save time, I recommend downloading the one file that holds all the recipes.

Subj: B&B Recipes
Date: August 29, 1994
From: JH Penguin
File: RECIPES.B&B (21483 bytes)
DL time: < 1 minute
Needs: Text reader

Where

Travel

Bed & Breakfast U.S.A.

Keyword

Bed & Breakfast

Select

File Library

Download

B&B Recipes

Vegetarian Journal

This file contains excerpts from the March/April 1994 edition of the *Vegetarian Journal*, published by the Vegetarian Resource Group (VRG). It includes an update on recent scientific papers relating to vegetarianism, Veggie Bits, the VRG's testimony to the USDA about school meals, and recipes from Debra Wasserman's book, *The Lowfat Jewish Vegetarian Cookbook— Healthy Traditions from Around the World*. You'll find excerpts from several issues of *Vegetarian Journal* using these directions.

Subj: Vegetarian Journal excerpt 3/94
Date: May 7, 1994
From: NurseBobbi
File: VJMAR94.TXT (28544 bytes)
DL time: < 1 minute
Author: Veg. Resource Group
Needs: Text reader

Where

Clubs & Interests

Cooking Club

Keyword

Cooking

Select

Cooking Library Center

ASCII Cooking Library

Download

Vegetarian Journal excerpt 3/94

Coffee Crisis?

It begins the day and concludes fine meals. The price goes up; the price goes down. A true coffee fan will do (almost) anything for the best cup around. Won't you join me for a steaming cup?

Coffee Hints

The Coffee Hints is a compilation of articles from a gourmet coffee newsletter, *The French Press*. The perfect brew and ideal storage conditions are revealed in this excerpt by Debra Caruthers. *The French Press* is sent to customers of the Arabica Gourmet Coffee & Tea Club.

This file includes information about the newsletter and personalized mail-order coffee service. Request more information via E-mail or the 800 number, and they will include some *free whole bean samples* with the literature.

Subj: Coffee Hints
Date: May 7, 1994
From: EBWATERS
File: Coffee.TXT (4307 bytes)
DL time: < 1 minute
Author: SPARKLESSS
Needs: Any system, text reader

Where

Clubs & Interests

Cooking Club

Keyword

Cooking

Select

Cooking Library Center

ASCII Cooking Library

Download

Coffee Hints

THE GRINDER

The Grinder is SCompany's coffee newsletter. Each month *The Grinder* profiles a specific coffee blend and grind, plus you get a two pot sample (either bean or ground) of the special profile coffee. You will also find articles on machines, filters, and procedures—you name it and they've provided the story.

To receive a sample issue, you need to send your snail-mail address via E-mail. You should expect your sample within two weeks.

E-Mail

SCompany

Coffee Resources

This is the Coffee Resources Guide from alt.coffee.rec.food.drink.coffee, and alt.drugs.caffeine newsgroups. It contains lists of mail-order coffee houses, sources for coffee related items, and a coffee bibliography.

Subj:	Coffee Resources Guide 3.01-TXT
Date:	August 4, 1994
From:	Ddenk
File:	CRG text only (38985 bytes)
DL time:	< 1 minute
Author:	Tim Nemec
Needs:	Mac or PC, text reader

Where

Newsstand

Chicago

Keyword

Chicago

Select

Download Libraries

Entertainment Guide Library

Download

Coffee Resources Guide 3.01-TXT

Gifts and Crafts

Not fruitcake again! In this topic I will provide you with ideas for gifts for holiday celebrations and for friends and neighbors. Read on for unique recipes and tips.

Holiday Gifts from the Kitchen

Fruit cake not withstanding, gifts of food are among the most popular holiday gifts. They're perfect personalized gifts for neighbors, teachers, and co-workers. In this file, you'll get the complete directions for Miss Maudie's Pumpkin Butter, Cranberry Conserve, Cranapple Jelly, Cranberry Ketchup, Herb Butters, Herbal Honeys, Pretty Peppers in Oil, Lemon Pick Me Up Tea, Spicy Feel Better Tea, After Turkey Dinner Tea, Drift into Sleep Tea, Honey Beer Mustard, Sweet Mustard, China

Moon Hot Chili Oil, and much more. Remember me on your gift list this year!

Subj: Holiday Gifts from the Kitchen
Date: December 14, 1993
From: EBWATERS
File: HOLGIFTS (14911 bytes)
DL time: < 1 minute
Author: Liz Waters
Needs: Text reader

Where

Clubs & Interests

Cooking Club

Keyword

Cooking

Select

Cooking Library Center

ASCII Cooking Library

Download

Holiday Gifts from the Kitchen

Recipe Holiday Gifts

Almost 100 recipes for gift giving or holiday use, including mustards, sauces, seasoned rice mixes, soup mixes, candies, cookies, cordials, vinegars, and oils, homemade salami, and simmering potpourri. Most recipes include tips for use and decorative packaging ideas.

Subj: RECIPE Holiday Gifts
Date: August 7, 1994
From: Martha2
File: HOLIDAYS.TXT (185867 bytes)
DL time: < 5 minutes
Author: Various
Needs: Text reader, MM or MC2

Where

Clubs & Interests

SeniorNet

Keyword

SeniorNet

Select

Showcase & Exchange

Download

RECIPE Holiday Gifts

Favorite Fudge

Fudge is another winter and holiday favorite. Your cookie tray won't be complete without it. This is an excellent recipe and it even includes instructions for the totally inept. This fudge is easy to cook and makes a delicious addition to all kitchens.

Subj: FUDGE: Fudge Recipe
Date: November 18, 1992
From: PCA Robin
File: FUDGE.ZIP (1435 bytes)
DL time: < 1 minute
Author: Unknown
Needs: UnZIPing program
Type: Public domain

Where

The complete sequence of steps through Computing can be found on page 15. Of course, you can save time and money by using the Keyword shortcuts.

Keyword

PC: File Search

Mac: PC Software

Select

>cook chocolate

Download

FUDGE: Fudge Recipe

The Celebrity Cookbook

The Celebrity Cookbook is a searchable database of recipes of the stars! Just input your favorite celebrity's name, an ingredient, a type of dish, or anything you want to match, and enjoy the results. Try these for representative results: Barbra Streisand, John Lennon, Frank Sinatra, Sophia Loren, and Dinah Shore.

Where

Clubs & Interests

Cooking Club

Keyword

Cooking

Select

Celebrity Cookbook

Search the Celebrity Cookbook

>search by celebrity name or type of food

Celebrity Diets

Would you like to be Princess Diana for a day? Lady Di's diet can be yours when you check the celebrity diets. Perhaps Mary Tyler Moore, Liz Taylor, or Ronald Reagan would appeal to your dietary senses?

Where

Clubs & Interests

Cooking Club

Keyword

Cooking

Select

Celebrity Diets

Read/Save

[name]

Light-Hearted Fare

And, now for some food related fun. When all else fails, head for the restaurant (and hope you get a table) or reach for the phone and order a pizza.

Dial for Pizza

A depiction of the Domino's Pizza logo! It has the red and white domino on the left and the wording, DOMINO'S PIZZA in white on a blue field on the right. The author suggests "I'm sure the company would like for this to be used with a communications program to call in an order for a large pepperoni, or more!" You can order pizza on the Internet, you know, but right now only for Pizza Hut.

Subj: ICO: Domino's Pizza Icon
Date: March 21, 1994
From: Robert5492

File: DPI.ICO (766 bytes)
DL time: < 1 minute
Author: Unknown
Needs: Windows 3.x or icon viewer
Type: Freely distributed

Where

Computing

PC Software

Keyword

File Search

Select

>pizza

Download

ICO: Domino's Pizza Icon

I Scream, You Scream . . .

Here's a good scan of a three-scoop ice cream cone. Great for menus, flyers, or other desktop-published items. You could also use it on the invitation for a child's birthday party.

Subj: PCX: Ice Cream Graphics
Date: September 1, 1993
From: MarkV20
File: ICECREAM.PCX (50808 bytes)
DL time: < 6 minutes
Author: Unknown
Needs: PCX viewer or DTP program
Type: Freely distributed

Where

The complete sequence of steps through Computing can be found on page 15. Of course, you can save time and money by using the Keyword shortcuts.

Keyword

PC: File Search

Mac: PC Software

Select

>ice cream

Download

PCX: Ice Cream Graphics

Seinfeld: Elaine's Chinese Food

This is the fifth in a series of six sound clips from Elaine from the show *Seinfeld*. All of these clips come from the show where Jerry, George, and Elaine wait, unsuccessfully, for a table at a Chinese restaurant.

Elaine: "It's not fair that people are seated first-come first-served. It should be based on who's hungriest." Use this with an alarm gizmo as a reminder to go to lunch.

Subj: Elaine's Chinese food SND #5.sit
Date: January 26, 1994
From: BKimmel
File: Elaine's Chinese food SND 5.sit (78126 bytes)
DL time: < 2 minutes
Author: Elaine, BKimmel
Needs: Sound application, AOL 2.0 or StuffIt Expander

Where

The complete sequence of steps through Computing can be found on page 15. Of course, you can save time and money by using the Keyword shortcuts.

Keyword

Mac: File Search

PC: Mac Software

Select

>Seinfeld food

Download

Elaine's Chinese food SND #5.sit

Wine Connoisseur's Cookbook

Get the corkscrew. This abbreviated electronic book version of the *Wine Connoisseur's Cookbook* contains recipes featuring wine as an ingredient. Included are recipes for appetizers, salads, soups, main entrees, and desserts. This "mini" version is distributed as freeware, a very nice and accessible color software. Each recipe includes ingredients and preparation, as well as suggested wines and accompanying foods. The graphical interface is easy use; simply click on the topics you wish to review.

Subj: WINE CONNOISEUR'S COOKBOOK
Date: July 6, 1994
From: DavidCG883
File: WCCB.ZIP (171353 bytes)
DL time: < 4 minutes
Author: David C. Guardia
Needs: PC, mouse, CGA+, PKUNZIP 2.04 G

Where

Clubs & Interests

Cooking Club

Keyword

Cooking

Select

Cooking Library Center

DOS Cooking Library

Download

WINE CONNOISEUR'S COOKBOOK

WINE & DINE ONLINE

The Newsstand section of *Wine & Dine Online* has a growing library of reference materials on a wide range of subjects. You may find articles in two ways: by searching for a word or by browsing through the articles by source. Increase your wine knowledge, select

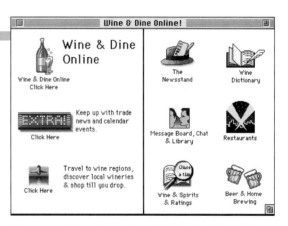

a wine for your Thanksgiving dinner, and read a series of wine book reviews.

Where

Clubs & Interests

Wine & Dine Online

Keyword

Wine

Select

The Newsstand

The Wine Dictionary

The online *Wine Dictionary* is an informal dictionary of common wine words. Goldwyn's Dine Base plans to expand this area to include food, cooking, beer, brewing, and spirits terms, as well.

Where

Clubs & Interests

Wine & Dine Online

Keyword

Wine

Select

The Wine Dictionary

Snacks Newsletter

Stop in at the Restaurant Reviews message board and find the folder marked About our E-mail Newsletter. Add your name to the list of those who receive *Snacks*, the Restaurant Reviews E-mail newsletter.

Where

Clubs & Interests

Wine & Dine Online

Keyword

Wine

Select

Message Board, Chat & Library

Restaurant Reviews

List topics

About our E-Mail Newsletter

What's Brewing

The "BrewNews" column from *All About Beer* Magazine can be found in *Wine & Dine Online*. Excerpts include Samuel Adams successes, meads for your brew, beer DNA, Japanese beer legislation, Breckenridge free beer recycling program, Coors earthquake relief efforts, and the impact of excise taxes on beer drinkers.

Where

Clubs & Interests

Wine & Dine Online

Keyword

Wine

Select

Beer & Home Brewing

All About Beer

Read/Save

What's Brewing [issue]

Beer Recipe Stack

The best home-brewed beers start here. This is a stack to index and collect recipes for brewing beer. Recipes can be grouped and sorted according to classes set up by the AHA, or you can make up your own. The author has included a couple of examples for Fruit Beer (made with raspberries) and Anne's Choice Christmas Ale to get you started.

Subj: Beer Recipe Stack
Date: September 14, 1991
From: EBrian
File: BeerRcp.stack (39963 bytes)
DL time: < 1 minute
Author: EBrian
Needs: Mac, HyperCard 2.0, StuffIt

Where

The complete sequence of steps through Computing can be found on page 15. Of course, you can save time and money by using the Keyword shortcuts.

Keyword

File Search

Select

[x] Hypercard

>beer

Download

Beer Recipe Stack

Huge Drink Collection

This just may be the most complete drink collection online. You'll find everything from college drinks (Bloody Brain, Vulcan Mind Probe, and Gilligan's Island) to coffee drinks. More drinks than you can shake a jigger at.

Subj: Huge Drink Collection in WORD format
Date: March 7, 1994
From: PK10661
File: The Huge Drink Book Word 5.0 (72182 bytes)
DL time: < 2 minutes
Author: Paul Kolenda
Needs: Capability to read Microsoft Word files

Where

Clubs & Interests

Cooking Club

Keyword

Cooking

Select

Cooking Library Center

Mac Cooking Library

Download

Huge Drink Collection in WORD format

Where to Find More Goodies

When you eat three times a day, food is never far away. There are more online sources to satisfy your cravings. If you're looking for cookbooks, read the *Books, Magazines, and Literature* section. Then check out Stacey's in the Mercury Center or the Online Bookstore (Keyword: Bookstore).

Given that there are three recipes sources within *San Jose Mercury News* (Keyword: Mercury), select Advertising and then Mercury Mall to reach Stacey's Bookstore and the Del Monte recipes. Or, select Bay Area Living and you'll find the Food & Wine library with recipes.

For cooking appliance information, turn to the *Around the House* section, which also has topics for creating grocery lists and managing your coupon supply. For online help with appliances, be sure to check Consumer Reports (Keyword: Consumer) and the Gadget Guru (Keyword: Gadget Guru).

FREE $TUFF

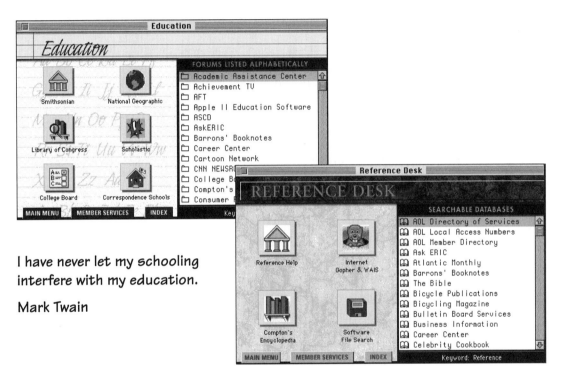

I have never let my schooling interfere with my education.

Mark Twain

Educational Ideas

With the advent of AOL's new multimedia user interface, the burgeoning Learning and Reference Department has been divided into two separate sections: Education and Reference. Education contains teaching references, tests, study guides, and education associations; Reference contains the more traditional "library" references—as only AOL can present them. Many sources, including Compton's Encyclopedia and the Library of Congress, fall within Reference. Don't be dissuaded. The Reference section is not merely a redundant version of your local public library, but rather a tremendous resource of online and downloadable data.

The range of educational opportunities begins with programs for babies (really) and continues through graduate school programs. Junior high and high school students, whether public, private or home schooled, will be able to take advantage of Smithsonian Online, Library of Congress Online, and National Geographic Online for project research, and teachers can request and utilize lesson plans and materials. All of these areas contain amazing photos, excerpts, and periodicals.

For the younger children play is educational. We've included pre-school programs in the Kid $tuff section.

Because of the overwhelming amount of educational material on AOL, this section focuses on information for older students— high school, college, and post-graduate. The *Kid $tuff* section covers preschool and grade school, and includes home schooling references. I think you'll be amazed at the variety of fun stuff I've found for you!

We'll be traveling together through the Education and Reference Departments just as we've progressed through our school lives. We'll also check a few far-flung areas with hidden educational goodies.

Are you ready for school? Yes? Well then, let's head to class!

Smithsonian Online

If you want history, the Smithsonian Institution has it, and Smithsonian Online, a service of the Smithsonian Institution in Washington, D.C., is no exception. The materials in this area are for the personal use of students, teachers, scholars, and the public.

The Smithsonian's services include:

- Information to help people plan their visits to Smithsonian museums
- Answers to commonly asked questions about the Institution and about its collections
- Resources for teachers and students
- Bulletin boards about Smithsonian museums
- Photographs of objects in its collections
- Notices of upcoming Smithsonian events, both in Washington, D.C. and in other communities
- Excerpts from *Smithsonian* and *Air & Space/Smithsonian* magazines, as well as subscription information
- Special online events, such as real-time chats with Smithsonian experts
- Catalogs of publications, museum shop products, and Smithsonian travel opportunities

Where

Education
Smithsonian Online

Keyword

Smithsonian

Periodicals for Teachers

You don't have your lesson plans ready and your principal just called to let you know that she'll be evaluating your class all day tomorrow? Don't sweat it; head to the Smithsonian Online. The Smithsonian Institution's Office of Elementary and Secondary Education publishes two periodical for teachers.

- *Art to Zoo* is the Office of Elementary and Secondary Education's quarterly journal for teachers of grades three to eight. Each issue provides background information, a lesson plan, classroom activities, and resources for further information on a science, art, or social studies topic. Three recent issues of *Art to Zoo* are currently available online.
- *Let's Go to the Smithsonian* is a quarterly newsletter highlighting exhibitions, resources, and publications of interest to teachers (grades pre-kindergarten through grade twelve) in the Washington, D.C. area. This guide helps teachers to decide which exhibits are appropriate for their students' grade levels and the curriculum. Parents may also want to review this before the next museum trip. The current issue of *Let's Go to the Smithsonian* is available online.

Where

Education

Smithsonian Online

Keyword

Smithsonian

Select

Smithsonian Education

About SI Education Services

Read/Save

Periodicals for Teachers

High School Curriculum Kits

Ahh, high school. You don't have good memories? Well, neither do your teachers. They spent their time arguing with the school board over what to teach you to make you a productive member of society. AOL and the Smithsonian Institution have helped this task along by providing teachers with the following high school curriculum kits free-of-charge:

- *Carbons to Computers: The Changing American Office*—This kit traces technological change and cultural values, from 1830 to the present, as they are reflected in offices.

- *Image and Identity: Clothing and Adolescence in the 1990s*—This book leads teachers and their students to examine the American adolescent's relationship with clothing.

- *Protest and Patriotism: A History of Dissent and Reform*—This kit examines the history of American protest through the study of three movements—populism, civil rights, and environmentalism.

Access this area for more information and to request these kits.

Where

Education

Smithsonian Online

Keyword

Smithsonian

Select

Smithsonian Education

About SI Education Services

Read/Save

High School Curriculum Kits

Resource Materials for Teachers

The *Resource Guide for Teachers* catalogs educational materials available from the Smithsonian Institution and several organizations affiliated with the Smithsonian including the National Gallery of Art, the Kennedy Center for the Performing Arts, and Reading Is Fundamental.

The *Guide* contains more than 400 entries, each of which is indexed in several ways. You can use these indexes to find the kind of material available on a subject at a particular grade level.

Each entry in the *Guide* is numbered and includes:

- A description of the material
- The grade level for which it is appropriate
- The cost (if any)
- The organization to contact when ordering; the organization is listed at the end of every entry

The address and phone number for each organization is listed in the section entitled "Where to Order Materials." For this file, check the Resource Guide Indexes.

Where

Education
Smithsonian Online

Keyword

Smithsonian

Select

Smithsonian Education
SI Education Resource Guide

Read/Save

Article Reprints
to
Videos & Films (Get it? Almost A to Z)

Library of Congress

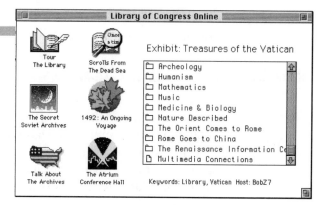

The Library of Congress Online is a pilot program involving the Library of Congress and America Online, Inc. At present, the Library does not have an online reference or information service.

The "virtual" library features several online special exhibits, including the *Scrolls from the Dead Sea*, *1492: An Ongoing Voyage*, *The Secret Soviet Archives*, and *Treasures of the Vatican*.

In addition to the special exhibits, there are several areas of interest to educators and scholars:

- Scholars' Exchange allows scholars to exchange materials about the exhibits and the events they cover. (Select: Talk about the Archives)

- Teachers' Exchange: allows teachers to exchange lesson plans and other classroom materials created in response to the exhibits. Free online time is awarded for the best contributions! (Select: Talk about the Archives)

- Renaissance Information Center is a special section for the new Vatican exhibit. Sign up for classes in astronomy, geometry, music, or Latin; get help with translations of the archives; look up featured figures in the online encyclopedia, discuss religious history and philosophy, or talk about the arts, play Renaissance-era fantasy games, and more. (Select: Renaissance Information Center)

Where

Education
Library of Congress Online

Keyword

Library

Select

See the bulleted items for specific selections

Scrolls from the Dead Sea

The *Scrolls from the Dead Sea* exhibit has been designed as a virtual museum tour. As you navigate the tour, you'll have the opportunity to visit the ruins, the caves, and the dig, as well as download GIFs of the artifacts. In itself, this is a fun archeology lesson. It's also a great preview if you are journeying to the "real" exhibit.

Where

Education
Library of Congress Online

Keyword

Library

Select

Scrolls from the Dead Sea

Go to Ruins

(or)

Go to Caves

(or)

The Dig

(or)

The People and the Place

Dead Sea Bowl

Want to eat your cereal in something special this morning? Well you can at least look at this picture while you separate Crunch Berries from the Cap'n Crunch. This deep bowl from the first century B.C. has a flat base, expertly turned on a lathe. Several concentric circles are incised in its base, and the rim of the bowl is rounded. Most wooden objects found in the Qumran area are of acacia tortilis, a tree prevalent in the southern valleys of Israel.

Subj: GIF: Bowl (R18 Color)
Date: April 24, 1993
From: Reuploader
File: REL_18.GIF (157385 bytes)
DL time: < 4 minutes
Needs: GIF viewer

Where

Education
Library of Congress

Keyword

Library

Select

Scrolls

Go to Ruins

Continue (not Object 1)

Bowl

Download

GIF: Bowl (R18 Color)

National Geographic Online

Within National Geographic Online, teachers and students will discover maps, lesson plans and articles pertaining to geography and culture. The three main sources within this forum are Geographic Education Program (GEP), NGS Kids Network, and NGS Online Atlas.

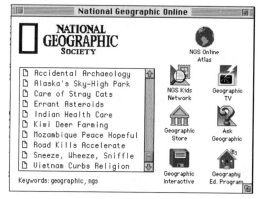

In the GEP online area, geography teachers can read articles from *Geography Education UPDATE*, the nation's leading newsletter for geography teachers; exchange ideas with other teachers on a geography teaching message board; network via the National Geographic Alliances; plan for the coming year with a regularly updated GEP calendar; exchange lesson plans in a Geography Teaching Lesson Plan Library; and hold conferences or have informal real-time chats with each other in the Explorers Hall conference room.

Where

Education

National Geographic Online

Keyword

NGS

Select

Geographic Education Program

Maps Online

Teachers and students: Check out this site and its wide selection of maps, which are both a teaching tool and a source of entertainment. Over 25 maps are available, including the continents, the United States, and places in the news. For current events lessons, select "In the News" to find up-to-date information on such hot spots as South Africa, Somalia, Macedonia, Croatia, Slovenia, Yugoslavia, and Bosnia.

Where

Education
National Geographic Online

Keyword

NGS

Select

NGS Online Atlas

Around the World

or From Another Angle

or In the News

Download

[your choice]

Geography Lesson Plan

Did you just get called to substitute for Mrs. Utley's Geography class again? As a seasoned veteran, you know that giving students busy work or showing filmstrips is a sure-fire way to make your day (and the students') miserable. Keep the students entertained while they learn with this lesson plan from the 1991 Geography Awareness Week teacher's handbook, published by the Geography Education Program of the National Geographic Society. The 1991 theme of the week, "Geography: New Worlds to Explore," emphasizes that geography—the study of the earth and its people—invites exploration.

Subj: Mountains Beneath The Sea
Date: September 24, 1991
From: Angela
File: lesson.plan3 (7348 bytes)
DL time: < 1 minute
Author: Lisa J. Rudy
Needs: PC or Mac, text reader

Where

Education
National Geographic Online

Keyword

NGS

Select

Geographic Education Program

Geographic Teaching Materials

Download

Mountains Beneath The Sea

Academic Assistance Center

Having a little trouble with logarithms in base 2? No need to worry. The Academic Assistance Center is designed for those who need additional reinforcement of concepts they are learning, help with their homework, or those who want to hone skills that have become rusty. Here is the place to find teachers who are dedicated to helping you achieve your academic goals.

You will also find assistance and guidance in preparing term papers through the Academic Research Service, and special help with end-of-term exams through the Exam Prep Center. For help with your study skills or if you are preparing for a standardized exam (GED, SAT, etc.), you can get help in the "Study Skills Instruction" area.

All of the boards in these areas are closely monitored—if you post a message on any of them and don't get a response within 48 hours, you'll get an hour of free time—the virtual equivalent of Domino's former 30 minutes or less motto.

In fact, with the teacher paging service, you'll be surprised at how fast you'll get a reply from a great tutor.

Where

Education

Academic Assistance Center

Keyword

Homework

The Exam Prep Center and the Exam Exchange Download Library are terrific resource areas for home schoolers as well as for traditional students and teachers! (Keyword: Homework)

Teacher Pager

The Teacher Pager allows grade school, high school, and college level students to get specific answers to and help with academic problems. The Teacher

Pager can be used to arrange a meeting with a teacher, ideally on the following day. There are even occasions when a teacher trained in the subject area you need will be immediately available.

If you're online in the evening (5:00 to midnight Eastern time), you should check first in the Homework Help Room (Keyword: Homework; Select: Academic Assistance). If there's no teacher available to help you, then use the Teacher Pager to schedule an appointment.

In general, it is best to use the Teacher Pager when you need assistance in less than 48 hours and there is no regularly scheduled session in your subject area within that time (check Keyword: AAC for the weekly schedule) and a teacher is not available to assist you in the Homework Help Room.

You'll generally meet the teacher in the Homework Help Room. If any room other than the main Homework Help Room is going to be the meeting place, you will receive E-mail before your meeting, telling you where to meet and how to get there.

Where

Education
Academic Assistance Center

Keyword

Teacher Pager

Select

Teacher Paging on the Mac

(or)

Teacher Paging on an IBM-compatible

Make a Page

>[Complete and send]

Mini-Lessons

With the mini-lessons, you may not even need to contact the Teacher Pager. The mini-lessons found in the libraries in the Teacher Pager area are an ever-growing compilation of the best responses made by the Interactive Education Services (IES) staff to questions asked through IES' Teacher Pager (a.k.a. the Exam Hotline). The mini-lesson libraries represent ideal answers to the most commonly asked questions by online students in all major subjects. Mini-lessons are great for elementary, junior high, and high school students, and provide good computer assignments to home schoolers as well. Nearly 1,000 mini-lessons are available. For example, whether you're talking about music or biographies, the Q&A on Andrew Lloyd Webber reveals the mastery of the composer and his music. His composition awards and accomplishments are included in this mini-lesson.

Subj: Andrew Lloyd Webber
Date: August 10, 1993
From: TeacherDN1
File: ALWEBER (1188 bytes)
DL time: < 1 minute
Author: Pamela2069
Needs: Any computer, text reader

Where

Education
Academic Assistance Center

Keyword

Homework

Select

Subject Specific Sessions
Mini-Lesson Library
Arts Mini Lessons

Download

Andrew Lloyd Webber

Study Survey

Could your study habits be improved? Do you know your strengths and weaknesses? Study patterns, schedules, note-taking, diagramming, highlighting, memorization, and test-taking are among the tested skills. By analyzing your study patterns, you'll know what you need to do to succeed!

Subj: Survey & Evaluation
Date: April 1, 1993
From: RussellM18
File: study.survey (5954 bytes)
DL time: < 1 minute
Needs: Text reader

Where

Education
Academic Assistance Center

Keyword

Homework

Select

The Study Skills Service

Study Skills Survey

Downloadable Survey & Evaluation

Download

Survey & Evaluation

Study Skills Lessons

We tested the Textbook Reading Lesson in the Study Skills Lessons and found it to be quite worthwhile. It's difficult to think back over one's years of education to determine when a tip or lesson was learned. The Study Skills Sessions are applicable for junior high and up—perhaps most appropriate for high school students. But the earlier we develop those good habits and skills, the better we'll do!

In the Textbook Reading Lesson, students begin by thinking about how the main points relate to the details presented. Once the book is open, the best students read introductions and summaries first, followed by survey topic markers.

The lesson includes a series of exercises and questions to be answered, all to reinforce the concepts presented.

Subj: Lesson 10:Textbook Reading (WORD)
Date: February 8, 1992
From: BKurshan
File: ss10 (23040 bytes)
DL time: < 1 minute
Author: Study Smart
Needs: Microsoft Word compatible software

Where

Education

Academic Assistance Center

Keyword

Homework

Select

Study Skills Lessons

Lesson & Chart Library

Download

Lesson 10 Textbook Reading

Tools and Tests

AOL's primary download libraries, accessed through *File Search, PC Software and Mac Software,* are home to thousands of files, several hundred of which have education applications. I've selected just a few to represent the best and the most unusual from the eclectic education collections.

IQ Test

Have you ever taken an IQ test? Well now you can in the privacy of your own home. This test automatically adjusts for age. The IQ tests your ability to reason and think logically compared to other people. A score between 95 and 105 represents an average IQ. As limited by the format, the test does not measure musical talent, manual dexterity, or a variety of other abilities. It only tests logical thinking, which is important to success in life. You might want to try this on your next date!

This test is shareware. If you like it, please send $8 to the address noted. For the fee, the author will provide the correct answers and the explanations as to why they are correct.

Subj: IQ Test sea
Date: June 29, 1994
From: Zappertron
File: IQ Test.sea (317146 bytes)
DL time: < 8 minutes
Author: Chris Athanas
Needs: Mac, hard disk, System 6.07 or later, 4Mb of RAM

Where

The complete sequence of steps through Computing can be found on page 15. Of course, you can save time and money by using the Keyword shortcuts.

Keyword

File Search

Select

>IQ

Download

IQ Test

IQ Testing in Windows

The Mac IQ test was so much fun I just had to find one for Windows users. A friend and I took this one together and we came up with a score of 144. Does that mean 72 each? Have fun and don't take this too seriously unless you are trained in IQ matters. IQ Test consists of 50 multiple-choice questions that you answer within a 30-minute timed period. You may also elect to finish the test prior to that time by clicking on the DONE button. The program will then calculate your answers, display your IQ score with "reasonable accuracy," and show you the question numbers that you answered incorrectly together with the right answers.

With payment of a fee, you can obtain the latest version of IQ Test plus a Color Preference Analysis test and a catalog of psychological and pre-employment testing programs.

Subj: IQTEST: V2.0 Windows IQ Test
Date: August 11, 1992
From: RBAKER PC
File: IQTEST.ZIP (17487 bytes)
DL time: < 1 minutes
Author: Terry Wilkins
Needs: UnZIPing program, Windows 3.x
Type: Freely distributed (see notes)

Where

The complete sequence of steps through Computing can be found on page 15. Of course, you can save time and money by using the Keyword shortcuts.

Keyword

File Search

Select

>intelligence IQ

Download

IQ Test:V2.0 Windows IQ Test

Science Graphics and Clip Art Sampler

The Science Graphics Collection is the fifteenth in School House Mac's SuperClipArt series collections of public domain graphics.

The Science Graphics Collection is comprised of over 87 paint files and 40 PICT files. This sampler contains 5 files from the complete Science Graphics Collection so you can see the quality of the graphics, as well as their size and style.

Subj: Science Graphics Sampler sea
Date: June 22, 1994
From: Charlie938
File: Science Graphics Sampler.sea (92729 bytes)
DL time: < 2 minutes
Author: Charles Doe/SchoolHouse Mac
Needs: Mac, HyperCard 2.x

Where

The complete sequence of steps through Computing can be found on page 15. Of course, you can save time and money by using the Keyword shortcuts.

Keyword

File Search

Select

>Science graphics

Download

Science Graphics Sampler

The Lion's Roar General Math Guide

The Lion's Roar General Math Guide is a math help book/simplified instruction manual for high school/SAT and beginning college students (or anyone who wants to learn "other math" with reduced struggle). It's now one file consisting of nine pages of step-by-step instructions culled from the author's tutoring of high school and junior college students. It's the cream of many hours of tutoring in an encapsulated format, and demonstrates the solutions with graphs and pictures.

You will find help with truth tables, matrix problems, euler circles, problems with sets and set notation, and SAT/Trig triangles.

Subj: General Math Help MSWord or ClarisWorks (2 versions)
Date: June 26, 1994
From: MikeG36776
File: General Math Help Book - Word (44544 bytes)
DL time: < 1 minute
Author: Michael Goldberger
Needs: Mac, Microsoft Word 5.1a or ClarisWorks

Where

The complete sequence of steps through Computing can be found on page 15. Of course, you can save time and money by using the Keyword shortcuts.

Keyword

File Search

Select

>General math help

Download

General Math Help MSWord

General Math Help ClarisWorks

Periodic Table

Every chemistry student needs a periodic table and you might as well have one on your computer. Who needs one in a book? This file contains two simple periodic tables: one of the tables has the "f" region included into the table; the second table has the quantum mechanical designations over each section. This file was created in Canvas 3.0 and converted to a PICT file.

Subj: Periodic Table
Date: October 26, 1993
From: MIKECHEM
File: QM Periodic Table (26642 bytes)
DL time: < 1 minute
Author: M. Luco
Needs: PICT viewer

Where

The complete sequence of steps through Computing can be found on page 15. Of course, you can save time and money by using the Keyword shortcuts.

Keyword

File Search

Select

>Periodic table

Download

Periodic Table

Word Use Skills

Is it *carat* or *karat*? *troop* or *troupe*? *luxurious* or *luxuriant*? *rout* or *route*? You will encounter words with similar sounds but different meanings, nonexistent words, and improper word forms. WordUse will develop your ability to use the correct word and *not* use an incorrect or nonexistent word (irregardless, ugh!).

You will be challenged to select the correct answer in a series of multiple-choice, sentence-completion questions. Your score histories are retained for subsequent comparison of your progress. To enrich the learning experience, many questions are derived from history and literature (". . . lend me your ears!"). This also makes a fun quiz/game for language trivia lovers!

Subj: WORDUSE: Word Use Skills
Date: March 4, 1994
From: SKILLWARE
File: WORDUSE.ZIP (169231 bytes)
DL time: < 4 minutes
Author: SKILLWARE
Needs: PC, UnZIPing program
Type: Shareware

Where

Education

Keyword

Education

Select

PC/MS-DOS Education Software

Quick Find

>Spelling

Download

WORDUSE: Word Use Skills

Win Free Time!

You may have won $10 million dollars! No, Ed McMahon is not beating down your door with a check, but you can access this area to get free time. Interactive Education Services in the Online Campus features four ongoing contests in Literature, Science, Math, and History.

Every few days new questions are posted and the first person to answer five questions correctly will be awarded one hour of free time. Credit for correct answers will only be given to the *first* person who posts the correct answer after the question. Check each day to see if your answer was correct and then answer the next question. Some questions and problems that have appeared in the past are:

- What is the title of the latest book by the author of *Jaws*?

- Who wrote the the screenplay for the mini-series based on Stephen King's novel *The Stand*?

- What was the difference between a Winchester .44 carbine and a Winchester .44 rifle?
- Why do most helicopters have two rotors?
- You need to retile the floor of your bathroom. The floor is a rectangle with a width equivalent to 15 tiles. You can only buy tiles in groups of 53. You guess at how many tiles you need, but when you return home you find to your dismay that you are one tile short. How many tiles long is your bathroom floor? (Assume that it is less than 80 tiles long.)

Where

Education
Interactive Education Services

Keyword

IES

Select

Coliseum 4.0

Literature Contest (or)

History Contest (or)

Science Contest (or)

Mathematics Contest

Barron's Booknotes

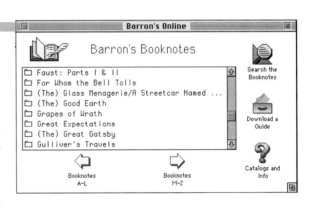

Barron's Inc. is one of America's leading publishers of education and business information. Barron's Booknotes are the company's popular guides to great works of literature—great help for students trying to read, understand, and write about these works, and also for all of us interested in—or in need of—hearing another voice, another perspective as we read the classics.

Each Booknotes guide is written by a respected academic and/or educator and includes classic literary criticism of the work in question, the author's biography, life, and work in context of the times, and detailed analyses of plot, character, and the literary qualities of the work.

The Booknotes can be read online or downloaded. I recommend you download the files to save your online time.

Where

Education

Keyword

Barrons

A TALE OF TWO CITIES

"It was the best of times, it was the worst of times . . . ." A Tale of Two Cities is one of Charles Dickens' great classics that millions of high school students encounter and enjoy each year. With a description of a brutal punishment carried out on a French boy, Dickens leads in to the two major themes that are woven through the historical novel: Fate and Death. With characters that seem to stand for entire social classes, the actions of Madame Defarge and Miss Pross represent a contest between the forces of hatred and of love. The Booknotes online will help your students to clarify the issues and prepare their own analysis of the plot and the characters.

Subj: Tale of Two Cities
Date: April 13, 1993
From: Edprod
File: btal.dbs.text (141122 bytes)
DL time: < 3 minutes
Needs: Text reader

Where

Education

Keyword

Barrons

Select

Download a Guide

Download

Great Expectations

Research Tips

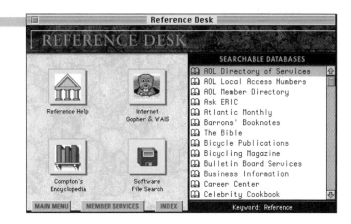

You'll find help and how-to files throughout AOL. This area is filled with useful tips to help students conduct research on AOL.

- *Compton's Encyclopedia*: *Compton's Encyclopedia* may provide some background on your subject. Remember to start out with a broad general search, then narrow your search to a specific topic. For example, if you were researching the school desegregation case Brown v. Board of Education, start out by searching on Black Americans, then The Civil Rights Movement, then check out Notable Black Americans, then Thurgood Marshall. Also, remember, the search function in Compton's does not accept wildcard entries—it searches on whole words and phrases only.

- *Academic Research Service*: If you are doing research for a school paper, you may want to post a message to the expert research staff in the Academic Research Service. From the Reference Desk, click on the Reference Help icon then select Academic Research Service.

- *Talk About Reference*: Would you like input from other AOL members about your research topic? Just click on the Talk About Reference message board icon in the Reference Help screen and select or create a folder about your subject. Then post a message asking America Online members to share their knowledge.

Academic Research Service

America Online's Academic Research Service provides research support for students in high school, college, or graduate school. The service is coordinated by Michael W. Popejoy, a college administrator, professor, researcher, and writer from Florida. Dr. Popejoy provides assistance, leads, basic information, sources of information, search strategies, and more, to assist in your research. To access the service and read the directions for use, follow these directions.

Where

Education
Academic Assistance Center

Keyword

Homework

Select

Online Research Service
Message Board
[Locate topic and add message]

E-mail

Check for a response in 24 to 72 hours

Test Dates

Planning your test schedule for the 1994-1995 academic year and you can't get an appointment with your guidance counselor? (Schools still have guidance counselors, don't they?) AOL can direct you to the SAT, ACT, LSAT, GMAT, and GRE test dates. Registration dates, test dates, and fees are all here. I've found two good sources . . . .

Where

Education
Princeton Review
/Student Access Online

Keyword

Student

Select

Test Preparation

Read/Save

[Select test information]

Where

Education
College Board Online

Keyword

College

Select

1994-1995 Test Dates

Read/Save

1994-1995 Test Dates

Financial Aid Guides

Admit it. Financial Aid is a mysterious, complicated, and potentially expensive topic. Effective college financing inevitably requires great effort and clever strategies on the part of parents, students, college administrators, and sometimes benefactors.

There are several guides to financial aid on AOL. I recommend that you read the next few—for a number of reasons. Financial aid is a complicated topic and the more you read, the more you'll know!

Where

Financial Aid Information

Keyword

College

Select

Financial Aid Package

Read/Save

[Financial Aid articles]

Where

Princeton Review/Student Access Online

Keyword

Education
Student Access Services

Select

Student Access Services
Financial Aid & Student Loans

Education in a Nutshell

Financial Aid in a Nutshell is a text document that describes the financial-aid process and provides general information for students and their families. This file provides a quick introduction to financial aid, and includes a general description that gives you an idea where to start looking and what is available. This article is somewhat more in depth than the articles featured above.

File: Financial Aid in a Nutshell (17536 bytes)
Date: March 10, 1994
DL time: < 1 minutes
Author: CllgFunder
Needs: Word processor (created in Microsoft Word)

Where

Education
Princeton Review/Student Access Online

Keyword

Student

Select

Students' Software

Mac Exchange

Download

Financial Aid in a Nutshell

Where to Find More Goodies

Elsewhere on AOL: Capital Connection (Keyword: Capital), The New York Times Online (@Times), Chicago Online (Chicago) and the Mercury Center (Mercury) are good places to check for supplementary information.

In this book, you'll want to refer to *Books, Magazines, and Literature, Kid $tuff, Government,* and *Science and Space.*

FREE $TUFF

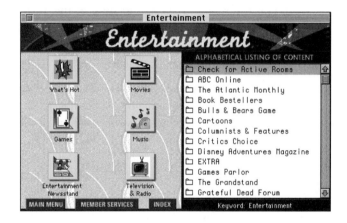

Television is now so desperately hungry for material that they're scraping the top of the barrel.

Gore Vidal

Entertaining AOL

Music, TV, movies, videos, cartoons, and comics come together in this fun-filled section. There's nothing too serious here except the access to the news. Together, we'll find clips from 1994's hot movies and historic scenes from yesteryear.

ABC and NBC both have prominent forums on America Online. You'll find their styles to be unique, like their programming. Fans of one network or the other will want to check in regularly, if not daily. Collectors of DC Comics will get to see the newest cover art as well as images from historic issues. You'll also get a chance to look at the Warner/Reprise Records Online and MTV forums to hear the scoop on the lastest in music, and Critics' Corner, Hollywood Online, and EXTRA will provide you with summaries and reviews of all the Hollywood hubbub.

And last, please keep in mind that media companies produce many of the terrific entertainment areas on AOL. Just as the television seasons change, the online content changes as well. At some point, the material in this section will be dated, but the content online will still be as hot as it gets.

Critics' Choice

Critics' Choice is a multimedia syndicate, specializing in reviewing entertainment. You'll find this forum to be an intelligent guidebook to to the cacophony of entertainment choices. They'll help you choose the best, and avoid the worst, *before* you commit your money and time.

Where

Entertainment

Critics' Choice

Keyword

Critic

Critics' Choice E-Mail

Members of the Critics' Choice E-mail list receive advance information about contests, articles, and reviews by private E-mail. This is a free service, designed to save you online time by letting you know what's up in Critics' Choice quickly and conveniently.

Where

Entertainment

Critics' Choice

Select

Contact Critics' Choice

Critics' Choice Contests

If you love trivia, test your knowledge here—you may win videos of new movies or receive tickets to concerts. Recent winners have been awarded the *Escape from Jafar* and *The Nightmare Before Christmas* videos while others have received tickets to see *Sugar* in concert. Often, you'll find more than one contest in Critics' Choice, usually awarding more than one prize. Stop in often to maximize your winning chances.

Where

Entertainment

Critics' Choice

Keyword

Critic

Select

CONTEST:[name]

Pssst . . . I Hear the Grateful Dead Is Playing Tonight . . .

There's no need to buy magazines and Sunday newspapers to keep up with the concert schedules for the major bands. Just log into AOL for the Critics' Choice up-to-date schedule of events. A current and comprehensive schedule is always available.

Where

Entertainment

Critics' Choice

Keyword

Critic

Select

Music & Concerts

Concert Dates

Read/Save

[performing artist or band]

Hot New Movies

What are the new movies? What are the story lines? Who are the stars? Do you know the release date for the new Disney film? Which ones are good? Each month you'll find the answers to these questions and you'll be the first to know which movies are worth the outrageous ticket price!

Where

Entertainment

Critics' Choice

Keyword

Critic

Select

Movie Features

Current Reviews

Read/Save

[movie name]

Select Coming Soon for information on movies that are due to appear on the big screen.

Classic Forrest Gump

Sitting on a bench as he tells his story, Tom Hanks stars as the title character in *Forrest Gump*. Now, you can have your very own picture of this "destined to be a classic" movie.

Subj: GUMP: Hanks on bench
Date: July 1, 1994
From: ArisC
File: HANKS1.GIF (47214 bytes)
DL time: < 1 minute
Author: Paramount Pictures
Needs: Any computer, GIF viewer

Where

Entertainment

Critics' Choice

Keyword

Critic

Select

Movie Features

Download Libraries

Pictures (8-bit)

Download

Gump

Quotes from Forrest Gump

Can you quote Forrest Gump? Now you can...with a little practice.

This file includes a collection of 14 sounds from the movie. These high-quality samples are presented in the System 7 sound format. You'll find such gems as "Same as everybody" and "What's my destiny?"

Subj: Forrest Gump Sounds SND
Date: August 10, 1994
From: Brian VDB
File: GumpSounds.sit (419130 bytes)
DL time: < 11 minutes
Needs: Sound application, AOL 2.x or StuffIt Expander 3.5

Where

Computing

Mac Software

Keyword

Mac: File Search
PC: Mac Software

Select

>Gump

Download

Forrest Gump Sounds SND

Entertainment News

Entertainment news, excerpted from *Studio Briefing*, is updated Monday through Friday. You'll find Disney, MCA, Home Shopping Network, takeover bids, media deals, corporate earnings, FCC rulings, TV ratings, hot videos, box office draws, new productions and castings, and more in each weekday's entertainment news.

Where
Entertainment
Critics' Choice

Keyword
Critic

Select
NEWS (Updated M-F)

Hollywood Online

Hollywood Online is an exciting service that features sneak previews of the hottest new motion pictures. Here you can sneak an exclusive look at the latest movie before you see it in the theater. The Pictures and Sounds library features downloadable pictures, while Movie Notes covers cast and production news. You can also download exclusive multimedia presentations, featuring sound bites and video clips.

Hollywood Online also offers drawings and contests through America Online, which afford members the opportunity to receive great promotional items from the movie studios, including movie posters and complimentary movie passes.

Movies and other projects rotate off line as new features become available, so if you see a clip that you'd like, don't wait because it may soon be replaced.

Where
Entertainment
Hollywood Online

Keyword
Hollywood

Select
Special [name] Promotion

Hot Ten Movies and Videos

What's a database without statistics? With all the lists on America Online, you'll never have to find out. Hollywood Online features two Hot Ten lists covering movies and videos. The movies list carries new openings and hot tips, while the videos list adds "new in the stores" and video hot tips.

Where

Entertainment

Hollywood Online

Keyword

Hollywood

Select

Inside Hollywood

Berlin's Hot Ten

Read/Save

Hot Ten Movies

Hot Ten Videos

Top 10 Lists

The EXTRA Top Ten features the top 10 box office movies, TV programs, video rentals, and albums for the prior week. Check here to gain trivia knowledge that's sure to liven up your next Tupperware party.

Where

Entertainment

EXTRA

Keyword

Extra

Select

Top 10

Read/Save

EXTRA TOP TEN [date]

Warner/Reprise Records Online

Warner/Reprise Records Online provides music fans with the latest information about artists on the Warner/Reprise family of labels, which includes Warner Bros., Reprise, Sire, American Recordings, Giant, Slash, 4AD, Qwest, Luaka Bop, Kinetic Records, The Medicine Label, and Maverick. You'll find all sorts of information here:

- **New Releases** contains release dates for new and upcoming albums, as well as personnel credits, track listings, and related information.

- **Artists On Tour** contains Warner artists' tour itineraries, including national and international concert dates.
- **Multimedia Library** contains graphic files, music samples, and self-contained multimedia presentations. The graphic files, which are in GIF format, include publicity photos, album cover art, band logos, and other interesting images.
- **Contests & Special Events** features contests in which users can win CDs, cassette tapes, t-shirts, and posters, among other items. It also provides information about special online events, such as live conferences with artists.
- **Music Categories**, featured in the scroll window, includes Alternative, Country, Gospel, Jazz (World Beat, New Age), Pop, Rap, Rock, and R & B. Within these folders you'll discover even more detailed information about selected artists, including bios, tour information, new/upcoming releases, and news bits.

Where

Entertainment

Warner/Reprise Records Online

Keyword

Warner

Select

Multimedia Library

Sound Samples

Download

[Artist/Group - song]

Madonna's Secret

Psssssttt—do you want to know Madonna's "secret"? Try this sound sample of Madonna's "Secret" from the album *Bedtime Stories*.

Subj:　Madonna "Secret"
Date:　September 14, 1994
From:　Max Warner
File:　SECRET.zip (497564 bytes)
DL time: < 13 minutes
Author:　Warner/Sire
Needs:　Mac, PC with soundcard, unZIPing program, WAV player

Where

Entertainment

Warner/Reprise Records Online

Keyword

Warner

Select

Multimedia Library

Sound Samples

Download

Madonna "Secret"

Warner Artists on Tour

With Warner/Reprise Records Online you can
stay on top of their artists' concert tours.

Where

Entertainment

Warner/Reprise Records Online

Keyword

Warner

Select

Artists on Tour

Read/Save

[Artist or Group]

Bound to Cover Just a Little More Ground

The Dead have been pumping out the tunes for over a quarter-century and now
even AOL has jumped on the bandwagon. Look here for a collection of all
things Dead—hot off of Usenet's rec.music.gdead newsgroup—from songlists
and special guests to Jerry's health and well being.

Subj: Useless Dead Stats 1993
Date: February 5, 1994
From: Elect Eye
File: useless dead stats (262688 bytes)
DL time: < 7 minutes
Author: Internet
Needs: Text reader

Where

Entertainment

Grateful Dead Forum

Keyword

Dead

Select

The Vault Dead Library

Vault

Download

Useless Dead Stats 1993

Cartoons

On America Online you have access to the newest form of cartoon entertainment. Download GIF-format cartoon files, and use a GIF viewer to see them on your own computer.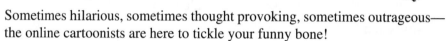

Sometimes hilarious, sometimes thought provoking, sometimes outrageous—the online cartoonists are here to tickle your funny bone!

Where

Entertainment

Cartoons

Keyword

Cartoons

CompuToon

CompuToon features the work of veteran cartoonist Charles Rodrigues. Charles produces cartoons regularly for *MacWEEK Magazine*, and has been doing cartoons for many other publications for years, including *Stereo Review* and *National Lampoon*.

A new cartoon is scheduled for release each Friday, depending on Charles' busy schedule. Be sure to sign on regularly and tune in to the outrageous Rodrigues view of the world!

Vasectomy

"Hey lady, it's okay . . . ." Perhaps some days you do need a flasher in your life! This GIF has over 15,000 downloads on record.

Subj: Vasectomy
Date: April 24, 1992
From: Tooner

File: Vasectomy.GIF (7717 bytes)
DL time: < 1 minute
Author: Charles Rodrigues
Needs: GIF file viewer

Where

Entertainment

Cartoons

Keyword

Cartoons

Select

CompuToon

CompuToon (again)

Download

Vasectomy

Dilbert

Everyone knows Dilbert—a United Feature Syndicate comic strip by Scott Adams. This new medium for Dilbert comes on the fourth anniversary of the comic strip, which was launched in 1989 by United Feature Syndicate and now appears in more than 130 newpapers. The AOL feature starts with the first syndicated Dilbert strip and will feature all the dailies in order.

Artist Scott Adams is available on America Online via screen name: ScottAdams.

Jury Selection

As juries are selected for today's trials, this Dilbert strip holds special meaning.

Subj: JURY SELECTION
Date: October 7, 1994
From: Caddy70
File: DIL01017.GIF (7423 bytes)
DL time: < 1 minute
Author: Scott Adams
Needs: GIF viewer

Where

Entertainment

Cartoons

Keyword

Cartoons

Select

Dilbert

Dilbert Comics

Download

JURY SELECTION

McHumor

Welcome to "McHumor" by Theresa McCracken. Theresa draws cartoons on just about everything under the sun, from "Anemic Astronauts to Zen Zoologists." A new McHumor cartoon is presented each week, covering a broad mixture of subjects. Add a little fun to your downloads.

"Pregnant too?"

When pickles and ice cream are the meal of the day, download this file for a hoot.

Subj: Pregnant
Date: April 3, 1993
From: Tooner
File: Pregnant.GIF (11758 bytes)
DL time: < 1 minute
Author: Theresa McCracken
Needs: GIF file viewer

Where

Entertainment

Cartoons

Keyword

Cartoons

Select

McHumor Cartoons

McHumor Library

Download

Pregnant

DC Comics Online

In a pioneering effort for a comic book publisher, DC Comics has created a customized area for AOL users. This is the first time a comic book publisher has partnered with an online service, and this successful venture has become a full-time DC Comics virtual convention.

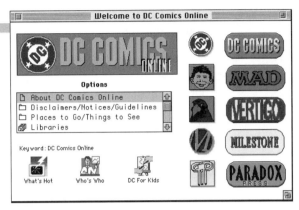

DC Comics has tons of stuff for America Online members. Check out these hot spots:

- To get a look at the actual comics before anyone else, hit the What's Hot Library and download the pictures that go with the articles. In these download files, you can even select covers that have already been shipped or those that are coming soon!
- Stop by the Who's Who photo-gallery sampler to see some of your favorite characters.
- Visit the archive section, where you can browse through samples of comic books you may never have seen before!
- Within the DC "neighborhoods," you can visit DC Comics, MAD Magazine, Vertigo, Milestone Media, and Paradox Press.

Where

Entertainment

DC Comics

Keyword

DC Comics

Calling Comic Creators

If you've ever wanted to be a comic creator, writer, or artist, you'll want to jump straight to the submission guidelines. In this section, AOL comic fans will learn what skills are required for artists and writers at DC Comics. Read this before submitting your work, because all requirements and changes will be noted here. Pencillers, inkers, letterers, and colorists, get your imaginations in gear.

Where

Entertainment

DC Comics

Keyword

DC Comics

Select

Disclaimers/Notices/Guidelines

Superman: Lois and Clark

From *The New Adventures of Superman* comes this photo of Superman (Dean Cain) and Lois Lane (Teri Hatcher). It's perfect for Superman fans to add to their collections.

Subj: Lois & Clark: Lois & Superman Pict
Date: October 6, 1994
From: DCOMLeib
File: LLSUP.GIF (109562 bytes)
DL time: < 3 minutes
Author: DC Comics Online
Needs: Mac, DOS or Windows, GIF viewer

Where

Entertainment

DC Comics

Keyword

DC Comics

Select

What's Hot

What's Hot DC Comics Graphics

Download

Lois & Clark: Lois & superman...

Batman Forever

Here is the logo for the upcoming film *Batman Forever*. It's mostly black, so perhaps you could use it for a screen saver.

Subj: Batman Forever Logo
Date: October 3, 1994
From: DCOMLeib

File: BTMNLG.GIF (26127 bytes)
DL time: < 1 minute
Author: DC Comics Online
Needs: Mac, DOS or Windows, GIF viewer

Where

Entertainment

DC Comics

Keyword

DC Comics

Select

What's Hot

What's Hot DC Comics Graphics

Download

Batman Forever Logo

Make It So!

For your collection of cover art, you'll want to download this shot from *Star Trek: The Next Generation*.

Subj: Ship 9/27: Star Trek: The Next Gen
Date: September 27, 1994
From: DCOMLeib
File: STNG.GIF (54414 bytes)
DL time: < 1 minute
Author: DC Comics Online
Needs: Mac, DOS or Windows, GIF viewer

Where

Entertainment

DC Comics

Keyword

DC Comics

Select

What's Hot

What's Hot DC Comics Graphics

Download

Ship 9/27: Star Trek: The Next Gen

Warner Bros. Studios/VIP Studio Tour Info

In a town known the world over for excitement and glamour, a town where celebrities can be seen almost everywhere you go, Warner Bros. Studios is a special place—one where movie magic is an routine occurrence.

Follow these directions for more information on tour schedules and reservations.

Where

Entertainment

DC Comics

Keyword

DC Comics

Select

Places to Go/Things to See

Warner Bros. Studios

Read/Save

Warner Bros. Studios VIP Studio Tour

Mouse Ears

A sample issue of *Mouse Ears*, the Disney newsletter, is available for download. Take a look to stay abreast of the changes at Disney's theme parks, be among the first to learn about the innovative new rides, and follow the explosive popularity of Disney videos. Both PageMaker and text versions are available.

Subj: MouseEars Sample
Date: September 21, 1994
From: MOUSE EARS
File: Mouse Ears v.1 n.8.sit (40043 bytes)
DL time: < 1 minute
Author: MouseEars
Needs: Mac, PageMaker 4.0 or higher

Where

Entertainment

Cartoons

Keyword

Cartoons

Select

Toon Talk

Toon Talk Archives

Download

MouseEars Sample

MouseEars Sample.txt

MTV Online

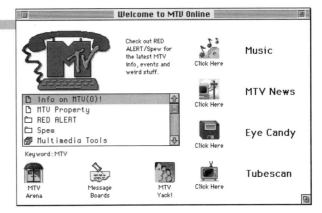

MTV Online is the ultimate interactive source for information, entertainment, and uninhibited self-expression. You can join the faithful MTV junkies who ritually log on to explore MTV's informative byways for music reviews and concert updates, MTV news, or images to download.

Talk Transcripts

Would you like to meet Tabitha Soren and other MTV personalities and guests? Check the MTV Arena Info and Schedules to find out who's coming next. After the hooha, you can download the transcript from the session. For a sample, take a look at this interview with Tabitha Soren.

Subj: Tabitha Soren
Date: August 24, 1994
From: Juliyap
File: TABCHAT.TXT (21763 bytes)
DL time: < 1 minute
Needs: Text reader

Where

Entertainment

Television & Radio

Networks

MTV Online

Keyword

MTV

Select
> MTV Arena
>
> MTV Arena Transcripts

Download
> Tabitha Soren

ABC Online

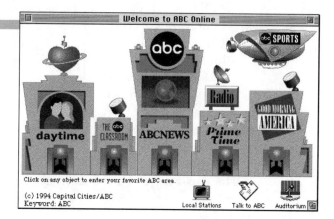

You'll find ABC favorites in ABC's attractive online forum. Within the city skyline, you can reach ABC News, Sports, Radio, Daytime, Prime Time, and Good Morning America.

Where
> Entertainment
>
> ABC Online

Keyword
> ABC

ABC News on Demand

ABC News on demand is a service provided by ABC News exclusively to the America Online community. It provides information about the major events of the day as this news team tracks goings-on around the world.

Where
> Entertainment
>
> ABC Online

Keyword
> ABC

Select
> ABC News

Read/Save
> ABC Newswire

On This Day . . . .

Curious to know what happened on your birthday back in 1912? Your daily dose of such trivia is available here. Start your day with On This Day and you'll know what battles were won, which famed person was born, and the importance of each of the 365 days during any given year.

Where

Entertainment

ABC Online

Keyword

ABC

Select

ABC News

Read/Save

On This Day

Tomorrow's News Today

You can forecast tomorrow's news with The Week Ahead. ABC will share news of the president's travels, sentencing for convicted criminals, demonstrations and rallies, and major world, national, and regional events.

Where

Entertainment

ABC Online

Keyword

ABC

Select

ABC News

Read/Save

The Week Ahead

Moments in History

ABC has captured thousands of moments in history since the network first went on the air in the 1950s. They've placed a selection online for your viewing. You're bound to open your memory's floodgates when you view this forum.

Where

Entertainment

ABC Online

Keyword

ABC

Select

ABC News

Library

Videoclips

Replays of History

Download

John Lennon

Berlin Wall Falls

Challenger Explodes

President Reagan Shot

The Royal Wedding

More Moments in History . . . A Royal Wedding to Remember

As Charles and Diana continue to make the news with their spats, books, and other joustings, Anglophiles may still enjoy a selection of perfect moments from the Royal Wedding. The clips include Diana entering the church, the once-happy Windsor family, and the poignant vows. A Mac version is also available.

Subj:　The Royal Wedding (Win)
Date:　October 14, 1994
From:　Jmpurdy
File:　ROYALWED.ZIP (1590807 bytes)
DL time: < 43 minutes
Author:　ABC News
Needs:　Windows 3.1, AVI player, sound card

Where

Entertainment

ABC Online

Keyword

ABC

Select

ABC News

Library

Videoclips

Replays of History

Download

The Royal Wedding (Win)

The Royal Wedding (MAC)

SoapBox

A daily update of the events in *General Hospital, All My Children, One Life to Live*, and *Loving*, is easily accessible online. Remote locations, behind the scenes scoops, and soap news are added to the day's storyline. Check back tomorrow to find out the latest news about your favorite soaps and stars. So, if you can't set the VCR, this is the place to find out what you've missed.

Where

Entertainment

ABC Online

Keyword

ABC

Select

Daytime

Read/Save

[date]

Soap Summaries

Do you want the news from all the soaps? Is Mary with Bob or Jim or Sue? Whose baby was switched? Has Hope come back to life? Follow these directions to the complete set of soap opera summaries.

Where

Entertainment

Television & Radio

Keyword

TV

Select

Soap Opera Summaries

Read/Save

Daytime Soaps

NBC Online

With NBC Online you can read bios and chat live with your favorite stars, check out production information for your shows, share your opinions with other viewers on the message boards, review the schedules for the week or season, and catch up on the history of a show by reading an About the Show document. If you've ever wanted to attend a taping or get programming information, this is your place.

Some of the local market affiliate stations have joined NBC Online, so you can voice your opinion of the local sports guy or ask questions of the charming local anchor through the discussion folders in the Local Channels area.

To check out this week's schedule, simply follow these directions

Where

Entertainment

NBC Online

Keyword

NBC

Select

NBC Announcements

Read/Save

NBC Prime-Time Schedule [dates]

NBC Contests

Throughout the year NBC will also be bringing advertising partners online so you can win unique and exciting promotional prizes. Click & Win is NBC Marketing's online promotional contest center. One recent contest with ad partner TGIFriday's featured a trip for two to London to visit a Friday's restaurant overseas. Another contest with McDonald's awarded $10,000 in computer equipment.

We encourage you to check NBC Online often and throughout the year so that you don't miss a once-in-a-lifetime opportunity.

Where

Entertainment

NBC Online

Keyword

NBC

When available, Click & Win contests will be featured on the main NBC screen.

Join the NBC Audience

NBC Online includes free ticket information for the network's most popular shows, including *Frasier*, *Seinfeld*, and the *Tonight Show with Jay Leno*.

Where

Entertainment

NBC Online

Keyword

NBC

Select

Ticket Info for NBC Shows

Read/Save

Blossom TICKET INFO

California Dreams TICKET INFO

Empty Nest TICKET INFO

Frasier TICKET INFO

Fresh Prince of Bel-Air TICKET INFO

Friends TICKET INFO

John Larroquette Show TICKET INFO

Late Night With Conan O'Brien TICKET INFO

Later With Greg Kinnear TICKET INFO

Leeza TICKET INFO

Mad About You TICKET INFO

Madman of the People TICKET INFO

Saturday Night Live TICKET INFO

Saved By the Bell TICKET INFO

Seinfeld TICKET INFO

The Martin Short Show TICKET INFORMATION

Tonight Show With Jay Leno TICKET INFO

Wings TICKET INFO

NBC Photo Gallery

Yes, it's really true: You can download photos of your favorite NBC stars. For the NBC soap *Days of Our Lives*, the most popular download is that of Deidre Hall. In NBC Online's first four months, Deidre Hall's photo was downloaded over 1,100 times and there were almost 7,000 downloads of an episode photo with the Seinfeld cast members!

The complete section of photos includes stars from virtually all NBC shows.

These photos are provided for your personal viewing and may not be used for public or commercial purposes.

Where

Entertainment

NBC Online

Keyword

NBC

Select

Photo Gallery

[Show]

Download

[your favorites]

TV Clips

Famous TV clips can be found throughout AOL and I've provided you with instructions to two of my favorites.

Classic Cheers Closing

From the final episode of *Cheers*, Frasier Crane screams, "Have you lost your freaking mind?" This file has been saved as a System 7 sound file.

Subj: Frasier Crane SND
Date: December 15, 1993
From: AFC Carey
File: HaveYouLost. . (FRASIER).sit (14525 bytes)
DL time: < 1 minute
Author: Kelsey Grammer
Needs: Sound utility if not running System 7

Where

The complete sequence of steps through Computing can be found on page 15. Of course, you can save time and money by using the Keyword shortcuts.

Keyword

Mac: File Search

PC: Mac Software

Select

>Frasier Cheers Sound

Download

Frasier Crane SND

I Love Lucy

Do you remember the opening music from *I Love Lucy*? This little treat will bring back memories of the Ricardos' and Mertzs' antics. Chocolate anyone?

Subj: WAV: Lucy Show Theme
Date: January 8, 1993
From: BruceB1670
File: LUCY.ZIP (98983 bytes)
DL time: < 2 minutes
Author: BMAN
Needs: UnZIPing program, Windows 3.1 or WAV file player

Where

The complete sequence of steps through Computing can be found on page 15. Of course, you can save time and money by using the Keyword shortcuts.

Keyword

PC: File Search

Mac: PC Software

Select

>Lucy Show

Download

WAV: Lucy Show Theme

Letterman's Top 10

Letterman's Top Ten lists are great fun and a definite day brightener. This file is a compilation of over 750 of Dave's Top Ten lists, dating back to the early 1980s.

Subj: TOP10: V1.0 Top Ten Lists
Date: August 5, 1994
From: AMelvis
File: TOP10.ZIP (907112 bytes)
DL time: < 24 minutes
Author: George White
Needs: UnZIPing program & Windows 3.1
Type: Freely Distributed

Where

The complete sequence of steps through Computing can be found on page 15. Of course, you can save time and money by using the Keyword shortcuts.

Keyword

File Search

Select

>Letterman

Download

TOP10: V1.0 Top Ten Lists

Where to Find More Goodies

If you're looking for theater productions, head for the Travel section of this book to find all the information you'll need on Broadway offerings.

The following magazines are accessible from the main Entertainment screen, and you can count on them for extensive entertainment coverage.

- *The Atlantic Monthly*
- *Disney Adventures* Magazine
- *The New Republic*
- *Omni Magazine Online*
- *Popular Photography Online*
- *Saturday Review Online*
- *Stereo Review Online*

FREE $TUFF

Anybody can win unless there
happens to be a second entry.

George Ade

Fun and Games

The innovative spirit of AOL and its members comes to life in a search for fun and games. Where else could you find a screen saver of eggs splattering as they hit? You'll also get a first-hand look at outrageous sound bites and gaming newsletters.

It's fair to say that five AOL users selected at random would choose completely different programs from the ones presented in this section. The files I've selected include just a few tidbits—representative of the 6,000+ PC DOS and Windows files and 7,000+ Macintosh files.

I'll start with PC games and proceed to Mac games. But don't gloss over a topic that isn't specific to your platform; there are plenty of cross-platform programs in each.

PC Games

In PC Games, you'll discover castles, crossword puzzles, chickens, and classics like Tic Tac Toe. Have a blast!

ATOMS: Find the Atoms

Shoot rays called "winons" into a grid and determine where the atoms are by watching where the winons bounce. This game can be quite complex and addicting as you add more atoms to the grid—fun for kids and adults.

Subj: ATOMS.ZIP: Find the Atoms...
Date: April 16, 1993
From: Susan G
File: atoms.zip (49878 bytes)

DL time: < 1 minute
Author: Mike McNamee, MP Software
Price: $5 or whatever you think it's worth

Where

The complete sequence of steps through Computing can be found on page 15. Of course, you can save time and money by using the Keyword shortcuts.

Keyword

Win500

Select

The Most of the Best

Download

ATOMS.ZIP: Find the Atoms...

Castle of the Winds 1.0

Castle of the Winds is a two-part graphical adventure game, loosely based on fantasy role-playing games, and drawing much inspiration from Norse mythology. Part one involves the character's efforts to avenge the deaths of his or her Godparents, who were murdered by unknown agents. Along the way, you will do battle with evil monsters, brave deadly traps, and collect the money and magical treasures guarded by dangerous foes. As the story unfolds, the character will also learn of his or her mysterious past, and the legacy left by the character's long-dead father.

You can choose the character's name and gender. And, as you set and vary the statistics (abilities and attributes) of your character, with each new game, an unlimited number of possibilities develop.

Subj: CASTLE: V1.0 Castle of Winds
Date: October 4, 1994
From: PCW Nancy
File: CASTLEOW.ZIP (409161 bytes)
DL time: < 12 minutes
Author: Rick Saada
Needs: UnZIPing program, Windows 3.x
Type: Shareware

Where

Newsstand

Multimedia World

Keyword

MMW

Select

The Library

Games & Entertainment

Download

CASTLE: V1.0 Castle of Winds

Crossword Anyone?

Crosswords Deluxe 1.0 is a Windows-hosted electronic crossword puzzle book. It includes such help features as clue assistance, answer peek, show correct words, and auto work save. This program comes with a puzzle book that you can solve on screen or print and work on the old-fashioned way. As you solve puzzles, your work is automatically saved to disk so that whenever you come back you can pick up where you stopped.

If you want to take the puzzles with you when you leave the computer, you can make printouts (up to four per page) of the puzzles with or without your work in progress.

The evaluation copy comes with a book of 25 puzzles. The registered version has 100 puzzles in your choice of Easy, Standard, Challenging, or Mixed.

Subj: Crosswords Deluxe v. 1.0
Date: July 20, 1993
From: PCW Eric
File: CWEVAL10.ZIP (169377 bytes)
DL time: < 4 minutes
Author: Edward E. Dellow
Needs: Windows 3.1

Where

Newsstand

PC World

Keyword

PC World

Select

Software Library

Windows Games

Download

Crosswords Deluxe v. 1.0

You Sunk My Battleship!

Destroyer for Windows is the electronic version of the classic board game "Battleship." You drop bombs on your opponent's battle grid, trying to sink his or her navy. Hits are recorded on the grid with one point scored for each hit made. This updated version includes a new screen, high score storage, awards of military rank, a smarter computer opponent, animated sinking ships, online help, and more gaming options.

Subj: DES4WIN: V2.0 Destroyer Game
Date: November 27, 1993
From: Acheron666
File: D4W20.ZIP (285195 bytes)
DL time: < 7 minutes
Author: Don Krafcheck (Timberline Software)
Needs: UnZIPing program, Windows 3.1
Type: Shareware

Where

The complete sequence of steps through Computing can be found on page 15. Of course, you can save time and money by using the Keyword shortcuts.

Keyword

File Search

Select

>destroyer games

Download

DES4WIN: V2.0 Destroyer Game

Mac Blaster

Blast the evil Mac invaders with rotten apples as they attack your PC! Save the workplace from the Mac invaders as you fire rotten apples at the four Macs at the top of the screen. You may have seen this cute dig on Macs in the June, 1992 "Exit Windows" section of *Windows Magazine.*

Subj: Mac Blaster Game v1.2
Date: August 31, 1993
From: WinMag1
File: MACBLA12.ZIP (20480 bytes)
DL time: < 1 minute
Author: Earl Gehr
Needs: Windows

Where
> Newsstand
>
> Windows Magazine

Keyword
> WinMag

Select
> Software Libraries
>
> Games

Download
> Mac Blaster Game v1.2

Mazemaker for Windows

Ever wonder how a mouse in a maze feels? Now you can find out. All but the easiest mazes are three-dimensional. And it is nearly impossible to work a maze from the end.

The Mazemaker guarantees that at least one solution is possible for every maze. Good luck finding the way out (or in)!

Subj: Mazemaker for Windows v2.01
Date: June 3, 1993
From: DonD0
File: MAZEM201.ZIP (78296 bytes)
DL time: < 2 minutes
Author: Custom Real-Time Software, Inc. (CRTS)
Needs: PC, Windows 3.0+

Where
> Newsstand
>
> PC World

Keyword
> PC World

Select
> Software Library
>
> Windows Games

Download
> Mazemaker for Windows v2.01

MJWIN: 1.0 Mahjongg Tiles Game

This is the new Windows version of Ron Balewski's immensely popular VGA Mah Jongg program (MJVGA, found in the Windows Games Forum Libraries).

Be sure to read the complete file description before downloading because the program's author has a number of graphics-related details to share.

Subj: MJWIN: V1.0 Mahjongg Tiles Game
Date: April 26, 1993
From: PCC JolieT
File: MJWIN.ZIP (258560 bytes)
DL time: < 7 minutes
Author: Ron Balewski
Needs: Mouse, VGA, unZIPing program, Windows 3.x
Type: Shareware

Where

The complete sequence of steps through Computing can be found on page 15. Of course, you can save time and money by using the Keyword shortcuts.

Keyword

File Search

Select

>mjwin games

Download

MJWIN: V1.0 Mahjongg Tiles Game

Tank Battle Action

In this demo version of Tank, a battle arcade game, you may choose from a small selection of prepared games. The registered version contains additional options, including the ability to use your own edited characters, maps, and tanks.

Subj: Tank Version 2.4
Date: June 30, 1994
File: TANK.ZIP (151122 bytes)
DL time: < 4 minutes
Author: Rockland Software
Needs: PC, 286+, EGA-VGA, mouse, PKZip 2.04G

Where

Marketplace

Kim Komando's Komputer Klinic

Keyword

Komando

Select

Komando Libraries

Demonstration Versions (WIN/DOS)

Games

Download

Tank Version 2.4

Tetris for Windows

TetWin is an excellent Windows 3.x Tetris clone with very good play action and colorful graphics. Watch out, TetWin is highly addictive, and your boss might not appreciate your diligence in trying to get to level 10!

Subj: TetWin (Tetris for Windows)
Date: March 6, 1993
From: PCW Eric
File: TETWIN.ZIP (30157 bytes)
DL time: < 1 minute
Author: Joseph Briatico
Needs: PC, Windows 3.x

Where

Newsstand

PC World

Keyword

PC World

Select

Software Library

Windows Games

Download

TetWin (Tetris for Windows)

Tic Tac Toe

This classic Tic Tac Toe game is presented with the Deco font. You use your mouse buttons to enter the X and O symbols. This one is sure to keep the kids busy for hours.

Subj: TTT—Tic Tac Toe Game
Date: March 28, 1994
From: Gary1028
File: TTT2.EXE (14086 bytes)
DL time: < 1 minute
Author: Gary Friedman
Needs: VBRUN300.DLL
Type: Shareware, $10

Where

Newsstand

Windows Magazine

Keyword

WinMag

Select

Software Libraries

Games

Download

TTT—Tic Tac Toe Game

Warhead

In this game, the object is to destroy the incoming enemy missiles with your anti-ballistic missiles, protect your cities from nuclear destruction, and score as many points as possible. Do you think the authors of this one also had a hand in formulating the Strategic Defense Initiative?

Subj: WARHEAD: V2.0 Arcade Game
Date: September 18, 1994
From: Steadle
File: WARHEAD2.ZIP (386001 bytes)
DL time: < 10 minutes
Author: Eric Lee Steadle, Brian C. Lowe
Needs: Sound card, unZIPing program, Windows 3.x
Type: Shareware

Where

Computing

Windows Forum

Keyword

Windows Forum

Select

Software Libraries

Games

Download

WARHEAD: V2.0 Arcade Game

Chickens from Hell Screen Saver

The Chickens from Hell screen saver features demented poultry on the war-path against your desktop. Configuration settings include: Egging Speed, Eggs Density, Animation Speed, Sound, Clear Screen, Password. Now you have a choice when you can start your day—with eggs or with the Chickens from Hell screen saver.

Subj: SCR: Chickens from Hell
Date: October 8, 1994
From: PCA Dan
File: CHICK.ZIP (103947 bytes)
DL time: < 2 minutes
Author: Diversified Computer Services
Needs: Sound card, unZIPing program, Windows 3.1
Type: Shareware

Where

The complete sequence of steps through Computing can be found on page 15. Of course, you can save time and money by using the Keyword shortcuts.

Keyword

File Search

Select

>chickens

Download

SCR: Chickens from Hell

Jeopardy

With the Jeopardy.WAV file, you too can have this sound bite from the semi-classical composition "Syncopated Clock," used as the timer on *Jeopardy*. Use this whenever you need a countdown clock!

Subj: WAV: Jeopardy: Theme
Date: December 13, 1992
From: PCA Jolie
File: JEOPARDY.WAV (167757 bytes)

DL time: < 5 minutes
Author: Unknown
Needs: Win 3.1 or WAV player
Type: Public domain

Where

The complete sequence of steps through Computing can be found on page 15. Of course, you can save time and money by using the Keyword shortcuts.

Keyword

File Search

Select

[x] sound

>game show

Download

WAV: Jeopardy: Theme

Pac-Man

Do you remember those gobbling, munching sounds that drifted out from arcades in the early 1980s? If you miss these Pac-Man sounds, you can have them back. This file is a collection of WAV files from the game *PAC-MAN* for the Atari 2600. The three sounds range from 1.59 seconds to 5.81 seconds.

These sounds are suitable for event association, so you may want to use them in place of warning beeps or at shutdown.

Subj: WAV: PAC-MAN
Date: August 8, 1993
From: Michae1882
File: PACMAN.ZIP (55567 bytes)
DL time: < 2 minutes
Author: Unknown
Needs: UnZIPing program, Windows 3.1 or WAV file player
Type: Public Domain

Where

The complete sequence of steps through Computing can be found on page 15. Of course, you can save time and money by using the Keyword shortcuts.

Keyword

File Search

Select

> Atari sound collection

Download

WAV: PAC-MAN

Newsletter for Gamers

Now gamers can receive *The New Shareware Games Newsletter* as a free service for the shareware game community, both for those making games and for those playing them. *The Newsletter*, which contains information on recently released and upcoming shareware games, is sent via Internet E-mail to a list of people who have asked to receive it.

This newsletter is published at least once a month and will save you time when searching for the best new files to download. You'll get a copy of the current issue within a week of subscribing, so you're sure to have the latest information.

E-Mail

mattdm@cedar.goshen.edu

Subject

Subscribe to Games Newsletter

Mac Games

In Mac Games you can glide an airplane, ski a race, create a puzzle, and challenge your skills. Just keep these games hidden behind your screen saver and you'll have a great day at work.

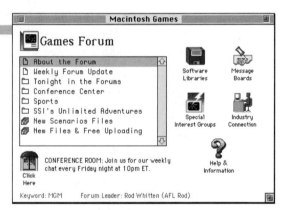

B14, B14

All Ages Bingo! is a multimedia rendition of traditional Bingo that can be played and enjoyed by all ages. For adults and older children, the program prints out randomly generated cards four to a sheet of 8.5" × 11" paper. All Ages Bingo then uses the Speech Manager to call out the numbers in user-selectable voices. You can also play traditional Bingo using onscreen cards against the Mac or a live friend. For younger kids, All Ages Bingo! has a special Shapes Bingo mode in which children match shapes and colors on a smaller Bingo card. With the shareware fee, you get a copy of another great program for kids, Coloring Book.

Subj: All Ages Bingo v.1.01
Date: September 15, 1994
From: AFA DaveAx
File: All_AGES_BINGO .sit (813181 bytes)
DL time: < 22 minutes
Author: Jim Allison
Needs: Color Mac with 13" display, System 7 for speech features
Type: Shareware, $18; fee includes a free copy of Coloring Book 2.0.1

Where

The complete sequence of steps through Computing can be found on page 15.
Of course, you can save time and money by using the Keyword shortcuts.

Keyword

File Search

Select

> Bingo games

Download

All Ages Bingo v.1.01

City Defense

This is a Missile Command-style game where you defend your cities against
nuclear destruction at the hands of the attacking hordes. Send your missiles up,
patriot-style, to blow up other incoming missiles.

Subj: City Defense
Date: July 13, 1992
From: Ventana500
File: City Defense.sit (6734 bytes)
DL time: < 1 minute
Author: unknown
Needs: System 6 or 7

Where

Computing

Computer Resources Center

Publications

Mac Shareware 500

Keyword

Mac 500

Select

Fun & Games

Download

City Defense

Countdown

Countdown 1.0.2 is the latest version of Rob Koch's politically incorrect software. This is a dittohead must. With Countdown, you can pass the time until "The Raw Deal" is over. Best yet, it's freeware.

Subj: Countdown v.1.0.2
Date: March 15, 1993
From: RobKoch
File: Countdown102.sea (29014 bytes)
DL time: < 1 minute
Author: Rob Koch
Needs: Mac, System 6.0.5+

Where

The complete sequence of steps through Computing can be found on page 15. Of course, you can save time and money by using the Keyword shortcuts.

Keyword

File Search

Select

>countdown games

Download

Countdown v.1.0.2

Deluxe Klondike

This is an updated version of Klondike Solitaire for the Mac. It's the computer version of the classic card game that most people simply call Solitaire. Deluxe Klondike uses large colorful cards on a full 640 x 480 screen, but will also work on 12-inch color monitors. Deluxe Klondike gives the player a choice of several different textured backgrounds and includes digitized sound effects. It plays both versions of Klondike—the player can turn one card up at a time or three at a time.

Subj: Deluxe Klondike v.1.4
Date: October 19, 1994
From: Network23
File: Deluxe Klondike.sit (398274 bytes)
DL time: < 10 minutes
Author: Glenn Seemann

Needs: System 6.0.7 or higher, 256 colors
Type: Shareware, $15

Where

The complete sequence of steps through Computing can be found on page 15. Of course, you can save time and money by using the Keyword shortcuts.

Keyword

File Search

Select

>Deluxe Klondike

Download

Deluxe Klondike v.1.4

Glider +

Glider is a fun game in which you guide your paper airplane through 15 rooms by using vents for uplift while avoiding candles, tables, and other objects that could cause you to crash. Glider is fairly easy to master and kids love it. Version 4.0 is commercially distributed by Casady & Greene.

Subj: Glider+ v.3.1.2
Date: May 16, 1991
From: SoftDoroth
File: Glider+3.1.2.sea (111052 bytes)
DL time: < 3 minutes
Author: Soft Dorothy
Needs: Mac, System 7 compatible, self-extracting
Type: Shareware, free

Where

The complete sequence of steps through Computing can be found on page 15. Of course, you can save time and money by using the Keyword shortcuts.

Keyword

File Search

Select

>glider games

Download

Glider+ v.3.1.2

Glider 4.0 Demos for Mac and Windows are available in Casady & Greene's forum in the Industry Connection (Keyword: Industry Connection).

MacSki

MacSki is a fantastic and fun skiing game, with expressive sounds and expertly animated graphics in both color and black and white. MacSki includes a wide variety of ready-to-ski courses, as well as a click-and-drag course editor that allows you to create your own. Before you hit the slopes, you can adjust the weather conditions or change your skis. MacSki features over a hundred different types of obstacles, including trees, rocks, fences, igloos, snow bunnies, moguls, photographers, wounded skiers, snowmobiles, snowballs, ski wax, sign posts, and several types of small animals.

Subj: MacSki v1.5
Date: October 4, 1994
From: StormImpac
File: MacSki v1.5.sit (552456 bytes)
DL time: < 15 minutes
Author: Storm Impact, Inc.
Needs: MacPlus+, 600K free RAM b/w, 1400K color, System 6.0.2+
Type: Shareware, $28

Where

The complete sequence of steps through Computing can be found on page 15. Of course, you can save time and money by using the Keyword shortcuts.

Keyword

File Search

Select

>MacSki

Download

MacSki v1.5

MacSki Colors.sit

With the same directions and another seven minutes, you can have the color art.

Mastermind

Here is the new version of the classic Mastermind board game. If you've never played before, you can learn in minutes. The concept is simple: Match four colored pegs to a hidden pattern, and you win. Be aware, though, it's hard to master. Mastermind features full-color graphics, a short download, and best of all, it's free!

Subj: Mastermind v.1.1
Date: May 17, 1993
From: Msiegal
File: Mastermind.sit (139449 bytes)
DL time: < 3 minutes
Author: Arthur Edelstein
Needs: Macintosh, 13" monitor

Where

The complete sequence of steps through Computing can be found on page 15. Of course, you can save time and money by using the Keyword shortcuts.

Keyword

File Search

Select

>Mastermind games

Download

Mastermind v.1.1

Monopoly

Psst . . . want to trade Boardwalk for Marvin Gardens? Have you contributed to the Community Chest? This is a great monopoly game for the Macintosh, but there's one problem—you can't cheat!

Subj: Monopoly v.4.05
Date: November 18, 1993
From: Raider18
File: monopoly. sea (89153 bytes)
DL time: < 2 minutes
Author: Thomas Fossom
Needs: Mac

Where

The complete sequence of steps through Computing can be found on page 15. Of course, you can save time and money by using the Keyword shortcuts.

Keyword

File Search

Select

> Monopoly games

Download

Monopoly v.4.05

Where to Find More Goodies

You can find more fun and games goodies in the *Kid Stuff*, *Computers*, and *Military and Aviation* sections of this book. *Kid Stuff* tells you where to find other coloring programs and fun dinosaur fonts. The *Computers* section explains where to find handy clocks and screen savers. Flight simulators are described in *Military and Aviation*.

Online, stay tuned to the major computing magazines (Keywords: Macworld, PC World, WinMag, and MMWorld) and the Mac and PC Games Forums (Keywords: MGM and PGM, respectively). Their software libraries are updated regularly with new games and fun utilities.

FREE $TUFF

All free governments are managed by the combined wisdom and folly of the people.

James A. Garfield

Government

America Online is a giant database without an index or a global word search function. You can spend hours trying to find all of the information on a certain topic. Consider a search for the U.S. Constitution. Will the Constitution include all amendments? Where will you find it? Is it in the White House Forum? C-SPAN? Washington Week in Review? Smithsonian? Compton's Encyclopedia? Will File Search find it? In this section, I'll point you in the right directions for many great freebies available from or about Uncle Sam and several state governments.

Starting at the Top

No doubt you've heard: The White House Forum is alive and it's on America Online. With a name like that, where else would the White House Forum be established?

The White House Forum contains the press releases from the White House, divided into these categories:

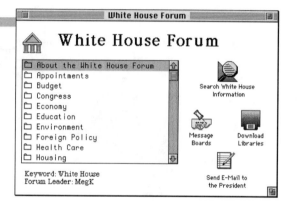

- Appointments
- Budget
- Congress
- Education
- Economy
- Foreign Policy
- Health Care
- Housing
- Labor
- Law and Order
- Meetings & Speeches
- Proclamations
- Technology
- Vice President

The White House Forum also features a message board so that you can discuss the releases with other AOL members, a searchable database for easy retrieval of releases that interest you, and two download libraries. One is comprised of releases from the White House, including all meaningful information and speeches from major events, the latest in health care, pending or recently enacted legislation, and information on major current events. The other library allows members to upload files of interest for fellow members.

Where
Clubs & Interests

Capital Connection

Keyword
White House

Clinton

 The White House files are formatted as *.sit* or *.zip* files. The .sit files are StuffIt files for Macs and the .zip files are for Windows and DOS users. Most of these files self-expand upon delivery, but you should have an un-zip file utility or StuffIt in your "toolbox."

White House FAQ

The White House has published White House Electronic Publications FAQ. It's the first stop (download) for serious government watchers. The FAQ covers searching and retrieving White House documents (primarily Internet), signing up for daily electronic publications, sending E-mail to the White House, and sending E-mail to Congress. Now you can make a difference!

Where
Clubs & Interests

Capital Connection

Keyword
White House

Select
Search White House Information

>Electronic Publications

Read/Save
White House FAQ

Washington Watcher

Media buffs and government watchers will treasure Washington Agenda for its compilations of Washington events and photo ops. If you want to peek at Hillary on the Hill or the President in the rose garden, this is the schedule to have! It's prepared a day or two in advance, so check daily if you're a Washington Watcher. Families and school groups preparing for a trip to Washington may find this fun, as well.

Where

Clubs & Interests

Capital Connection

Keyword

Capital

Select

Washington Agenda

Read/Save

White House/Administration

Federal Agencies

Courts

Senate Committees

House Committees

General News Events

Presidential Access

Have you ever thought about writing to the President? Is it just too hard to find the pen, paper, and postage stamp—and let's not forget the etiquette book with the correct forms of address. With the Write the White House icon in the White House Forum, you're ready to draft that dispatch. Here's what I'd like to see:

Dear Bill,

Please do something about our taxes, crime, health care, the military, international relations, acid rain, free trade, the deficit, the budget, teenage pregnancy, education, Congress members who waver, the economy's cycles, and one Vice President who plays basketball...and probably shouldn't.

—a constituent

Dear Al,

Sorry to hear you hurt your Achilles Tendon. Hope you received good care at Bethesda. They fixed the correct one, didn't they?

Always, Hillary

If you'd like to add the President and the Vice President to your E- mail lists, use these addresses:

President@WhiteHouse.GOV
Vice.President@WhiteHouse.GOV

Where

Clubs & Interests

Capital Connection

Keyword

White House

Select

Send E-mail to the President

Highway to the Hill: E-Mail to Congress

Currently, forty Members of the U.S. House of Representatives have been assigned public electronic mailboxes that can be accessed by their constituents. The nature and character of the incoming electronic mail have demonstrated that this capability will be an invaluable source of information on constituent opinion. The program is continuing to be expanded to include other members of Congress—as technical, budgetary, and staffing constraints allow. If your Representative is not yet online, please be patient and check monthly for an updated list.

Likewise, you will find several committees of the U.S. House of Representatives that are able and willing to receive your electronic hurrahs or grievances.

Subj: Email to House Reps
Date: August 4, 1994
From: MegK
File: C_EMAIL.TXT (10145 bytes)
DL time: < 1 minute
Author: House of Reps
Needs: Text reader

Where

Clubs & Interests

Capital Connection

Keyword

White House

Select

Download Libraries

>Information

Download

E-mail to House Reps

Write to Congressional Committees

If you're feeling feisty and it's time to make your opinion—which no doubt is the right one—known, then contact your representatives in Washington. How do you know just who should be listening? We've found the definitive list of House and Senate committees for you.

Now go to it!

Where

Capital Connection

Washington Week in Review

Keyword

WWIR

Select

Capital Facts

Read/Save

Senate Committees

House Committees

Branch Out . . . Executive Branch, That Is!

When your congressional representative or senator just won't do, head straight to the top and try one of the key departments in the Executive Branch. The President's Cabinet Members are also on this list.

Subj: Executive Branch Address

Date: May 4, 1994

From: Westie2993
File: EXECUTIV.TXT (2770 bytes)
DL time: < 1 minute
Needs: Text reader

Where

Clubs & Interests

Capital Connection

CSPAN

Keyword

CSPAN

Select

Viewer Services

Software Library–Transcripts

Download

Executive Branch Address

It's Your House, Too

Did you forget your camera? Or do you just want to impress your friends? Either way, if you want a full-color photo of the White House on a sunny day in Washington D.C., I've found it for you.

Subj: GIF: White House
Date: October 29, 1992
From: FID2
File: W_HOUSE.GIF (129184 bytes)
DL time: < 3 minutes
Author: Unknown
Needs: A GIF viewer
Type: Public domain

Where

The complete sequence of steps through Computing can be found on page 15. Of course, you can save time and money by using the Keyword shortcuts.

Keyword

PC: File Search

Mac: PC Software

Select

[x] Graphics>President Monument

Download

GIF: White House

When Abe Saved the Day

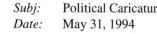

Civil War buffs will want to add this photo of Abe Lincoln to their collection. Head to this site to see a scan made with Thunderware's LightningScan 400 on a Mac SE/30.

Subj: Abe Lincoln B&W GIF
Date: July 20, 1991
From: WilliamW33
File: Lincoln.GIF (21020 bytes)
DL time: < 1 minutes
Author: Bill Warnement
Needs: GIF converter or GIF display

Where

The complete sequence of steps through Computing can be found on page 15. Of course, you can save time and money by using the Keyword shortcuts.

Keyword

PC: Mac Software
Mac: File Search

Select

>Lincoln

Download

Abe Lincoln B&W GIF

The 1996 Race

Interested in investing in future collectibles? These four caricatures from a series "CrabbyRay" created for *World News* magazine on likely Presidential candidates Bob Dole, Phil Gramm, Ross Perot, and Pat Buchanan may not be worth anything now, but you just never know.

Subj: Political Caricatures GIF
Date: May 31, 1994
From: CRABBYRAY

File: CHARICATURES.GIF (27980 bytes)
DL time: < 1 minute
Author: CRABBYRAY
Needs: GIF viewer

Where

The complete sequence of steps through Computing can be found on page 15. Of course, you can save time and money by using the Keyword shortcuts.

Keyword

PC: Mac Software
Mac: File Search

Select

>President Candidates

Download

Political Caricatures

Bill and Hillary, Al and Tipper

This is a picture of Bill Clinton with his wife and Al Gore with his wife. Great picture to frame and place in an appropriate spot—whatever *that* means to you. I'm not sure when it was taken or who took it, but Clinton fans will enjoy it!

Subj: Clinton President PICT
Date: May 12, 1993
From: Ludwig77
File: Clinton.sea (99706 bytes)
DL time: < 2 minutes
Author: None
Needs: Paint Viewer or Superpaint 3.0

Where

The complete sequence of steps through Computing can be found on page 15. Of course, you can save time and money by using the Keyword shortcuts.

Keyword

PC: Mac Software
Mac: File Search

Select

[x] Graphics

>President Clinton

Download

Clinton President PICT

Ask Not . . .

This is a recording of JFK's famous words: "And so, my fellow Americans, ask not what your country can do for you. Ask what you can do for your country." Perfect for all inaugurations and Kennedy Kodak moments.

Subj: WAV: JFK: Ask Not What
From: MarcoM4
File: KENNEDY.ZIP (88302 bytes)
DL time: < 2 minutes
Author: MarcoM
Needs: Windows 3.1 or WAV File Player
Type: Public Domain

Where

The complete sequence of steps through Computing can be found on page 15. Of course, you can save time and money by using the Keyword shortcuts.

Keyword

PC: File Search

Mac: PC Software

Select

[x] Sound>Kennedy

Download

WAV: JFK: Ask Not What

Nixon's Resignation Speech

It's cast into the hearts and minds of many— that August day of infamy. NIXON.WAV is a 3.00 second sound bite of former President Richard M. Nixon saying, "I shall resign the presidency effective at noon tomorrow." This clip is suitable for your own resignation or for your Windows exit. Perhaps you could add it to your outgoing voice mail message on April Fool's Day.

Subj: WAV: Nixon: Resigning
Date: July 24, 1994
From: FRESHIAM
File: NIXON.WAV (33168 bytes)
DL time: < 1 minutes
Author: Michael Ross-Lang
Needs: Windows 3.1 or WAV file player
Type: Public domain

Where

The complete sequence of steps through Computing can be found on page 15. Of course, you can save time and money by using the Keyword shortcuts.

Keyword

PC: File Search

Mac: PC Software

Select

>Nixon

Download

WAV: Nixon: Resigning

Out of Context?

This sound bite from President Bill Clinton's press conference of August 4, 1994, proves the impact editors have when they select a single phrase or sentence for the evening news. According to the author, this is a direct quote and has not been edited in any way. The President says, "First of all, keep in mind that most of our problem is with working Americans." Open your next union meeting with that one!

Subj: WAV: Bill Clinton: Our Problem
Date: August 5, 1994
From: EASYCHEEZ
File: PROBLEM.WAV (219912 bytes)
DL time: < 6 minutes
Author: EASYCHEEZ
Needs: Windows 3.1 or WAV File Player

Where

The complete sequence of steps through Computing can be found on page 15. Of course, you can save time and money by using the Keyword shortcuts.

Keyword

PC: File Search

Mac: PC Software

Select

[x] Sound

>President

Download

WAV: Bill Clinton: Our Problem

Who Is the Governor of Arkansas?

Thinking of relocating to another state and state politics are top on your list in limiting your search? With this ASCII file you can contact the governors of all 50 states and find out just how their states stack up against each other. Their party designations and phone numbers are included.

Subj: Governors of the 50 States
Date: June 23,
File: GOVS.TXT (2949 bytes)
From: Westie2993
DL time: < 1 minute
Author: C-SPAN
Needs: Text reader

Where

Clubs & Interests

Capital Connection

C-SPAN

Keyword

CSPAN

Select

Download Libraries

Members of Congress

Download

Governors of the 50 States

We the People . . . .

I've found a copy of the U.S. Constitution and the amendments, including the Bill of Rights. It might be helpful to have this along side your *TV Guide* when you are watching the commentaries on Sunday morning. American Government students should keep this on their hard drive.

Subj: U.S. Constitution
Date: June 2, 1994
File: CONSTITU.TXT (53364 bytes)
From: Westie2993
DL time: < 1 minutes
Author: Bicentennial Comm.
Needs: Text reader

Where

> Clubs & Interests
>
> Capital Connection
>
> C-SPAN

Keyword

> CSPAN

Select

> Download Libraries
>
> Historic Documents

Download

> U.S. Constitution

Supreme Court

Over 100 Justices have served on the Supreme Court. Five men—John Rutledge, Edward D. White, Charles E. Hughes, Harlan F. Stone, and William Rehnquist—have served as both Associate and Chief Justice. Check this site out to find such vital information as this:

- Justice Rutledge was appointed in 1795 to succeed John Jay as Chief Justice, and he presided as a recess appointee over the Court's August term. But that December, the Senate rejected his nomination.

- Do you know how many justices Franklin D. Roosevelt nominated? How about Ronald Reagan?

This is a great file for history buffs and students alike.

Subj: Supreme Court Justices List
Date: June 27, 1994
From: Westie2993
File: JUSTICES.TXT (5260 bytes)
DL time: < 1 minute
Needs: Text reader

Where

> Clubs & Interests
>
> Capital Connection
>
> C-SPAN

Keyword

> CSPAN

Select

Download Libraries

Members of Congress

Download

Supreme Court Justices List

Fun Downloads from Washington

Need to spruce up your mantle with photos other than the ones that were already in the frames when you bought them? Look here to find photos of all current Supreme Court Justices, the Declaration of Independence, and Washington Week in Review Commentators/Panelists. Think anyone will be fooled into thinking Sandra Day O'Connor is your close personal friend?

Where

Clubs & Interests

Capital Connection

Washington Week in Review

Keyword

WWIR

Select

Image Bank

[image name]

Lincoln's Gettysburg Address

Lincoln's Gettysburg Address is just one of a treasure of documents that can be found online. Next time you have to give a speech, you can grab a one-liner from any of these gems—make sure to give proper credit, though:

- Washington's Farewell Address (1796)
- Lincoln's Emancipation Proclamation (1862)
- Lincoln's First Inaugural Address
- Clinton's Inaugural Address
- Clinton's State of the Union Address (Pt. 2)
- Clinton's State of the Union Address (Pt. 1)
- Lincoln's Second Inaugural Address

- King: I Have a Dream
- The Mayflower Compact
- Kennedy's Inaugural Address
- Henry: Give Me Liberty Or Give Me Death
- The Declaration of Independence of the Thirteen Colonies
- The Constitution Of The United States Of America, 1787
- The United States Bill of Rights

Where

Clubs & Interests

Capital Connection

Washington Week in Review

Keyword

WWIR

Select

Capital Facts

American History

Read/Save

[document name]

National Debt

Are you worried about the national debt? Do you wonder if anyone's keeping track of it? For those of us who have difficulty just keeping an eye on our savings account, I've found a little gem that tracks the debt for you! (I've also found a few gems for your personal finances, but that's another section.)

Subj: US National Debt (WIN)
Date: April 19, 1994
From: Komando
File: USDEBT$.ZIP (10083 bytes)
DL time: < 1 minute
Author: Chris Riley
Needs: Windows 3.1 and PKZIP 2.04G

Where

Marketplace

Kim Komando's Komputer Clinic

Keyword

Komando

Select

Komando Libraries

Kool Shareware & Stuff (WIN/DOS)

Download

US National Debt (WIN)

State House Central

Residents of Utah, Massachusetts, and Michigan now have greater access to their state governments. Business Assistance, Employment Development Programs, Tourism, Consumer Affairs, Education, and Technology Development are among the departments featured in each state's forum.

Where

Clubs & Interests

Capital Connection

Keywords

Mass

Utah

Michigan

Michigan Madness

Residents of Michigan should discover the Michigan Governor's Forum. A few of the best downloadable freebies are listed below:

Where

Clubs & Interests

Capital Connection

Michigan Governor's Forum

Select

Download Library

Download

MI School Report (choose DOS/Window or Mac)

State of State (choose TEXT, Windows or Mac)

Utah's Best

Utah is also on the leading edge when it comes to communicating with the state's citizens. State facts, history, recreation, relocation information, and business assistance can be found here.

Where

Clubs & Interests

Capital Connection

Utah Forum

Keyword

Utah

Rush Limbaugh: Where Are You?

Just about everyone wants to know how to contact Rush Limbaugh to tell him something or just tell him off!

Use the Internet Mail Gateway and send him E-mail at the following address:

70277.2502@compuserve.com

Think Tanks and Magazines

Have you ever wondered about the Heritage Foundation? Do you need a transcript from Washington Week in Review? What's scheduled for C-SPAN this evening?

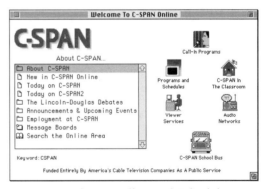

If you're a politics and news junkie, you'll probably want to know the full range of coverage in America Online. Political commentaries from newspapers, magazines, radio, and television are available online with transcripts, excerpts, and complete forums.

Inside the Beltway

It's possible that government fascinates you, and the daily summaries of government in action just aren't enough. Through C-SPAN Online, you'll have maximum contact coverage!

C-SPAN's audience has access to the live gavel-to-gavel proceedings of the U.S. House of Representatives and the U.S. Senate, and to other forums where public policy is discussed, debated and decided—all without editing, commentary, or analysis. You'll also notice a balanced presentation of points of view. C-SPAN Online provides the the perfect complement to the cable coverage with transcripts and legislative summaries.

Where

Clubs & Interests

Capital Connection

C-SPAN

Keyword

CSPAN

The McLaughlin Group

The award winning program The McLaughlin Group is a weekly television panel of five of America's most popular and respected columnists who tackle—no-holds-barred—the major issues of the day. John McLaughlin is the host and moderator. Regular panelists include Jack Germond, Eleanor Clift, Mort Kondracke, Clarence Page, and Fred Barnes.

The transcripts from each weekly show are available in The McLaughlin Group's forum.

Where

Clubs & Interests

Capital Connection

McLaughlin Group

Keyword

McLaughlin Group

Select

Transcripts

Download

[date of broadcast]

National Public Radio

Every week, more than 14 million men and women tune to NPR member stations. NPR's news and cultural programming attracts an audience distinguished by its level of education, professionalism, and community involvement. They are motivated citizens involved in public activities, such as voting and fundraising. They address public meetings, write letters to editors, and lead business and civic groups. This loyal and devoted following can take part in NPR's daily broadcasts through NPR Online.

NPR's news programs have won millions of loyal listeners and every prestigious broadcast journalism award in the country by offering national and international news coverage, analysis, features, and commentary seven days a week.

Where

Education

NPR Outreach

Keyword

NPR

Select

Talk of the Nation (to participate)

Policy Review

Published by The Heritage Foundation, America's leading conservative think-tank, *Policy Review* translates the bedrock conservative principles—freedom, responsibility, family, tradition, and opportunity—into successful political strategy. Articles from current and past issues are available for your perusal.

Articles include:

- "Let's Pull the Plug on Federal Energy Programs"
- "What Feminists are Doing to Rape"
- "The Case for the Bachelor Army"
- "Health Care: You Better Shop Around"

Where

Clubs & Interests

Capital Connection

Keyword

Capital

Select

Heritage Foundation/Policy Review

Read/Save

[article]

THE NEW REPUBLIC

The judges of last year's National Magazine Awards presented *The New Republic* with the award for General Excellence. The judges proclaimed, ". . . The New Republic offers lucid analysis, sophisticated reporting, and the zest of a good argument . . . ."

When you visit the TNR Issues Forum, you will be able to match wits and share ideas with fellow TNR readers about the issues discussed in the magazine. From time to time, TNR editors also host real-time conferences on a variety of important political and social topics. *The New Republic* message board allows online readers to exchange information on a whole range of interests. Start a discussion folder about a topic of your choice, or search for TNR readers who share your interests and activities! Turn to "Search TNR Archives" to browse articles or search for subjects of particular interest.

Recent articles include:

- "Our Babies, Our Selves"
- "A Multiethnic Utopia?"
- "Governor Weld's Welfare Dodge"
- "The Fallacy of Unrestricted Travel"
- "Woodstock Postcard"

Where

Clubs & Interests

Capital Connection

New Republic

Keyword

TNR

Select

[article]

COLUMNISTS AND FEATURES ONLINE

The Newspaper Enterprise Association's (NEA) *Columnists and Features Online* is the electronic way to read some provocative newspaper columnists and communicate with them online.

NEA syndicates distinguished writers and political columnists to newspapers nationwide. Among NEA's best-known alumni are Carl Sandburg, Jimmy Breslin, Isaac Asimov, Herblock (who won his first Pulitzer for an NEA cartoon) and Ira Berkow.

The text of 29 NEA columns and features appears on America Online in three Columnists & Features categories: Commentary, Entertainment, and Lifestyles.

Each column appears the same day it is released to newspapers and remains online one week.

In addition, past columns are available and can be searched by keywords.

Here is a list of some of the columns/columnists you'll find:

Hodding Carter: State Department spokesman for Jimmy Carter's administration, Hodding Carter III offers sharp opinions on today's issues from the perspective of a respected insider and noted partisan of strong, active government.

The Conservative Advocate **by William Rusher:** Written by the former publisher of *The National Review*, *The Conservative Advocate* jabs and lampoons liberals and the left, mixing humor and political commentary in this popular voice of the American right.

Nat Hentoff: As one of the foremost authorities on the First Amendment, Nat Hentoff, whose column appears in *The Washington Post*, examines how legislative decisions affect our basic freedoms to speak, write, think, and assemble.

News Focus **by Howard Siner:** An in-depth look at off-beat current events.

Sarah Overstreet: Sharp, spirited observations on everything from the latest Supreme Court decision to the role of make-up in the business world.

Joseph Perkins: Opinion writer for the *San Diego Union-Tribune*, Perkins brings a conservative view to long-standing issues.

Ian Shoales: Amusing social commentary from this popular National Public Radio and *San Francisco Examiner* humor columnist.

Martin Schram: Politics with a liberal perspective from this frequent commentator for CNN's "The Capital Gang."

Ben Wattenberg: Astute analysis of demographic trends, their political impact, and America's global influence.

Where

Newsstand

Keyword

Columnists

Select

Commentary Columnists & Features

Read/Save

[Selected Column]

Where to Find More Goodies

Within this book you'll find more goodies in *The Law* section, especially files pertaining to the current president's legal challenges.

When you're looking for detailed reports on major national and international events, go to the Capital Connection (Keyword: Capital) and start with the White House Forum (White House), Washington Week in Review (WWIR), and C-SPAN (CSPAN).

The best places to search for useful material for reports on government or history topics are White House Forum (White House), Washington Week in Review (WWIR), C-SPAN (CSPAN), and Compton's Encyclopedia (Comptons—no apostrophe).

Be sure to check Travel & Shopping (Travel), Smithsonian Museums and Popular Museum Subjects (Smithsonian) and don't miss Capitol Facts Visitor Information in Washington Week in Review (WWIR). It's a virtual Washington Tour Guide!

FREE $TUFF

The only way to keep your health is to eat what you don't want, drink what you don't like, and do what you'd rather not.

Mark Twain

Health and Family

In this section, we'll take a peek into family life from family planning to the great beyond. You'll find information on both traditional and alternative medicine, as well as pertinent sources for support groups, adoption information, and health reform information.

Before I get carried away with the health information sources on AOL, I must remind you that this information should not be considered as medical advice nor instruction. I hope it makes you a better health care consumer, but this information should not replace appropriate consultation with a qualified health or medical expert.

Self-Help Informatics Coalition

America Online currently has more self-help group meetings than any other national service—due in part to AOL's affordable pricing and to the efforts of Todd Daniel Woodward in making hundreds of AOL members aware of these many (over 70) weekly opportunities! Self-Help Informatics Coalition is intended to be the nation's first online self-help clearinghouse, meeting mostly the needs of members on AOL, but always researching ways to reach out to the Internet and its side roads. Self-Help Informatics Coalition's comprehensive listings not only increase membership in these groups but encourage others to start new groups on AOL. One of the fascinating growth characteristics of these groups is that the majority are being started voluntarily by ordinary AOL members.

For more information send E-mail to SHIC, or use the Keywords listed next to explore particular forums that have a number of group meetings.

E-Mail

SHIC

[Request support group information and schedules.]

Keywords

IMH = Issues in Mental Health forum

Health = Better Health & Medical forum

GLCF = Gay & Lesbian Community forum

PIN = Parent's Information Network

Better Health & Medical Forum

The Better Health & Medical Forum is provided for consumers and health professionals alike. This forum is for all AOL members interested in health—

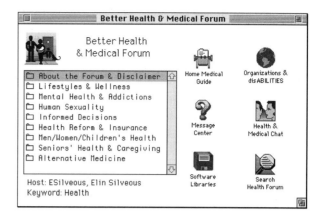

both those seeking information and support with specific health topics and for health professionals interested in networking with others.

The message boards are a great place to start because they are very extensive. To become familiar with them, you should select List Topics to view all of the topics in all of the folders. There are hundreds, if not thousands, of informed patients who can share their experiences. Medical professionals often stop in to share their knowledge as well.

The download files should be checked regularly because new documents are often added on such topics as prevention, diseases, tests, medications, assistive technologies, and health reform.

Where

Clubs & Interests

Better Health & Medical Forum

Keyword

Health

Medical Info Always Available

Do you need to know the difference between an optometrist and an ophthalmologist? A quick dictionary of medical specialities is available to help you resolve these kinds of questions.

Where

Clubs & Interests

Better Health & Medical Forum

Keyword

Health

Select

Patient's Rights

Read/Save

Medical Specialists: Who's Who?

Medical Terminology

If you spend any time in the Better Health & Medical Forum, you'll find a great bunch of folks who believe strongly in advocating a patient's right to ask questions of their health professionals. There's one problem—to challenge the "experts" you need to be able to ask the right questions and pronounce the big words!

This tutorial was designed for anyone working or studying in the medical field, but we can all use it to learn how to correctly spell, pronounce, and define commonly used medical terms; recognize word elements and their meanings; and understand the rules for formulating medical terms.

Subj: Medical Terminology Tutor
Date: August 10, 1992
From: PaulP37
File: MEDTUTOR.ZIP (76985 bytes)
DL time : < 2 minutes
Author: Hoyle W. Dabbs
Needs: UnZIPing program
Type: Shareware

Where

The complete sequence of steps through Computing can be found on page 15. Of course, you can save time and money by using the Keyword shortcuts.

Keyword

PC: File Search
Mac: PC Software

Select

>Medical Terminology

Download

Medical Terminology Tutor

Informed Consent

Do you know what the term "informed consent" means? In these times of advanced medical treatments and aggressive medical care, the explanations due the patients have been lacking. Informed Consent Laws have been enacted to establish and protect your right to information pertaining to your medical care. This document will help you to become a stronger health consumer.

Where

Clubs & Interests

Better Health & Medical Forum

Keyword

Health

Select

Patient's Rights

Read/Save

Informed Consent & Your Rights

Health Associations

The health associations online are sources for very targeted information. Associations representing cerebral palsy, multiple sclerosis, disabilities, and the mentally ill are present with full forums. You'll find them cross-referenced under both the Clubs & Interests department and in the Better Health & Medical Forum.

Where

Clubs & Interests

Keyword

Clubs

Select

United Cerebral Palsy Associations, Inc.

National Multiple Sclerosis Society

National Alliance for the Mentally Ill

Issues in Mental Health

disAbilities

Doctor's Hippocratic Oath

The Hippocratic Oath is still taken by many graduating medical students. It provides interesting commentary on subjects such as euthanasia and abortion.

Should you ever find yourself in need of surgery, you might want to memorize this portion of the oath and recite it as you are prepared to receive general anesthesia. "While I continue to keep this oath unviolated may it be granted to me to enjoy life and the practice of the art, respected by all men at all times but should I trespass and violate this oath, may the reverse be my lot."

Subj: Doctor's Hippocratic Oath
Date: August 10, 1991
From: AnchorMan3
File: HIPPOATH.TXT (1969 bytes)
DL time: < 1 minute
Needs: Text reader

Where

Capital Connection

Keyword

Capital

Select

Software Libraries

General Download Library

Download

Doctor's Hippocratic Oath

THE CHICAGO TRIBUNE's Health Series

The Chicago Tribune Reference Desk Library contains a number of hard-hitting medical articles, including the Pulitzer Prize winning Brain series. You will also find articles on breast cancer, Medicaid, the abortion pill, and kids having kids.

Where

Newsstand

Chicago Tribune

Keyword

Chicago

Select

Download Libraries

Download

The Abortion Pill

Kids Having Kids Series

Breast Cancer Series

Pulitzer-Winning Brain Series

Medicaid Series

One a Day

Consumer Reports took a hard look at vitamins in their September 1994 issue. Read this before you decide if supplements are worth it—but I'm not giving away the story here.

Where

Newsstand

Consumer Reports

Keyword

Consumer

Select

Home/Workshop

Read/Save

Taking Vitamins, September 1994

Buying Vitamins, September 1994

Baby Talk

The variety of baby-related information available online makes a great example about how much you can learn about each life stage. If you think there's a lot of baby stuff, you should see all the files on gastrointestinal disorders!

Baby Planner

The Smart-N-Easy Baby Planner will help with every aspect of planning for your new baby. It can be useful for new parents both before and after the baby's birth. You can count on this program to help you:

- Calculate your expected due date
- Manage your medical bills, insurance claims, and expenses
- Keep track of doctor appointments, tests, results, doctor's advice, among other things
- Print a list of questions to ask your doctor on your next visit
- Display or print a progress chart on Mom's weight gain
- Create a list of gifts you hope to receive
- Keep track of gifts received by person or occasion
- Print mailing labels for thank-you notes

- Record your experiences, thoughts, plans, and ideas in the Diary/Journal
- Select baby names
- Track your baby's first year
- Find helpful hints and solutions

Subj: BABY: V1.0 Baby Planner
Date: January 26, 1994
From: Hi Tech NE
File: BABYPLAN.EXE (346362 bytes)
DL time: < 9 minutes
Author: Automated Systems
Needs: 640K RAM, hard drive, floppy drive for install
Type: Shareware

Where

The complete sequence of steps through Computing can be found on page 15. Of course, you can save time and money by using the Keyword shortcuts.

Keyword

PC: File Search
Mac: PC Software

Select

> Family Pregnancy Parents

Download

BABY: V1.0 Baby Planner

Parenthood 101

Parents are always concerned about the progress of their children. They memorize the percentile scores at each well baby or well child visit. With this program, you can also track your children at home.

Parents can plot the height and weight for boys and girls. Each chart has the normal range to allow for a simple determination of whether the growth is within the expected range. This is a useful screening tool for a dentist, school nurse, or concerned parent.

Note: This program should not be considered a replacement for regular checkups.

Subj: Growth Charts SIT
Date: August 15, 1993
From: StevenAS

File: Growth Charts (207329 bytes)
DL time: < 5 minutes
Author: S.A. Seelig
Needs: HyperCard 2.1, StuffIt 1.5.1

Where

The complete sequence of steps through Computing can be found on page 15. Of course, you can save time and money by using the Keyword shortcuts.

Keyword

File Search

Select

>growth charts

Download

Growth Charts SIT

Picture This . . . Baby

It's not your average ultrasound photo. This is actually an X-ray of a baby with congenital (neonatal) pneumonia. The X-ray was photographed with the Logitech Fotoman digital camera and processed on a Macintosh LCII with Aldus Digital Darkroom. Text was added with Expert Color Paint and the resulting TIFF file was converted to a GIF file.

Subj: Neonatal Pneumonia.GIF
Date: January 16, 1994
From: DRMIKE4118
File: NeoPneum.GIF (39817 bytes)
DL time: < 1 minute
Author: Michael Weinstein, M.D.
Needs: GIF viewer

Where

Clubs & Interests

Better Health & Medical Forum

Keyword

Health

Select

Health Mac Library

Download

Neonatal Pneumonia.GIF

Checklist for New Mothers

Being a new mother can be extremely overwhelming. This file may be able to remove some of the stress by providing a checklist from the American College of Obstetricians and Gynecologists. This file can help you select a pediatrician, buy an infant car seat, stock the refrigerator, and lots more!

Subj: Checklist for New Mothers
Date: August 7, 1994
From: Gyndok
File: Checklist for New Mothers (2448 bytes)
DL time: < 1 minute
Author: ACOG
Needs: Text reader

Where

Clubs & Interests

Better Health & Medical Forum

Keyword

Health

Select

Health Mac Library

Download

Checklist for New Mothers

Does Anyone Here Know CPR?

This is a CPR demo program that presents questions and answers on the administration of the CPR technique. It's a very educational program and is well worth the download time.

Subj: CPR Demo SIT
Date: July 26, 1989
From: AFA LindaS
File: CPR SIT (24447 bytes)
DL time: < 1 minutes
Author: Robert E. Neville
Needs: StuffIt 1.5

Where

The complete sequence of steps through Computing can be found on page 15. Of course, you can save time and money by using the Keyword shortcuts.

Keyword

File Search

Select

>CPR

Download

CPR Demo SIT

911 Emergency First Aid

911 Emergency First Aid provides immediate access to correct first-aid procedures and emergency phone numbers. An index is displayed of 290 possible emergencies in alphabetical order. Select the emergency that fits your situation and get a detailed description of the proper first-aid procedures to follow. This program is not intended as a substitute for actual first-aid training.

Subj: 911: V1.3 Emergency First Aid
Date: November 18, 1992
From: RBAKER PC
File: 911v13.exe (125758 bytes)
DL time: < 3 minutes
Author: Emerald Coast Software
Type: Shareware

Where

The complete sequence of steps through Computing can be found on page 15. Of course, you can save time and money by using the Keyword shortcuts.

Keyword

PC: File Search
Mac: PC Software

Select

>Medical rescue

Download

911: V1.3 Emergency First Aid

Medical Clip Art

Over two dozen selections of medical clip art are included in this PCX file, which was converted from Print Shop. These small graphic images are appropriate for patient newsletters and reminders. The images include beakers, a first-aid kit, a hypodermic needle, a microscope, a doctor, nurses, poison, a prescription, research, a stethoscope, and X-ray films.

Subj: Medical Graphics
Date: January 18, 1994
From: ESilveous
File: MEDPCX.ZIP (17066 bytes)
DL time: < 1 minute
Author: Unknown
Needs: PCX image viewer, unZIPing program
Type: Public domain

Where

Clubs & Interests

Better Health & Medical Forum

Keyword

Health

Select

Health PC Library

Download

Medical Graphics

Is Your Body Fat?

This handy HyperCard stack calculates the percentage of fat in your body, based on height, weight, and measurements. You'll determine your total fat, lean body mass, and ideal weight.

Subj: Find %Fat in your body
Date: July 21, 1993
From: SwamiG
File: Your Fat %.sit (5808 bytes)
DL time: < 1 minute
Author: SwamiG
Needs: HyperCard 2.1, StuffIt Expander or AOL 2.0 to unstuff

Where

The complete sequence of steps through Computing can be found on page 15. Of course, you can save time and money by using the Keyword shortcuts.

Keyword

File Search

Select

>health body fat

Download

Find %Fat in your body

National Institutes of Health

Where can you find information on diseases currently under investigation by NIH or NIH-supported scientists, major NIH research areas, and important health-related topics? From the National Institutes of Health. This index lists hundreds of diseases and organ systems related to human health. Each entry shows what component of the National Institutes of Health works on that area and provides a telephone number for further information.

Subj: NIH Information Index
Date: November 14, 1993
From: DennisR48
File: NIHINDEX.ZIP (24006 bytes)
DL time: < 1 minute
Author: DennisR
Needs: Text reader, PKZIP 2.04c or later

Where

Clubs & Interests

Better Health & Medical Forum

Keyword

Health

Select

Software Libraries

Health PC Library

Download

NIH Information Index

Medical BBSs

This is a listing of medical and related BBSs within the scientific community. This extensive list contains hundreds of hospitals, AIDS information lines, scientists, medical special interest groups, medical centers, and universities.

Subj: Medical & Related BBSs
Date: September 25, 1993
From: DRTLJ
File: TMED.FON (34453 bytes)

DL time: < 1 minute
Needs: Text reader

Where

Clubs & Interests

Better Health & Medical Forum

Keyword

Health

Select

Software Libraries

Health PC Library

Download

Medical & Related BBSs

SCIENTIFIC AMERICAN

Scientific American Online includes the well researched and pertinent medical articles for which the magazine is renowned. This is a terrific source to check each month for the latest updates in the medical community.

Where

Newsstand

Scientific American

Keyword

SciAm

Select

Downloaded Articles & Images

Text Files

Read/Save

Meningitis Epidemics

Why Kids Talk to Themselves

Controlling Health Costs

Prozac Spurs Tumors?

Sepsis Can Be Fatal

Disarming Lyme Disease

To view the Meningitis images, select Image Files, and then How Meningitis Attacks.JPG or How Meningitis Attacks.GIF.

Boxing Fracture

If you want to see what could happen to a boxer's ungloved fist, take a look at this boxer's fracture sustained by a teenager who had a "fight" with the wall.

Subj: BoxerFracture.GIF
Date: January 16, 1994
From: DRMIKE4118
File: Boxer's Fracture.GIF (83085 bytes)
DL time: < 2 minutes
Author: Michael Weinstein, M.D.
Needs: GIF reader

Where

Clubs & Interests

Better Health & Medical Forum

Keyword

Health

Select

Software Libraries

Health Mac Library

Download

BoxerFracture.GIF

Parent and Child Agreement

Perhaps if the teenager whose fist was X-rayed above had an agreement with his parents, the destruction to the wall and his hand could have been avoided. The agreement is a one-page document that functions as a contract between a parent and child and helps to improve the relationship and communication. Trust, sharing, understanding, and respect just might be better fostered in your home with this agreement.

Subj: A Parent and Child Agreement
Date: October 7, 1994
From: JVCraw
File: PARCHLD.WPS (1570 bytes)
DL time: < 1 minute
Author: Jack V. Crawford
Needs: Text reader

Where

Clubs & Interests

Issues in Mental Health

Keyword

IMH

Select

IMH Library

Download

A Parent and Child Agreement

Fertility Book Excerpt

Here's another gem unearthed from the download libraries: It's a file with excerpts from Peggy Robin's *How to Be a Successful Fertility Patient*. This extensive text file provides general advice on how to select the right doctor for infertility treatment. In over 20 text pages, you'll learn the basics of infertility treatment and determine if this is the right book for you.

Subj: Infertility Book
Date: September 12, 1993
From: AdlerBooks
File: FERTILIT.TXT (73663 bytes)
DL time: < 2 minutes
Author: Bill Adler
Needs: Text reader

Where

Clubs & Interests

Better Health & Medical Forum

Keyword

Health

Select

Software Libraries

Health PC Library

Download

Infertility Book

Adoption

For those who are building families through adoption, the Adoption Forum is a terrific resource. You'll find many parents and prospective parents sharing information on the adoption process, birth mothers, home studies performed by agencies, searches for birth parents, and subsidies that may be available.

You can save online time by downloading archived message boards found in the Adoption Library. Once you've read a few of the message files, you may want to join in on the active message boards.

Where

Education

Parents' Information Network

Adoption Forum

Keyword

Adoption

Select

Adoption Library

Download

10/16 Orphan AIDS adoptions folder

09/25 Agency Adoption—folder archive

09/03 Homestudies-folder archive

07/31 Expectations of B-mom folder

07/26 Why Adopt? (Sect.2)

07/26 Why Adopt? (Sect.1)

05/22 Transracial Adoption

05/10 Grandparents adopting folder

05/04 AFA Books on Adoption

05/04 ACC Books on Adoption

I Feel Good!

The goal of all those who seek health information on AOL can be summarized with James Brown's signature line, "I Feel Good!" This 4.22 second sound bite would be a terrific way to start the day. Try it for your computer's start-up greeting.

Subj: WAV: James Brown: I Feel Good
Date: July 16, 1994
From: ChuenA
File: FEELGOOD.WAV (93738 bytes)
DL time: < 2 minutes
Author: ChuenA
Needs: Windows 3.1 or WAV file player
Type: Public domain

Where

The complete sequence of steps through Computing can be found on page 15. Of course, you can save time and money by using the Keyword shortcuts.

Keyword

PC: File Search

Mac: PC Software

Select

>Feel Good

Download

WAV: James Brown: I Feel Good

Seniors & Genealogy

AOL covers the health spectrum from pre-natal to gerontology. In fact, you'll find a significant number of informative files for senior citizens. AOL has a strong following of senior citizens who are enjoying their online connections. You'll find them in Senior Net, AARP, and the Genealogy Forum.

Alzheimer's Information

Understanding Alzheimer's Disease may be a bit easier with this fact sheet on Alzheimer's disease prepared by the National Institute on Aging. This paper contains beneficial information for the families of patients, and it concludes with Eldercare and Alzheimer's Association contact numbers.

Subj: Alzheimer's Disease Facts
Date: May 27, 1994
From: DennisR48
File: ALZHFACT.TXT (10927 bytes)
DL time: < 1 minute

Author: DennisR48
Needs: Text reader

Where

Clubs & Interests

Better Health & Medical Forum

Keyword

Health

Select

Software Libraries

Health PC Library

Download

Alzheimer's Disease Facts

A Senior's Guide to Good Nutrition

"A Seniors' Guide to Good Nutrition" by Suzanne Havala, MS, RD originally appeared in the *Vegetarian Journal*, published by the Vegetarian Resource Group. This guide to vegetarian nutrition for seniors provides valuable information for any senior looking to improve their diet whether or not they are vegetarian. Ms. Havala is the primary author of the American Dietetic Association's position paper on vegetarian diets.

Subj: Seniors' Nutrition Guide
Date: February 16, 1994
From: NurseBobbi
File: SENIOR1.TXT (29860 bytes)
DL time: < 1 minute
Author: Sue Havala, MS, RD
Needs: Text reader

Where

Clubs & Interests

Better Health & Medical Forum

Keyword

Health

Select

Software Libraries

Health PC Library

Download

Seniors' Nutrition Guide

Death with Dignity

An AOL member downloaded this Death with Dignity statement from another BBS to share with AOL members. This reads very similarly to an advanced directive that I recently read in a hospital. Basically, this document specifies that no life-sustaining procedures are to be used in the event of a terminal condition.

Subj: Death With Dignity
Date: October 23, 1994
From: Dave 000
File: Death with Dignity.sit (4627 bytes)
DL time: < 1 minute
Needs: Text reader

Where

Clubs & Interests

Better Health & Medical Forum

Keyword

Health

Select

Software Libraries

Health Mac Library

Download

Death With Dignity

Genealogy Forum

One of the most popular corners of America Online is the Genealogy Forum. The forum provides a place to exchange knowledge and experiences while providing any needed guidance in the search of ancestry.

Where

Clubs & Interests

Genealogy Forum

Keyword

Roots

Select

Genealogy Libraries

IBM PC Compatible Software Library (or)

Macintosh Software Library

Download

10/24 genealogical ftp-sites

08/29 treedraw for windows ver 1.0

08/29 family tree maker/windows 1.0

09/12 genealogy stack 1.2 (mac)

09/12 Family Tree Stack (MAC)

American Association of Retired Persons

The American Association of Retired Persons (AARP) is a nonprofit, nonpartisan organization dedicated to helping older Americans achieve lives of independence, dignity, and purpose.

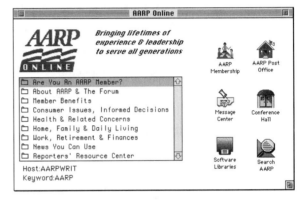

Founded in 1958 by the late Dr. Ethel Percy Andrus, AARP is the nation's oldest and largest organization of older Americans, with a membership of more than 33 million. Membership is open to anyone age 50 or older, both working and retired.

You'll find terrific health, genealogy, and Social Security articles in AARP's Software Libraries.

Where

Clubs & Interests

AARP Online

Keyword

AARP

Select

Download Libraries

Member Exchange

Download

10/14 Retirement & Social Security

10/14 Survivors Benefits & Social Security

10/14 Disability & Social Security

10/14 Medicare & Social Security

10/14 Women & Social Security

10/14 Supplemental Security Income

10/14 Figure Your SS Retirement Benefit

10/07 Understanding Social Security

10/07 Earning Credits & Social Security

10/07 Self Employment & Social Security

10/07 Military Service & Social Security

09/15 Social Security Appeals Process

09/15 Test Your Aging I.Q.

09/15 Forms For Genealogy

09/15 Alzheimer's Disease

Test Your Aging I.Q.

Take this quiz about aging and you'll find out whether you can teach an old dog new tricks. This ASCII document contains a quiz about aging prepared by the National Institutes of Health. This quiz challenges test-takers with common facts and fallacies about aging.

Subj: Test Your Aging I.Q.
Date: September 15, 1994
From: ESilveous
File: AGINGIQ.TXT (7080 bytes)
DL time: < 1 minute
Author: NIH
Needs: Text reader

Where

Clubs & Interests

AARP Online

Keyword

AARP

Select

Software Libraries

Member Exchange

Download

Test Your Aging I.Q.

Medigap Consumer's Guide

Medigap, or Medicare supplement insurance, is designed to cover some of the costs not paid by Medicare and is purchased by more than 20 million older Americans. AARP would like to help you through the Medigap maze and introduce you to recent changes. This article describes Medicare, private health insurance, and Medicaid. It also provides guidance on policy comparison, and includes a glossary of terms and a list of additional resources. Perhaps even more useful than knowing what Medicare covers is knowing what it doesn't cover. You can review the list included in this file to see where coverage gaps exist.

Subj: Medigap Consumer's Guide
Date: September 16, 1994
From: ESilveous
File: 70.TXT (35450 bytes)
DL time: < 1 minute
Author: AARP
Needs: Text reader

Where

Clubs & Interests

AARP Online

Keyword

AARP

Select

Software Libraries

Info from AARP

Download

Medigap Consumer's Guide

Where to Find More Goodies

If you're looking for more goodies that relate to health, I suggest that you review the *Cooking* section. After all, you can't have good health without good nutrition!

Many, many goodies, too numerous to count, can be found in the message boards in the Better Health & Medical Forum. Health professionals will find job postings, and health consumers will even find one board filled with 800 numbers for associations and health research.

You'll find health-reform reading in several areas. Whenever our leaders in Washington put forth a new proposal, you'll find transcripts, commentary, and summaries online. The best place to start is the Health Reform Library within the Software Libraries of the Capital Connection (Keyword: Capital).

Of course, there's always great reading at the Newsstand: It's safe to say that you'll find hundreds of health and insurance related articles in the following selections from AOL's Newsstand.

Title	Keyword
Longevity	Longevity
Consumer Reports	Consumer
Chicago Online	Chicago
The New Republic	TNR
Time	Time
San Jose Mercury News	Mercury
Scientific American	SciAm

FREE $TUFF

The best way to make children
good is to make them happy.

Oscar Wilde

Kid $tuff

Today's kids are growing up with computers. Just think of the stories we'll be able to tell them about life before remote controls, fax machines, call waiting, and CDs. What will they think when we tell them CDs were originally banking instruments? That'll confuse them.

Seriously, though, this chapter should be written by a ten-year-old and not this thirty-something-year-old. I took my first programming course in college, just prior to the advent of the PC. In my first post-college job, I worked with punch cards—Ancient stuff!

I'll bet you're acquainted with a computer-literate kid—you know, the pre-teen in your house who's running up the online bills and you're happy about it because at least you know where he is!

Crammed into this section are games for toddlers, kindergarten concepts, elementary lessons, and tools for teachers. I'll use an age-sensitive format (so politically correct) and conclude with tools for teachers.

If the topics in this section are important to you, make sure you at least scan the *Education* section as well.

AOL contains loads of things that you won't find in this book, so make sure to research this topic more.

So, where *is* all this good stuff? You'll find it where you'd most expect it and again where you'd least expect it:

- Library of Congress (Keyword: Library)
- National Geographic (Keyword: NGS)
- Kids Only Online (Keyword: Kids)
- Education (Keyword: Education)
- Reference (Keyword: Reference)
- National Public Radio (Keyword: NPR)
- Chicago Online (Keyword: Chicago)
- The New York Times Online (Keyword: @times)
- Disney Adventures (Keyword: Disney)

You're about to discover the fun and the serious, newsletters and games, coloring books and GIFs, and lots more!

This section is dedicated to all the girls and boys whose parents are trying to guide them into being socially-adept and computer-literate kids. For Carly, Kathryn, Elizabeth, Katie, T.J., Josh, Brian, and Daniel . . . and all of the others to come!

The National Parenting Center

Are the kids getting to you—*again*? The National Parenting Center (TNPC) is the premier resource for parents on America Online. Their newsletter *ParenTalk* features articles pertinent to all parents.

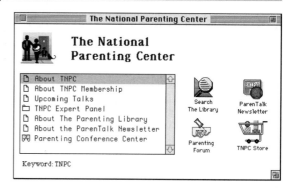

Membership in TNPC is discounted for AOL members. Those with a Parenting Center Membership are also eligible for special discounts in the TNPC store, which features baby products, toddler toys, and educational software.

Where

Education

Parents Information Network

The National Parenting Center

Keyword

TNPC

Read/Save

About TPNC Membership

PARENTALK Newsletter

ParenTalk is the award-winning newsletter published each month by The National Parenting Center. *ParenTalk* features columns of advice and information for today's parents ranging from pregnancy through adolescence. The columns are written by TNPC's world-renowned panel of child-rearing experts. The topics cover issues from behavioral to medical, as well as educational matters and practical parenting support tips to help make your day run a little smoother.

To browse through past columns by age group, click on the ParenTalk Newsletter icon, select an age group, and find a topic of interest. To find a specific topic, click on the Browse Library icon and follow the instructions on the screen.

Where

Education

Parents Information Network

The National Parenting Center

Keyword

TNPC

Select

ParenTalk Newsletter

Articles on Pregnancy

Articles on Newborns

Articles on Infancy

Articles on Toddlers

Articles on Pre-Schoolers

Articles on Pre-Teens

Articles on Adolescents

Read/Save

[selected article]

College Costs: Better Start Saving Now

As soon as the kids come along, you start tallying the cost of diapers, wipes, formula, clothes, the bigger car, the bigger house, and, don't forget, college looms in the future. You'll find more budget aids in the Personal and Home Finance section, but you may want to start with one of these!

College Savings

Little Herman Broderbeast Smythe IV has arrived! He has been "showered" prior to his arrival, and the gifts just keep pouring in. His father tallies the sums of money that have arrived, sure that they will allow little Hermie to attend the finest university of his choice. The rest of us must *save* for the day our Johnnies and Sallys leave for college. If you're not Hermie's father, you'll want to try this Excel spreadsheet! It will help you figure out the monthly and annual investment required to fund your child's college expenses. All you enter is five key assumptions.

Subj: College Savings
Date: January 27, 1993

From:	Tom North
File:	College Savings.sit (3847 bytes)
DL time:	< 1 minute
Author:	Tom Northenscold
Needs:	Mac, Excel 3.0, StuffIt 1.5

Where

The complete sequence of steps through Computing can be found on page 15. Of course, you can save time and money by using the Keyword shortcuts.

Keyword

File Search

Select

>college savings

Download

College Savings

For more college planning software, try the *Personal Finance* section.

Guide to Preschool Children with Disabilities

This file contains a parents' guide to the development of preschool children with disabilities. Parents of preschool children with visual or physical disabilities will find in this reference circular a wide range of information to assist them in promoting the development of their child from infancy to age five. The listing includes organizations, producers, and distributors who offer materials or services at the national level. The referenced materials include:

- Specially formatted materials—braille, cassettes, large print, and records
- Educational games, toys, and play equipment
- Articles, books, magazines, and pamphlets
- National organizations concerned with infants, toddlers, and preschool children with disabilities

Subj:	Parents Guide
Date:	October 16, 1992
From:	RussellM18
File:	PARENTS (33374 bytes)
DL time:	< 1 minute
Author:	Library of Congress
Needs:	Text reader

FREE $TUFF from America Online

Where

Education

Library of Congress

Keyword

Library

Select

Tour the Library

National Library Service (NLS)

Library Research Guides

Download

Parent's Guide

Baby Wipes and Other Freebies

Kids take up an incredible amount of time, but help is on the way. This area will save you both time and money by supplying money saving tips, newsletters, formula coupons, catalogs, and more. I've found the message boards with the savvy consumers who know where to find more savings. Some tips include 800 numbers for your convenience, and there are lots of terrific ideas!

Where

Education

Parent's Information Network

Keyword

Parent

Select

Parent Exchange

Parent to Parent Message Board

Read/Save

The Penny Pinchers

Classifieds for this Board

Better yet, use your system log to copy this section as you read it!

Pre-School

For little kids, everything is an educational experience. After you get past those food fight "lessons" and Johnny has learned to put away his toys, you should see what AOL has in store.

Baby Keys

The author of Baby Keys has created a program for the curiosity of even the youngest children. This program is designed for little ones between 6 months and 24 months. When Baby Keys is running, all your child has to do is hit the keys on the keyboard. (This comes naturally, trust me!) The computer will produce a variety of sounds accompanied by graphical images that will capture your child's attention (at least for a few minutes).

Subj:	BABYKEYS: Baby Keys for Young Children
Date:	March 15, 1993
From:	Sky Manor
File:	BABYKEYS.ZIP (119505 bytes)
DL time:	< 3 minutes
Author:	Multi Computing
Needs:	PC, unZIPing program

Where

The complete sequence of steps through Computing can be found on page 15. Of course, you can save time and money by using the Keyword shortcuts.

Keyword

File Search

Select

>pre-school baby keys

Download

BABYKEYS: Baby Keys for Young Children

No More Coloring on the Wall

In Coloring Book 2.01, children color areas of pictures by selecting a color from the palette and clicking on the various items, such as layers in a birthday cake. Hidden within the pages are surprising animations and enjoyable sounds. Coloring Book has received rave reviews in publications from several of the largest Mac users groups. More importantly, it has been delighting children (and a few adults) around the world for the past two years.

When you send in your $16 shareware fee, you will receive a double-sized version of the program with 10 additional pages including: Multiplying Rabbits, A Space Adventure, A Counting Game, Things that Begin with B, Electronic "Paper Dolls," A Robot Construction Set, A Very Active Apple Tree, An Octopus with Fancy Spots, and A Basketball Game in Which The Home Team Never Misses.

Subj: Coloring Book 2.01 SIT
Date: April 23, 1994
From: AFA DaveAx
File: Coloring Book.sit (829306 bytes)
DL time: < 22 minutes
Author: Jim Allison
Needs: Mac w/13" or larger color monitor, AOL 2.x or StuffIt Expander 3.x

Where

The complete sequence of steps through Computing can be found on page 15. Of course, you can save time and money by using the Keyword shortcuts.

Keyword

File Search

Select

>coloring book

Download

Coloring Book 2.01

A PC Coloring Book

Here is a coloring book that you can use with your PC. With this program, children can select the image they want to color and then pick from a full range of colors to bring the image to life. The cursor even changes to the shape of a crayon. Kids can color, erase, and otherwise change their image. The images colored can be saved as .PCX files. This is an excellent program that will supply hours of fun and learning.

Subj: ECBPREVU: Kids Coloring Book
Date: January 11, 1992
From: ArielB3
File: ECBPREVU.ZIP (229670 bytes)
DL time: < 6 minutes
Author: KINDERWARE, INC.
Needs: PC, unZIPping program, EGA monitor, mouse

Where

The complete sequence of steps through Computing can be found on page 15. Of course, you can save time and money by using the Keyword shortcuts.

Keyword

File Search

Select

>coloring book

Download

ECBPREVU: Kids Coloring Book

Colorforms Computer Fun Set Demo

Do you remember those little rubbery, plastic-like Colorforms that have always been popular among kids? This is my favorite download in this entire book! This great, usable demo will capture your attention (and your child's) for hours. Long before you master the farm module, you'll be ready to purchase the complete software, which includes three additional modules: Alphabet, Ocean, and Play Shapes.

Best of all—it's available in both Mac and Windows versions!

Subj: Colorforms CFS Demo
Date: August 18, 1994
From: GryphonSW
File: COLORFMS.ZIP (1155521 bytes)
DL time: < 31 minutes
Author: Gryphon Software Corporation
Needs: Windows 3.1, VGA, mouse

Where

The complete sequence of steps through Computing can be found on page 15. Of course, you can save time and money by using the Keyword shortcuts.

Keyword

Gryphon

Select

Software Library – Mac

Software Library – PC

Download

Colorforms CFS Demo

ABC 123

I've found this simple and enjoyable program for your preschooler. When a letter appears on the screen, the child picks the matching letter from the keyboard. If you like the program, the author suggests a $10 registration fee.

Subj: ABC_123: Education -Pre-School
Date: August 17, 1994
From: BillW10167
File: ABC_123.ZIP (45228 bytes)
DL time: < 1 minute
Needs: PC (EGA or better), UnZIPing program

Where

The complete sequence of steps through Computing can be found on page 15. Of course, you can save time and money by using the Keyword shortcuts.

Keyword

File Search

Select

>ABC

Download

ABC_123: Education -Pre-School

Chores for Kids

Regina Folse is an innovative mom who created a chore chart with dollar incentives to share the work and encourage responsibility among her children. These files include weekly and daily chore charts that have been successfully used with her 6-and 9-year-old children.

She devised individual chore fees by taking what she was paying her housekeeper at the time, and dividing it between the jobs needing to be done daily.

This is a *two-part* download.

Subj: Chore Chart For Kids - Part 1
Date: July 9, 1994
From: ReggiF892
File: CHORE.TXT (5154 bytes)
DL time: < 1 minute
Needs: Text reader

Subj: Chore Chart For Kids - Part 2
File: DAILYCH.TXT (4240 bytes)
DL time: < 1 minute

Where

Education

Parents Information Network

Keyword

Parent

Select

Parents' Libraries

Just for Parents

Parent to Parent

Download

Chore Chart For Kids - Part 1

Chore Chart For Kids - Part 2

Kids' Software Review in HomePC Online

HomePC Online has thousands of of reviews of kids' software programs. When you're looking for a review, there's no need to page through back issues of your computer magazines; simply go to HomePC Online and search their very complete files!

Where

Newsstand

HomePC

Keyword

Homepc

Select

Search Children's Database

Search Children's Software Finder

>Fatty Bear

Read/Save

Fatty Bear's Birthday Surprise

Fatty Bear's Birthday Surprise Demo

This is a playable demo of Fatty Bear's Birthday Surprise, a comic book-like adventure. Children move through a house solving puzzles and searching for clues.

Subj: Fatty Bear's Birthday Surprise
From: Mia HPC
File: FBDEMO.EXE (1408890 bytes)
DL time: < 38 minutes
Author: Humongous Entertainment
Needs: PC, sound card helpful, not required

Where

Newsstand

HomePC

Keyword

Homepc

Select

Home PC Library

Download

Fatty Bear's Birthday Surprise

Barney Collection

You may love him or hate him, but Barney is still popular among preschoolers. Here's a collection of WAV files from the popular and *very* rich purple dinosaur. The ZIP file includes: "Hey, this reminds me of a fun song," Barney laughing, "I'm glad you came to play," "Oh boy!" and "Each and every one of you is very special!" With an unZIPing program, it's suitable for both Mac and Windows users.

Subj: WAV: Barney Collection
Date: March 13, 1994
From: PCC Ted
File: BARNEY.ZIP (38875 bytes)
DL time: < 1 minute
Needs: PC or Mac, unZIPing program, Windows 3.1 or WAV file player

Type: Public domain

Where

The complete sequence of steps through Computing can be found on page 15. Of course, you can save time and money by using the Keyword shortcuts.

Keyword

PC: File Search
Mac: PC Software

Select

>dinosaur sound

Download

WAV: Barney Collection

Disney Fun

I've found some first-rate images and sounds in the Disney areas. The images are great fun when they "magically" pop up on the screen and pre-schoolers also like printed copies that can be colored with crayons.

```
┌─────────── Disney Adventures Magazine ───────────┐
│                                                  │
│              ╔═══════════════╗                   │
│              Adventures                          │
│              THE MAGAZINE FOR KIDS               │
│                                                  │
│  ┌ About Disney Adventures              ▲        │
│  ▦ The Odeon Auditorium                           │
│  ⬥ Disney Adventures Readers' Survey              │
│  ▢ D.A. Live Schedule!                            │
│  ▢ Animals                               ▼        │
│                                                  │
│   👥       📖       ✎        💾        📝         │
│  D.A.   Search D.A.  Message   D.A.    Subscribe │
│  Live    Articles    Board    Library  To D.A.   │
│                                                  │
│  Keyword: Disney                                  │
└──────────────────────────────────────────────────┘
```

Little Mermaid

This is a BMP file that can be used with Windows 3.1. It's a great image of Ariel, the little mermaid, sitting off to the right side of the screen.

Subj: WINDOWS: Little Mermaid .BMP
Date: November 12, 1994
From: DaveDisney
File: MERMAID.BMP (153718 bytes)
DL time: < 4 minutes
Author: Disney Software
Needs: PC, Windows 3.1

Where

The complete sequence of steps through Computing can be found on page 15. Of course, you can save time and money by using the Keyword shortcuts.

Keyword

Disney

Select

Disney Software

Disney Images

Download

WINDOWS: Little Mermaid BMP

The Lion King

This is a great Lion King picture. It shows Simba standing on a mountain overlooking his kingdom. He's looking at you smiling. The background is at dawn with the sun just coming over the horizon. The phrase *Disney's The Lion King* is shown in big red letters. An excellent picture.

Subj: The Lion King
Date: August 27, 1994
From: ZimboTek
File: Lion King (Smba & Bkgnd).sit (17207 bytes)
DL time: < 1 minute
Needs: Mac, graphics program that can view Mac PICT; 256 colors

Where

The complete sequence of steps through Computing can be found on page 15. Of course, you can save time and money by using the Keyword shortcuts.

Keyword

Disney

Select

Disney Software

Disney Images

Download

The Lion King

The Lion King WAV

This is a sound clip of the song *Hakuna Matata* from Disney's *The Lion King*. Because this song translates as "no worries," you might find it suitable for error messages or when Windows starts successfully. You may need to rename this file when you download it, due to the fact that it starts with a period.

Subj: .wav Lion King
Date: July 4, 1994
From: WesLan
File: MATATA.WAV (130868 bytes)

DL time: < 3 minutes
Needs: PC or Mac, Windows 3.1 or .WAV file player

Where

Education

Education Industry Connection

Disney Software

Keyword

Disney

Select

Disney Software

Disney Sound Source

Download

.wav Lion King

Elementary

There's nothing like the first day of school—every year. In the topics ahead, I'll share a few goodies for elementary students and their parents.

Kindergarten Expectations

From the time a child is born, parents start thinking about that first day of school. And, depending on where you live, children can start at age four, five, or six. Many parents have worries about their child's readiness and future successes. This file indicates the grade level expectations for kindergarten. The file provides some ideas for future lesson plans—that is, what the children are expected to do for math, science, language arts, and so on.

Subj: Kindergarten Expectations txt
Date: December 11, 1993
From: AFL Cheryl
File: K_expect.txt (2171 bytes)
DL time: < 1 minute
Needs: Text reader

Where

Education

Teachers' Information Network

Keyword

TIN

Select

Lesson Plan Libraries

Pre-School

Download

Kindergarten Expectations txt

Kindergarten Readiness

I have found a concise *Kindergarten Readiness* article that will help parents everywhere.

Question: My son is going to be 5 on September 26. Is he too young to start kindergarten?

Answer (in part): Readiness is a term used to describe preparation for what comes next: readiness for kindergarten involves both the child and the instructional situation. Any consideration of the preparation a child needs to be successful in kindergarten must take into account the kindergarten program and the teacher's expectations of the child.

The complete answer includes one ERIC Digest and a list of organizations to contact for more information.

Where

Education

AskERIC

Keyword

ERIC

Select

For Parents

Download

What Should be Learned in Kindergarten?

Free E-Mail for Kids

If your kids like AOL and envy your E-mail, they can take part in KidDesk Penpals! Your children just need to decide what kind of penpal they would like to have: male or female, age, location, interests, etc.

Your child should then tell the potential penpal a little about himself/herself. Post the message in the appropriate folder in the KidDesk Penpal area, then wait for a reply. Your penpal will send E-mail to your personal mailbox. The response will not be posted in the KidDesk Penpal area.

Where

Education

Education Industry Connection

Edmark Corporation

Keyword

KidDesk

Select

KidDesk Penpals

Read/Save

Read this First

Look Out Kitchen

This is the recipe from Weekend ATC, 8/13/94. It's a kid's recipe for muffins. See the muffins.gif file for kids' picture versions of this recipe. Kids will enjoy making these muffins under parents' guidance. Just make sure they share!

You will also find instructions for how to get other recipes.

Subj: Kid's Muffins recipe
Date: August 18, 1994
From: Raydeeoh
File: muffin recipe (3534 bytes)
DL time: < 1 minute
Author: WATC/Mollie Katzan
Needs: Text reader

Where

Education

NPR Outreach

Keyword

NPR

Select

NPR Studios

Download

Kid's Muffins recipe

or GIF: Kid's Muffin Recipe (WATC)

Activities for Children in New York

@Times, the online service of *The New York Times*, includes articles on activities for children. Swimming pools, ferry rides, the Brooklyn Dodgers exhibit at the Brooklyn Historical Society, and Summergarden concerts at The Museum of Modern Art are typical of the encapsulated tips. Science, theater, and art workshops are included, too.

Where

Newsstand

The New York Times Online

The Arts

Keyword

Times Arts

Read/Save

For Children

Family Explorer Newsletter

This area holds the text-only version of the June issue of the *Family Explorer* newsletter of science and nature activities written for the parents of school-age children. Unfortunately, this text-only version does not include illustrations and the star chart. For information on the printed version, you can reach the author through the Internet address provided within the text version.

Subj: Science/Nature newsletter
Date: June 3, 1994
From: LarryS8548
File: JUNE_FE.TXT (23198 bytes)
DL time: < 1 minute
Needs: Text reader

Where

Education

Parents Information Network

Home Schooling Forum

Keyword

Home School

Select

Home Schooling Library

Download

Science/Nature newsletter

Jungle Book

The Jungle Book is an all-time favorite among youngsters. This downloadable lesson includes several learning objectives for young people. The children will learn to describe the behaviors of animals, distinguish between the activities and the lifestyles of humans and animals, and discuss the meaning of friend-ship and identify the characteristics of a friend.

Subj: The Jungle Book
Date: November 7, 1991
From: TFA DP
File: jungle book (1739 bytes)
DL time: < 1 minute
Author: Dr. Deborah Isom
Needs: *The Jungle Book* video or pictures, text reader

Where

Education

National Principals' Center Online

Keyword

Principal

Select

Educational Libraries

Lesson Plan Libraries

Elementary/Grade School

Language Skills

Download

The Jungle Book

Check the *Education* section for information on using the Teacher Pager (Key-word: Teacherpager) and the Academic Assistance Center (Keyword: Home-work). Elementary students can take advantage of these, too!

Show Me Math

One of the all-time top downloads, Show Me Math, trains students from age four through college pre-algebra in hundredss of math skills. This file contains thousands of step-by-step problem demonstrations.

Subj: SM_MATH: v2.2 Show Me Math
Date: October 21, 1993
From: McBain
File: SM_MATH.ZIP (651679 bytes)
DL time: < 17 minutes
Author: R. Webster Kehr
Needs: PC, unZIPing program

Where

Education

Keyword

Education

Select

Education Software

PC/MS-DOS Educational Software
Top Picks

Download

SM_MATH: v2.2 Show Me Math

Words Alive

Learning to read is fun, Fun, FUN. WRDALIVE contains three state-of-the-art games that grab your child's attention with colorful, fully animated pictures, popular children's tunes, a clock, and excellent-quality speech produced through the internal PC speaker (*does not* require a sound card). Games are easily adjusted to various difficulty levels, from letters and case recognition all the way to spelling and telling time. This one's great fun!

The keyboard speed was especially adjusted for kids' slow rate of typing. A new key (letter) is accepted only after a previous letter has been displayed and pronounced by the computer.

Subj: WRDALIVE: Spelling Game
Date: April 22, 1993
From: MikeK62
File: WRDALIVE.ZIP (365898 bytes)
DL time: < 10 minutes
Needs: PC (EGA or better), voice option requires 8MHz 286 +, unZIPing program

Where

Education

Keyword

Education

Select

Educational Software
PC/MS-DOS Educational Software
Top Picks

Download

WRDALIVE: Spelling Game

Kids Only

The Kids Only department is a place for children to interact with other kids and to find age-appropriate information. Kids Only is made up of six departments, and a Fun Features listbox. Parents are invited to monitor their child's online interaction and to explore the Kids Only content. However, parents are asked to not post on message boards nor participate in the real-time chat games, interviews, and chats.

The Kids Only departments include:

- *Kids News and Sports*: An interesting collection of information about these subjects to help you keep up with the world, the scores, and what the weather will be in your area. Here, you may also discuss current events on the TIME for Kids message boards.

- *Search and Explore*: Education aids for students and for the curious. You will find Compton's Encyclopedia, National Geographic, The Academic Assistance Center, Homework Help, and more.

- *Games and Computers*: Here you will find information relating to computers of all kinds. There are libraries available of programs that will interest you—from programming help to games to graphics and art. Download only.

- *Kids Only Library*: Use your computer skills to create stories, games, poems, and art to be loaded into the Kids Only Library. This library is where kids share their computer accomplishments. Upload and download.

- *Hobbies and Clubs*: Also known as Special Interest Groups. If you collect something or have a particular interest in something—this is the place to find it.

- *TV, Movies, and More*: TV, Movies, Books, Music, Magazines, Radio. See what these special areas have to offer, and add your review to the Kids Only Reviews message board.

- *Kids Connection*: This is the place for live conversation, games, special guests, and special topics. There's always something going on here, and it's a good idea to check the calendar to see just what is happening.

Where

Kids Only

Keyword

Kids

Select

Kids News and Sports (or)

Search and Explore (or)

Games and Computers (or)

Hobbies and Clubs (or)

TV, Movies, and More (or)

Kids Connection

Stuff for Teachers

Inspiration for teaching creativity can have many sources. Amed with clipart and dinosaurs, your lessons will enthrall the Nintendo Generation.

Teachers Desktop Publishing Sampler

Teachers Desktop Publishing Sampler contains samples of the graphics, projects, ideas, and articles available in the nearly 1500K stack from SchoolHouse Mac. This particular sampler gives you an idea of the topics, projects, and tutorials that the larger stack contains.

Teachers Desktop Publishing with HyperCard came about because of HyperCard's power and flexibility. The combination of graphics and writing tools, along with the capability of creating stacks of varying sizes and printing in different sizes, makes HyperCard an excellent basic desktop-publishing program for teachers.

Instructions for these projects, and working with HyperCard in connection with them, are included. The author has included some simple suggestions for creating your own art and working with HyperCard's graphics tools.

Subj:　Teachers Desktop Pub.Sampler sea
Date:　May 12, 1994
From:　Charlie938

File: Teachers Desktop Pub.Sampler (134579 bytes)
DL time: < 3 minutes
Author: Charles Doe/SchoolHouse Mac
Needs: Mac, HyperCard 2.x or player

Where

Education

EDUCATIONAL SOFTWARE

Keyword

Education

Select

Educational Software

Mac Educational Software

Miscellaneous

Download

Teachers Desktop Pub.Sampler sea

Three Dozen Goodies

SchoolHouse Mac has placed over 40 educational tools on America Online. Clip art themes include: TinyClipArt, Transportation, Holiday, 2nd Semester, Halloween, NASA, Science Fiction, and many more. Reading/Language and Science/Health programs are also on the list.

Where

The complete sequence of steps through Computing can be found on page 15. Of course, you can save time and money by using the Keyword shortcuts.

Keyword

File Search

Select

>Charlie938

Download

[Your choice of over 40 programs!]

Sound Lesson Plans for Kindergarten and Pre-School

These are some simple lesson plans on teaching concepts about sound to kindergarten and pre-school age children. They may be helpful in giving you ideas about your own lessons. The lessons include sounds made by containers commonly found around the house, vibrations, voice noise, and animal sounds.

311

Subj: Sound Lesson Plans
Date: December 27, 1993
From: Langelote
File: SOUNDS.TXT (16122 bytes)
DL time: < 1 minute
Author: Langelote
Needs: Text reader

Where

Education

Teachers' Information Network

Keyword

TIN

Select

Lesson Plan Libraries

Pre-School

Download

Sound Lesson Plans

Dinosaur Mania

Kids love dinosaurs no matter what type: animated, stuffed, or in museums. This next section includes dinosaur fonts, sounds, and a lesson plan.

Dinosotype

This very exclusive font (available in both TrueType and Type 1 format) contains very live dinosaurs—original pictures ready to print, A through Z and a through z. Dinosotype is shareware and upon registration, you will receive 50 more fonts, including many other original and foreign fonts (Japanese Kata and Hiragana, Russian, Slovak, Armenian, ancient Greek, Hebrew, and more).

Subj: Dinosaurs pictures chars (TT or T1)
Date: December 5, 1993
From: MichelChap
File: DINOS-TT.sit (111041 bytes)
DL time: < 3 minutes
Author: M.Bujardet, Match Software
Needs: Mac, high-res printer, AOL 2.0 or StuffIt Expander, System 7

Where

The complete sequence of steps through Computing can be found on page 15. Of course, you can save time and money by using the Keyword shortcuts.

Keyword

File Search

Select

>dinosaurs

Download

Dinosaurs pictures chars (TT)

Dinosaurs pictures chars (Type 1)

Dinomania Font

Dinomania is a font where the lowercase characters are images of 26 different species of dinosaurs, from flying species like the Pteranodon to swimming varieties like the Mosasaurus. In order to make them clearer at small sizes, the images are all done as silhouettes, but the species are still clearly identifiable. To make it even more interesting, they are scaled proportional to their actual size with a silhouette of a Scotsman included to give an idea of their size relative to a human being.

Pre-schoolers will enjoy the printed samples they can paint or color. Aside from amusing toddlers, these dinosaurs make great little decorations or embellishments in letters or other documents.

This font is shareware and you'll get even more goodies when you send your fee!

Subj: Dinomania Font (True Type or Type 1)
Date: August 27, 1994
From: RagnarokGC
File: DinomaniaTT.sit (115946 bytes)
DL time: < 3 minutes
Author: Dave Nalle/SFL
Needs: Mac, System 7 or TT Init/Postscript -Type 1

Where

The complete sequence of steps through Computing can be found on page 15. Of course, you can save time and money by using the Keyword shortcuts.

Keyword

File Search

Select
>dinosaurs

Download
Dinomania Font (True Type)

Dinomania Font (Type One)

I Am Dinosaur, Hear Me Roar!

Look here to find a Jurassic Park sound clip of a T-Rex roar. For a longer file try Jurassic Park #17 SND. Rooooaaaarrrrrr!

Subj: Jurassic Park #19 SND
Date: June 21, 1993
From: LorettaT
File: T-Rex roar.sit (43949 bytes)
DL time: < 1 minute
Author: LorettaT
Needs: Sound utility, AOL 2.0, StuffIt Expander

Where

The complete sequence of steps through Computing can be found on page 15. Of course, you can save time and money by using the Keyword shortcuts.

Keyword
File Search

Select
Software Libraries

Software Search

>Jurassic Park dinosaur

Download
Jurassic Park #19 SND

Dinosaur Lesson Plan

Children love dinosaurs and this lesson plan caters to that kid appeal by integrating dinosaurs and geography. This Geoguide lesson plan supplements the article on dinosaurs from the January 1993 issue of *National Geographic* magazine. Seven activities are outlined and are adaptable to a range of ages. Best for students from kindergarten through sixth grade.

Subj: Dinosaurs Geoguide Lesson Plan
Date: June 22, 1994
From: EalyGEP

File: Dinosaurs Geoguide.txt (10908 bytes)
DL time: < 1 minute
Author: National Geographic Society
Needs: Text reader

Where

Education

National Geographic

Keyword

NGS

Select

Geography Education Program

Geography Teaching Materials

Download

Dinosaurs Geoguide Lesson Plan

Where to Find More Goodies

In this book, you'll want to take a look at *Education* and *Science and Space* for parents' programs and related files. Plus, in *Around the House* and in *Cooking*, you'll find directions to find fascinating kids crafts.

On AOL, you can access the Internet in search of more free stuff for children and their parents. Did you know that there are 11 Internet newsgroups for or about kids? Try the Keyword Newsgroups, and select Search All Newsgroups. Type **kids** and you'll find all the current kids newsgroups—misc.kids is very popular. On any given day, 200 to 400 new messages will be posted. Stay tunecd often.

Once again through the magic of America Online, I've found multiples of tools and toys for kids of the electronic persuasion. The best places to start are Education, Kids Only, Parent, Newsstand—and all over AOL. The next time you're looking for something for kids, be sure to start in the main areas we've featured in this chapter.

FREE $TUFF

It is the spirit and not the form of
the law that keeps justice alive.

Earl Warren

The Law

The Law is all around us. No, that doesn't imply the police are at the front door, nor does it imply that we'll soon have one ID card to replace the wallet full of identifiers. It's inescapable. We encounter the law and its ramifications throughout our day.

That's what this section is for—to show you the law in all the ways it affects you:

- You'll see the major trials found on Court TV and on Court TV online.
- You'll find online samples of leases, deeds, wills, and contracts.
- You'll find an employment application template and the complete text and implications of the Americans with Disabilities Act.
- If you're thinking about Law School or have graduated already, you'll find directions to an LSAT simulator and a Bar Exam simulator.

Finally, I promise you the fascinating Last Will and Testament of a rich and famous individual—a scoop that's not even in *People Magazine*.

MULTIMEDIA LAW HANDBOOK

This material is a selection from the recently published *Multimedia Law Handbook*. Five text files are included, encompassing Copyright law, use of pre-existing works, and distribution agreements. Subtopics include using music, clearing rights, and obtaining licenses.

Subj: MMLAW: Multimedia Law Handbook
Date: April 8, 1994
From: PC BillP
File: MMLAW.ZIP (24454 bytes)
DL time: < 1 minute
Author: J. Dianne Brinson
Needs: UnZIPing program, text reader

Where

The complete sequence of steps through Computing can be found on page 15. Of course, you can save time and money by using the Keyword shortcuts.

Keyword

PC: File Search
Mac: PC Software

Select

>Multimedia Law

Download

MMLAW: Multimedia Law Handbook

Patent Copyright Trademark Primer ©

ClinicStax is a folder containing seven "freeware" HyperCard stacks. The stacks provide practical information about patents, trademarks, and copyrights for programmers, artists, independent inventors, and small business owners.

The stacks were written by Professor Thomas G. Field, Jr., Director of the Innovation Clinic of Franklin Pierce Law Center (Concord NH) based on almost 20 years of experience in answering questions. Well over 80,000 copies of these stacks have been distributed in booklet form by the Law Center and the U.S. Small Business Administration.

Here are the stack descriptions:

- *Information* is a general index to the stacks.
- *So You Have an Idea* is a basic review of the relationship between patents and the market value of inventions. This stack discusses the need for counsel in making outside submissions, the need for prior art searches, invention promoters, and other matters of special interest to independent inventors—particularly from a cost standpoint.
- *Seeking Cost-Effective Patents* addresses ways to evaluate intellectual property options in view of the nature of an invention and its market value. This stack contains specific strategies for controlling ever-increasing patent costs in the face of market uncertainty.
- *Trademarks and Business Goodwill* is a discussion of strong versus weak marks, the need for searches, the value of state and federal registrations and other matters of importance to owners of small businesses.
- *Avoiding Patent, Trademark and Copyright Problems* is written primarily for owners of small businesses.
- *Copyright in Visual Arts* and *Copyright for Computer Authors* address the importance of copyright registration and notice, works for hire, deposit requirements, registration of multiple works, the need for counsel in licensing and other matters of interest to freelance artists, computer authors, craftspeople, and small entrepreneurs.

Subj: Patent Copyright Trademark Primer
Date: February 22, 1994
From: Mouser 28
File: Patent_____Stacks.sit (212436 bytes)
DL time: < 5 minutes

Author: Prof. Thomas G. Field, Jr.
Needs: Mac, HyperCard, UnStuffIt or AOL 2.0

Where

The complete sequence of steps through Computing can be found on page 15. Of course, you can save time and money by using the Keyword shortcuts.

Keyword

File Search

Select

>Patent

Download

Patent Copyright Trademark Primer

For additional information on copyrights, go to the Library of Congress (Keyword: Library). Once there, select Tour the Library, and then The Copyright Office.

Software Agreements

Got the killer program ready to put on the market? Take a look at this article first. You will find information on the proper use of contracts in software development by Attorney Steve Fishman, author of *Software Development: A Legal Guide*. This article appeared in the Winter 1993 issue of the *Nolo News*.

Subj: Software Agreements (text)
Date: May 1, 1994
From: Nolo Press
File: NN93SW.TXT (13449 bytes)
DL time: < 1 minute
Author: Nolo Press
Needs: Text reader

Where

The complete sequence of steps through Computing can be found on page 15. Of course, you can save time and money by using the Keyword shortcuts.

Keyword

Legal SIG

Select

Legal SIG Download Library

Download

Software Agreements (text)

Employment Focus Newsletter

The law firm of Gibney, Anthony & Flaherty (NYC) publishes a quarterly newsletter on employment, immigration, and benefits issues. Gibney, Anthony & Flaherty is a 40 lawyer full-service firm with specialties in labor and employment, employee benefits, immigration, trademark (especially anti-counterfeiting), trusts and estates, customs, international tax, real estate, government relations, and litigation. The newsletter is primarily for employers, corporate executives, human resource officers, and lawyers concerned with employment issues. To see a sample issue, download the ASCII version of *Employment Focus Newsletter*. If you're interested in a free subscription, send E-mail to Ruffino with your name, company/firm name, and mailing address.

Where

The complete sequence of steps through Computing can be found on page 15. Of course, you can save time and money by using the Keyword shortcuts.

Keyword

Legal SIG

Select

Legal SIG Download Library

Download

Employment Focus Newsletter

E-mail:

Ruffino—*include your name, company/firm name, and mailing address*

Gibney, Anthony & Flaherty (NYC) has also posted their *AlbanyFocus* lobbying newsletter, which will be of interest to NewYorkers. Follow the Employment Focus Newsletter download directions.

Starting a Business in the United States

Gibney, Anthony & Flaherty (NYC) also offers a guide to the legal issues involved in starting a business in the United States. This 70-page guide, entitled *Starting a Business in the United States, A Practical Guide to Legal Issues*, tells the story of a foreign manufacturer that brings its business to the United States. You'll follow the establishment and growth of the business through three distinct stages: Entering the United States market, establishing a presence, and expanding

United States operations. The guide provides summaries of U.S. laws on corporate tax, trademark and copyright, licensing and distribution, business organizations, immigration, litigation, and much more! The guide is offered for business owners and corporate executives. If you're interested in a free subscription, send E-mail to Ruffino with your name, company/firm name, and mailing address.

E-mail:

Ruffino—*Include your name, company/firm name and mailing address*

Legal Bytes

Computer and technology law are addressed in this download of Legal Bytes. The file includes the first three issues of a legal newsletter written by the Austin, Texas law firm of George, Donaldson & Ford.

This file is a compilation of three issues, so there are several topics in this download, including electronic BBS operators liability for their users' libelous statements, when a computer program is a copy, theft of trade secrets, contracting for confidentiality, *fair use* by schools and non-profit organizations, and advertising by lawyers on the Internet.

Subj:　Legal Bytes (ZIP)
Date:　August 3, 1994
From:　Rich Dunn
File:　LGLBYTES.ZIP (48010 bytes)
DL time: < 1 minute
Needs:　UnZIPing program, text reader

Where

The complete sequence of steps through Computing can be found on page 15. Of course, you can save time and money by using the Keyword shortcuts.

Keyword

Legal SIG

Select

Legal SIG Download Library

Download

Legal Bytes (ZIP)

Pass the Bar

A shareware version of the popular multistate bar exam simulator—The Para Mason's Bar Review Series 4.0 with artificial intelligence—for the PC. It places you in a real-time exam taking mode. All questions and answers are based upon the Black Letter Law. You can actually take a torts exam. The commercial version is available for DOS, Windows, and Macs at $295.

Subj: Bar Exam Simulator (ZIP)
Date: April 13, 1994
From: PARA MASON
File: PARA_PC.ZIP (187736 bytes)
DL time: < 5 minutes
Author: Bill Flowers
Needs: PC, UnZIPing program

Where

The complete sequence of steps through Computing can be found on page 15. Of course, you can save time and money by using the Keyword shortcuts.

Keyword

Legal SIG

Select

Legal SIG Download Library

Download

Bar Exam Simulator (ZIP)

The *San Jose Mercury News* publishes a list of individuals who pass the California Bar exam. If you live in California and want to see who's new in the legal field, try this source. With the following directions you're on the freeway to the list.

Keyword

Mercury

Select

Communications

Software Library

Mercury Library

Bar Exam Feb. 94 (Alpha or ZIP)

The Legal Research FAQ

This document presents an overview of the standard resources and tools used in conducting legal research on state and federal law in the United States. It also provides an overview of the structure of the various state and federal court systems, and describes the primary legal sources (case reporters, statutory and

regulatory compilations) where the law *per se* can be located. It is written for the layperson, not lawyers; no prior legal knowledge or research experience is assumed.

The author is an attorney admitted to practice in the both State of New York and the Commonwealth of Massachusetts.

Subj: The Legal Research FAQ (ZIP)
Date: April 4, 1994
From: Rich Dunn
File: RESEARCH.ZIP (26076 bytes)
DL time: < 1 minute
Author: Mark Eckenwiler
Needs: Any computer, UnZIPing program, text reader

Where

The complete sequence of steps through Computing can be found on page 15. Of course, you can save time and money by using the Keyword shortcuts.

Keyword

PC: Mac Software

Mac: File Search

Select

>Legal research

Download

The Legal Research FAQ (ZIP)

In Re Macintosh Newsletter

In Re Macintosh is an electronically distributed newsletter for legal professionals who use or are considering using the Macintosh computer to automate their law practice. In addition to the articles on the use of Macs in the law office, readers will discover BBSs of interest to lawyers, and reviews of pertinent hardware and software.

Subj: In Re Macintosh 1.5 (Mac)
Date: May 15, 1994
From: JPSMAC
File: InReMac1.5.sea (248082 bytes)
DL time: < 6 minutes
Author: Jonathan P. Sullivan
Needs: Mac, 1Mb free memory

Where

The complete sequence of steps through Computing can be found on page 15. Of course, you can save time and money by using the Keyword shortcuts.

Keyword

Legal SIG

Select

Legal SIG Software Library

Download

In Re Macintosh 1.5 (Mac)

Apple's LEGAL SOLUTIONS GUIDE

This is the latest version of Apple's *Legal Solutions Guide*. It lists tons of products that might be of interest to an attorney or legal professional. With 80-plus pages, the guide extensively covers legal research, litigation support, document processing, case management, legal forms, docket and calendaring, client databases, time and billing, document management, law-office management, text scanning, accounting, desktop publishing, electronic mail, file transfers, modems and networking. Pass the Bar then get the guide.

Subj: Legal Solutions Guide (SIT)
Date: July 16, 1993
From: RBS
File: Legal Solutions Guide.sit (76699 bytes)
DL time: < 2 minutes
Author: Apple
Needs: Microsoft Word

Where

The complete sequence of steps through Computing can be found on page 15. Of course, you can save time and money by using the Keyword shortcuts.

Keyword

PC: Mac Software
Mac: File Search

Select

>legal solutions

Download

Legal Solutions Guide (SIT)

Country Lawyers Forms - Word 4

A set of simple forms demonstrating the usefulness of Word in the law office. The forms are designed for use in Arkansas but you may be able to modify them for use in your jurisdiction. The forms include a warranty deed, a bill of sale, a divorce waiver, a subpoena, a federal court summons, a speed note, and a simple will for a male.

Subj: Country Lawyers Forms - WORD4
Date: June 17, 1990
From: JohnP213
File: CountryLawyersKit (21548 bytes)
DL time: < 1 minute
Author: John Purtle
Needs: Mac, StuffIt, Word 4, Times, Helvetica, London fonts

Where

The complete sequence of steps through Computing can be found on page 15. Of course, you can save time and money by using the Keyword shortcuts.

Keyword

PC: Mac Software
Mac: File Search

Select

> law forms

Download

Country Lawyers Forms - WORD4

Law Office Macros

Is your workday set on express? An AOL user has posted his law office macros as freeware. Take advantage of these macros that can be easily modified for your uses. Some are specific to legal applications, for example, writing court orders; while others are more general, for example, creating memo and letter closing formats.

Subj: Law Office Macros
Date: April 26, 1994
From: Picass9879
File: LawOfcGenericMacros (23395 bytes)
DL time: < 1 minutes
Author: Michael J. Walter
Needs: Mac, WordPerfect 2.1.x

Where

Computing

Industry Connection

[Choose WordPerfect Corporation]

Keyword

WordPerfect

Select

WordPerfect Mac Technical Support

Software Libraries

WP Macros

Download

Law Office Macros

Legal Forms-Revised

Legal Forms-Revised is a file containing five standard legal forms. This download includes a Pledge of Personal Property, a General Release, a Contract Clause for Property Damaged or Destroyed, Assignment of Accounts Receivable, and a Consulting Agreement. The file description includes the directions for ordering 35 more forms on disk or via E-mail—including Demands, Notes, Guarantees, Joint Property, Letter of Credit, Power of Attorney, and Capital Investment— in ASCII format for only $6.

Subj: LEGAL FORMS-REVISED
Date: December 13, 1993
From: RUSS4HAM
File: FREE LEGAL$$ (13730 bytes)
DL time: < 1 minute
Needs: Text reader, printer

Where

The complete sequence of steps through Computing can be found on page 15. Of course, you can save time and money by using the Keyword shortcuts.

Keyword

PC: Mac Software

Mac: File Search

Select

>legal forms

Download

LEGAL FORMS-REVISED

Nolo Catalog

Answers to many—if not most—of the questions commonly asked in the Legal SIG Forum can be found in books by Nolo Press, the leading publisher of self-help law products since 1971.

Nolo currently publishes more than 80 book and software titles. Although the books are written by lawyers and other experts, they are specifically designed to be used by laypeople. Nolo books de-mystify the law, explain legal rules in plain English, and set out legal procedures in an easy-to-follow, step-by-step manner.

Download this text file to read descriptions of all of Nolo's book and software titles, as well as reviews of their products. Information on how to order is included in the stack.

Subj: Nolo Catalog - Fall 94 (SIT)
Date: September 9, 1994
From: Nolo Press
File: NOLOCAT.sit (30675 bytes)
DL time: < 1 minute
Author: Nolo Press
Needs: Mac, StuffIt, text reader

Where

The complete sequence of steps through Computing can be found on page 15. Of course, you can save time and money by using the Keyword shortcuts.

Keyword

Legal SIG

Select

Legal SIG Software Library

Download

Nolo Catalog - Fall 94 (SIT)

WordPerfect Legal Sampler

WordPerfect has compiled the WP Legal Sampler folder full of documents and macros that work with WordPerfect 3.0 and the ExpressDocsx Stationery documents. You can add the legal macros to your library.

Subj: Legal Sampler
Date: December 25, 1994
From: MIKE WP
File: Install Legal Sampler (269968 bytes)
DL time: < 7 minutes
Author: WordPerfect Corporation
Needs: Mac, WordPerfect 3.0

Where

Computing

Industry Connection

[Choose WordPerfect Corporation]

Keyword

WordPerfect

Select

WordPerfect Mac Technical Support

Software Libraries

WP Macros

Download

Legal Sampler

Legal Documents

Look here to find a collection of over 80 legal documents and letters that you can easily import into your favorite word-processing program and modify to meet your needs. This download includes deeds, leases, titles, powers of attorney, business documents, purchase agreements, proxies, promissory notes, leins, foreclosures, liability waivers, contracts, letters of credit, bills of sale, escrow documents, employment agreements, affidavits, and more. Whew! The text files list all documents by filename and by description to make it easy for you to find what you need.

Subj: LEGAL: Legal Documents
Date: September 27, 1993
From: Frodo
File: LEGAL.ZIP (80979 bytes)
DL time: < 2 minutes
Author: Joe Simon
Needs: UnZIPing program, text reader

Where

The complete sequence of steps through Computing can be found on page 15. Of course, you can save time and money by using the Keyword shortcuts.

Keyword

PC: File Search

Mac: PC Software

Select

> legal documents

Download

LEGAL: Legal Documents

Bankrupt? At Least You Have Your Mac

Bankruptcy Mac 3.0 is set of FileMaker Pro 2 templates for filing Chapter 7, 11, and 13 bankruptcy petitions. This is the fully functional product—not a demo version. You may use the program only to review it in house for five calendar days. You may not use the product for any other purpose—to do so is a copyright violation. If you decide to purchase the program you can do so by following the instructions in the file description. Registration is $69.

Subj: Bankruptcy Mac
Date: April 11, 1994
From: Cakey
File: Bankruptcy Mac.sea (470345 bytes)
DL time: < 12 minutes
Author: Clayton P. Osting
Needs: 2 Mb RAM, hard disk, FileMaker Pro 2.0

Where

The complete sequence of steps through Computing can be found on page 15. Of course, you can save time and money by using the Keyword shortcuts.

Keyword

PC: Mac Software

Mac: File Search

Select

>bankruptcy

Download

Bankruptcy Mac

Prenuptial Agreements

Make sure you get a fair deal both before and after the marriage. This is a text file describing how to prepare and write a prenuptial agreement. You will find a copy of the applicable Florida statutes, a case study, and a sample prenuptial agreement. While this information is based on Florida's laws, it may be useful for those in other states.

Subj: PA: V1.0 Prenuptial Agreements
Date: November 29, 1993
From: GATEWAY466
File: MARRIAGE.ZIP (25792 bytes)
DL time: < 1 minute
Needs: UnZIPing program, text reader, GIF or PCX viewer (optional)

Where

The complete sequence of steps through Computing can be found on page 15. Of course, you can save time and money by using the Keyword shortcuts.

Keyword

PC: File Search

Mac: PC Software

Select

>marriage

Download

PA: V1.0 Prenuptial Agreements

Sound Off on Marriage

Can you believe Rush Limbaugh, President Clinton, and tax increases combined in a 14.75 second sound bite? With a background of the song *Liar, Liar*, President Clinton, in a speech excerpt, says, "I will not raise taxes on the middle class to pay for these programs. I am not gonna raise taxes on the middle class to pay for these programs." Rush interjects, "Marriage tax. Marriage tax. Wait'll you see it." Just call it an Election Day special.

Subj: WAV: Limbaugh: Marriage Tax
Date: January 16, 1994
From: KenPercell
File: BILLSLIE.WAV (162702 bytes)
DL time: < 4 minutes
Needs: Any computer, Windows 3.1 or WAV file player

Where

The complete sequence of steps through Computing can be found on page 15. Of course, you can save time and money by using the Keyword shortcuts.

Keyword

PC: File Search

Mac: PC Software

Select

>marriage music

Download

WAV: Limbaugh: Marriage Tax

Divorce Procedures

Looking to get unhitched? You might want to take a look at this short text file, which describes the process of divorce. This information is specific to Washington State. Topics covered include how to dissolve a marriage, residence requirements (so that Washington state laws would apply), child support, spousal support, custody, division of property, responsibility for debts and what to expect from lawyers. Divorce laws vary from state to state. While this information is general in nature, it may not apply to your own state.

Subj: DIVORCE: Divorce Procedures
Date: August 8, 1993
From: Gopher007
File: DIVORCE (18313 bytes)
DL time: < 1 minute
Author: Brent Knapp (Synergy Operating Systems)
Needs: Text reader

Where

The complete sequence of steps through Computing can be found on page 15. Of course, you can save time and money by using the Keyword shortcuts.

Keyword

PC: File Search
Mac: PC Software

Select

>divorce

Download

DIVORCE: Divorce Proceedures

Living Will

This is a text file consisting of state-approved living will forms for over 40 states, as well as a model form for those states that do not have an approved form. Living wills allow you to set forth directions on life-support level medical care in the event you are incapacitated or unable to communicate your desires. These forms are part of a book, *The Guide to Living Wills*, written by an attorney, which is intended to help you to understand and prepare a living will. Ordering information is included.

Subj: LIVEWILL: Living Will Guide
Date: December 30, 1993
From: PCC Op
File: LIVEWILL.ZIP (21216 bytes)
DL time: < 1 minute
Needs: UnZIPing program, text reader

Where

The complete sequence of steps through Computing can be found on page 15. Of course, you can save time and money by using the Keyword shortcuts.

Keyword

PC: File Search
Mac: PC Software

Select

>will

Download

LIVEWILL: Living Will Guide

Simple Will

Last week I received a phone call from a telemarketer with a special on cemetery plots. I informed her that my husband and I had no desire to spend our eternal resting days in Maryland. Seriously, that was a jarring phone call and a reminder to update my will! If you don't yet have a will, you may want to try this blank simple will that has been provided as shareware ($19 fee). Make sure you leave your PC to someone deserving.

Subj: A simple Will
Date: November 2, 1993
From: LegalSWare
File: Will_93.TXT (simple) (3903 bytes)

DL time: < 1 minute
Needs: Any computer

Where

The complete sequence of steps through Computing can be found on page 15. Of course, you can save time and money by using the Keyword shortcuts.

Keyword

PC: Mac Software

Mac: File Search

Select

>simple will

Download

A simple Will

Revocable Living Trust

Did you know that all of your assets, including your business, can be passed on to your heirs without the need to go through probate court? All property can be placed into a Revocable Living Trust which, upon death, transfers property to your beneficiaries quickly, privately, and often at much lower cost than settling a will. Be careful when you're looking for this: The file name is misspelled.

Subj: "Revokable Living Trusts"
Date: September 26, 1994
From: MegaSource
File: LT1.TXT (12398 bytes)
DL time: < 1 minute
Needs: PC, text reader

Where

Personal Finance

Microsoft Small Business Center

Keyword

MSBC

Select

Software Library

Strategies for Business

Download

"Revokable Living Trusts"

Immigration Law Compliance

The Immigration Reform and Control Act (IRCA) was passed in 1986. This act requires all employers to verify that all employees hired on or after Nov. 6, 1986 are legally authorized to work in the US. This law applies to organizations of any size and of any number of employees. The Immigration Law Compliance (ILC) software gives employers a quick easy way to qualify employees and to comply with federal law. The unregistered version prints a sample completed I-9 form and provides textual guidelines for complying with the IRCA of 1986.

The registered version ($19) provides these additions: A full-featured I-9 filler program, full form printing capabilities, a records database to store completed forms, an *I-9 Worksheet* form, a detailed user manual, and a sample "Immigration Law Compliance" employee policy.

Subj: ILC: V1.0 Immigration Law Compliance
Date: April 2, 1994
From: CAP
File: ILC11.ZIP (120104 bytes)
DL time: < 3 minutes
Author: Dean Charron
Needs: UnZIPing program
Type: Shareware

Where

The complete sequence of steps through Computing can be found on page 15. Of course, you can save time and money by using the Keyword shortcuts.

Keyword

PC: File Search
Mac: PC Software

Select

>immigration

Download

ILC: V1.0 Immigration Law Compliance

Police Car GIF

Look here for a colorful GIF file of a police car. It even has a small inscription added from *The Bible*, specifically from Romans 13. Keep this one around to ward off the criminals.

Subj: GIF: Police Cruiser
Date: December 21, 1991
From: WalterBAU
File: POLICE.GIF (4024 bytes)
DL time: < 1 minute
Author: Walter H. Bauer, Jr.
Needs: Any computer, GIF viewer

Where

The complete sequence of steps through Computing can be found on page 15. Of course, you can save time and money by using the Keyword shortcuts.

Keyword

PC: File Search

Mac: PC Software

Select

>police cruiser

Download

GIF: Police Cruiser

10 Codes

When a life-threatening situation arises, emergency crews need to quickly communicate information. Police and Fire Departments use the 10-code system for such situations. There are several codes systems in use today, and this file contains four of the more common code systems. Take a look at the following samples before you ease into your Lazy-Boy for the umpteenth rerun of *Adam-12*.

10-4 Acknowledgment (OK)
10-14 Prowler Report
10-16 Domestic Problem
10-32 Man with Gun
10-52 Ambulance Needed
10-70 Fire Alarm
10-79 Notify Coroner
10-98 Prison/Jail Break

Subj: Police "10" Codes
Date: February 24, 1994
From: DS Squared
File: TenCode.txt (8579 bytes)

DL time: < 1 minute
Author: DS Squared
Needs: Text reader

Where

The complete sequence of steps through Computing can be found on page 15. Of course, you can save time and money by using the Keyword shortcuts.

Keyword

PC: Mac Software

Mac: File Search

Select

>police code

Download

Police "10" Codes

Law & Order Sound File

This file contains the breakaway to/from commercial sound used in the TV show *Law & Order*. It has a fairly quick play time, so you could use this to substitute for your current system beep or quack.

Subj: Law & Order. FSSD
Date: February 28, 1992
From: N Miller
File: Law & Order.sit (26631 bytes)
DL time: < 1 minute
Needs: Sound Utility, StuffIt

Where

The complete sequence of steps through Computing can be found on page 15. Of course, you can save time and money by using the Keyword shortcuts.

Keyword

PC: Mac Software

Mac: File Search

Select

> Law and TV

Download

Law & Order. FSSD

Vintage TV—Car 54

CAR54.WAV is a 3.95 second sound bite from the TV series, *Car 54 Where Are You*, Just a little bit of nostalgia for you.

Subj: WAV: Car 54 Where Are You?
Date: June 25, 1994
From: Zippy Kurt
File: CAR54.WAV (87292 bytes)
DL time: < 2 minutes
Author: Zippy Kurt
Needs: Windows 3.1 or WAV file player
Type: Public domain

Where

The complete sequence of steps through Computing can be found on page 15. Of course, you can save time and money by using the Keyword shortcuts.

Keyword

PC: File Search

Mac: PC Software

Select

> TV and Police sound

Download

WAV: Car 54 Where Are You?

Read 'em Their Rights—Dragnet Sound Bite

From *Dragnet*, this is Joe Friday reading some criminal his rights, in that classic Joe Friday monotone. If you suspect something illegal or unethical in your office (or even if you just want to get a few laughs) you might make the involved parties paranoid with this one!

Subj: Read 'em Their Rights, Joe! SND
Date: May 25, 1994
From: WMaho
File: Read'emTheirRights,Joe.sit (118453 bytes)
DL time: < 3 minutes
Author: Jack Webb
Needs: Sound utility, AOL 2.0 or StuffIt Expander

Where

The complete sequence of steps through Computing can be found on page 15. Of course, you can save time and money by using the Keyword shortcuts.

Keyword

PC: Mac Software

Mac: File Search

Select

>Dragnet

Download

Read 'em Their Rights, Joe! SND

Also try Dragnet Police Officers SND. You'll hear Joe Friday saying "We're police officers, Ma'am."

Court TV Online

Millions of Americans already know about Court TV from its extensive coverage of the Menendez brothers' or William Kennedy Smith's trials. Court TV is an around-the-clock cable legal news network dedicated to reporting on the U.S. legal and judicial systems. When the news is filled with legal issues, check with Court TV Online for valuable issue-oriented information.

Where

Entertainment

Television & Radio

Networks

Court TV

Keyword

CourtTV

Last Will and Testament—Jacqueline Onassis

Interested in what Jackie O. bequeathed to her loved ones? Here's the last will and testament of the ever popular but very mysterious lady, as filed in probate court in the state of New York. Who was left what? How were the residences in New York, Newport, RI, and Martha's Vineyard distributed? How many trusts were established? Who received art work and a signed copy of JFK's inaugural address? What will the John F. Kennedy Library receive? The details, in-depth, are in this file.

Subj: Will of Jacqueline K. Onassis

Date: August 16, 1994

From: CourtTV

File: ONASSIS (74023 bytes)
DL time: < 2 minutes

Where

Entertainment

Television & Radio

Networks

Court TV

Keyword

Court TV

Select

Court TV Download Library

Download

Will of Jacqueline K. Onassis

Do You Recognize This Signature?

She's no longer with us, but she continues to be a mystery. This is the notarized signature of Jacqueline Kennedy Onassis as it appears on page 36 of her Last Will & Testament dated March 22, 1994 in New York City. Jackie died just 59 days later at her Fifth Avenue apartment on May 19, 1994 at the age of 64. The will was filed with the probate court 13 days later on June 1, 1994.

Randy Clark scanned Jackie's signature at 1200 dots-per-inch from an original court-certified copy he obtained directly from the New York County probate court where the original of Jackie's will is on file.

This GIF is in the public domain. Probated wills are considered public records and copies are available from the probate courts where they are on file. The courts charge a copying/search fee, but they will provide a copy to any member of the public willing to pay the court fees. The will itself is not copyrighted. The court fee for the Jackie O. will is $215 ($5 per page, plus $25 search fee).

The notarized signatures from the original court-certified copies of the wills of JFK, Richard Nixon, and Elvis Presley will soon be available courtesy of RClark@aol. Randy welcomes E-mail from anyone with questions about the wills or other celebrity documents.

Subj: Jacqueline Onassis Signature GIF
Date: July 5, 1994

From: RClarkJKO
File: JKOSIG.GIF (169652 bytes)
DL time: < 4 minutes
Needs: GIF viewer

Where

The complete sequence of steps through Computing can be found on page 15. Of course, you can save time and money by using the Keyword shortcuts.

Keyword

PC: Mac Software

Mac: File Search

Select

> Signature or celebrity

Download

Jacqueline Onassis Signature GIF

Elvis Presley Signature GIF

JFK Signature GIF

Richard Nixon Signature GIF

O.J. Simpson's Legal Troubles

Court TV has posted transcripts from Simpson Grand Jury proceedings that are available for download. They are public documents on file with the Court Reporter's office in Los Angeles. You could request a copy and pay over $200 plus shipping for a transcript hard copy or a disk with the ASCII file, but Court TV has done the work and covered the bill for you. Innocent or guilty, you'll likely discover that you didn't get the whole story from the network news!

Subj: Simpson Grand Jury Transcripts
Date: August 4, 1994
From: CourtTV
File: GRANDJ.ZIP (186614 bytes)
DL time: < 5 minutes
Author: Court TV
Needs: UnZIPing program

Where

Entertainment

Television & Radio

Networks

Court TV

Keyword

Court TV

Select

Court TV Download Library

Download

Simpson Grand Jury Transcript

O.J. Simpson Mugshot GIF

Here it is! Unfortunately for O.J. this is probably the most well-known photograph of him. You've seen it on the news-magazines, now view it on your screen.

Subj: O.J. Simpson Mugshot GIF
Date: July 22, 1994
From: Semprin179
File: oj-mug.gif (77742 bytes)
DL time: < 2 minutes
Author: Semprin179
Needs: Mac, GIF viewer

Where

The complete sequence of steps through Computing can be found on page 15. Of course, you can save time and money by using the Keyword shortcuts.

Keyword

PC: Mac Software
Mac: File Search

Select

>Simpson graphics

Download

OJ Simpson Mugshot GIF

Clinton Legal Expense Trust

Here is the trust fund established by President Clinton to raise money for the Clintons' legal expenses. If you're planning to contribute to Bill and Hillary's trust, this document provide the legal details on the trust. The trustees are an impressive collection; they include a former cabinet member and several university presidents. Psst...the fund was established with $1,000 from William

Jefferson Clinton and $1,000 from Hillary Rodham Clinton.

Subj: Clinton Legal Expense Trust
Date: August 25, 1994
From: CourtTV
File: TRUST.TXT (12428 bytes)
DL time: < 1 minute
Author: Court TV

Where

Entertainment

Television & Radio

Networks

Court TV

Keyword

Court TV

Select

Court TV Download Library

Download

Clinton Legal Expense Trust

Did He or Didn't He?

This is a copy of the complaint filed in federal court on May 6, 1994 by Paula Corbin Jones against William Jefferson Clinton and Danny Ferguson.

Complaint, jurisdiction, venue, parties, facts, counts, relief, and the demand for a jury trial are all set forth in the complaint. The counts include: deprivation of constitutional rights and privileges, conspiracy to depriving person of equal protection of the law, intentional infliction of emotional distress, and defamation. Both PC-ZIP and Mac files are available.

Subj: Paula Jones Complaint (ZIP)
Date: June 5, 1994
From: Rich Dunn
File: HEYPAULA.ZIP (10803 bytes)
DL time: < 1 minute
Author: Paula Jones
Needs: UnZIPing program, text reader

Where

Computing

Special Attractions

Special Interest Groups

Business

Legal

Keyword

Legal SIG

Select

Legal SIG Software Library

Download

Paula Jones Complaint (ZIP)

Where to Find More Goodies

For more files on the Rostenkowski indictment, Paula Jones versus William Jefferson Clinton, and OJ Simpson, stop in at Court TV and the Legal SIG. You may find a PC file at one source and a Mac file at another location. Chicago Online has an extensive download library. Try Keyword: Chicago, followed by selecting Download Library and the Reference Desk Library.

Within *Free $tuff from America Online*, there are two additional sections for you to scan: *Business* and *Personal Finance*.

FREE $TUFF

A young man who does not have what it takes to perform military service is not likely to have what it takes to make a living.

John Fitzgerald Kennedy

Military and Aviation

Some (like my husband) would say I shouldn't combine military and aviation into one topic. After all, there's more to fighting a war than just jets! I understand, but what makes for a more breathtaking picture: a haze gray ship on the horizon or a mid-air refueling? In this section, you'll find military insignias, spectacular photographs, dynamic flight simulators, and military news sources. And, there's one superb photo of a ~~boat~~, oops—ship.

Military City Online

At Military City Online, military members and their families can find news and information concerning jobs, careers, and benefits, as well as fellow service members and their families. Of course, if you just want to know more about military life, you can stop in too.

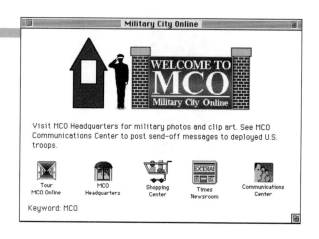

Where

Clubs & Interests

Military City Online

Keyword

MCO

Times Newsroom

The Times Newsroom area includes weekly news highlights from four Times papers: *Army Times*, *Air Force Times*, *Navy Times*, and *Navy Times Marine Corps Edition*. The current issue of each paper is available online and you can also review issues as far back as May 1994. However, back issues can only be searched by topic and not by date, so you'll have to use those acronyms and buzzwords in your search.

Where

Clubs & Interests

Military City Online

Keyword

MCO

Select
Times Newsroom

Early Bird News

For a quick update on daily news affecting military and defense issues, check out the Early Bird Headlines, Military City Online's listing of the articles appearing in the Pentagon's clipping service. *The Current News Early Bird* is a daily publication of the American Forces Information Service of the Department of Defense. The information service compiles and reprints news articles from a variety of newspapers for use by armed forces personnel. Each day's listing provides the headlines and the respective newspapers for further research.

Where
Clubs & Interests

Military City Online

Keyword
MCO

Select
MCO Headquarters

Early Bird Headlines

Read/Save
[date]

Installation Guide

Where is Sub Base Bangor, and what's there? All bases in the continental U.S. (CONUS) are listed in this database. Type in the name of the base or the city and state location and you'll see all you need to know about the number of housing units on base, what recreation facilities are available, and what commands are located there. The Installation Guide offers information on all CONUS installations with more than 300 assigned personnel. You'll also get another perspective of base closings from this list.

Where
Clubs & Interests

Military City Online

Keyword
MCO

Select

MCO headquarters

Military Installations

[service branch]

Read/Save

[installation name]

Service Seals

Be a patriot and download these Army, Navy, Air Force, Marines, and Coast Guard seals surrounding a U.S. flag. This file is in full color and in GIF format.

Subj: Service seals
Date: August 8, 1994
From: MCOSPE
File: SERVICES.GIF (16736 bytes)
DL time: < 1 minute
Author: Larry51
Needs: GIF viewer, 16 colors
Type: Public domain

Where

Clubs & Interests

Military City Online

Keyword

MCO

Select

MCO headquarters

Library

Cartoons, Drawings, Graphics

Read/Save

Service seals

Armored Vehicles Clip Art

And you thought armored vehicles were only for transporting money. Check out these PCX files of 50 armored vehicles from various countries, including U.S. and the former Soviet Union. The files were created in PC Paint Brush in VGA mode and are black and white. The ReadMe file carries the identification of each of the vehicles.

Subj: Armored vehicles clip art
Date: August 5, 1994
From: MCOSPE
File: ARMORPCX.ZIP (138404 bytes)
DL time: < 3 minutes
Author: James Snoke
Needs: PCX viewer, UnZIPing program
Type: Shareware

Where

Clubs & Interests

Military City Online

Keyword

MCO

Select

MCO headquarters

Library

Cartoons, Drawings, Graphics

Download

Armored vehicles clip art

Cruiser Fires!

This is a stunning photograph of one of the last 5"/38 gun mount firings: A live fire exercise on board the nuclear cruiser Long Beach (CGN-9) during her final operational cruise in April 1994 in the Western Atlantic. This gun mount—built in 1944—was subsequently sent to the China Lake Naval Testing Center in California following the cruiser's deactivation.

Subj: Cruiser Long Beach fires
Date: October 5, 1994
From: MCOSPE
File: BEACH.GIF (25131 bytes)
DL time: < 1 minute
Author: C.P. Cavas
Needs: GIF viewer

Where

Clubs & Interests

Military City Online

Keyword

MCO

Select

MCO headquarters

Library

Photographs

Download

Cruiser Long Beach fires

Ship's Bells and Sonar

Now your computer can make ship noises just like mine. These two sounds—
a ship's dinner bell and submarine sonar ping—make great beep sounds for
your computer. Now all you have to do is add water . . . well, on second thought,
a dry computer is a happy computer!

Subj: ShipsBell.FSSD
Date: January 11, 1990
From: FF Pollux
File: ShipsBell.sit (19076 bytes)
DL time: < 1 minute
Author: W.Lyons
Needs: Sound utility, AOL 2.0, or StuffIt

Where

The complete sequence of steps through Computing can be found on page 15.
Of course, you can save time and money by using the Keyword shortcuts.

Keyword

Mac: File Search

PC: Mac Software

Select

> ship alarm bell

Download

ShipsBell.FSSD

Sonar Ping SND

Marine Corps Graphics

Marine Corps graphics have been combined into this significant collection.
Marines and other service members will find these graphics helpful for adding
interest to newsletters, reunion notices, and announcements.

This is a very large file. It's obviously appreciated as it has had 260+ downloads.

Subj: Marine Graphics
Date: May 26, 1994
From: THE GUNNY
File: MARINE.EXE (1033821 bytes)
DL time: < 28 minutes
Author: Gunny (The Gunny)

Where

Clubs & Interests

Military City Online

Keyword

MCO

Select

MCO headquarters

Library

Cartoons, Drawings, Graphics

Download

Marine Graphics

DL time

Navy Ships

Is granddad's old ship still floating? Where is the new aircraft carrier, USS John F. Kennedy, homeported? Well now you can answer those pesky questions with one of these two ship lists found in Military City Online. One is an alphabetical listing of Navy ships and the other is a list of ships with their homeports and types. So, was that a cruiser or a battleship?

Subj: List of Navy Ships
Date: August 23, 1994
From: MCOSPE
File: SHIPLIST.TXT (36871 bytes)
DL time: < 1 minute
Author: U.S. Navy
Needs: Text reader

Where

Clubs & Interests

Military City Online

MCO Headquarters

Keyword
MCO HDQ

Select
Library

Text

Download
List of Navy Ships

List of USN ships by port, type

Coast Guard Emblem

Protect our shores and show your support for the U.S. Coast Guard by emblazoning your PC screen with this Coast Guard emblem. This distinctive insignia was created in Adobe Illustrator.

Subj: Coast Guard Emblem
Date: April 16, 1994
From: RSMuller
File: CG.Emblem.BW.gif (34873 bytes)
DL time: < 1 minute
Author: USCG files
Needs: Any GIF view

Where
Clubs & Interests

Military City Online

Keyword
Military

Select
Images, Photos & Graphics Files

Download
Coast Guard Emblem

F-14 Over San Diego

From San Diego, California you'll have an air-to-air right side view of a Fighter Squadron 194 (VF-194) F-14A Tomcat aircraft near Naval Air Station Miramar. Tom Cruise and Top Gun fans know this place as Fightertown USA. It's an official U.S. Navy photo.

Subj: F-14 over San Diego
Date: October 7, 1994

From: MCOGRA
File: F14.GIF (117843 bytes)
DL time: < 3 minutes
Author: Lt. Cmdr. Art Legare
Needs: GIF viewer

Where

Clubs & Interests

Military City Online

Keyword

MCO

Select

MCO Headquarters

Library

Photographs

Download

F-14 over San Diego

F-16 Refueling

What's volatile, critical, and life-saving at the same time? A mid-air refueling of a fighter jet. In this photo, you'll witness an Air Force F-16 getting some gas from a KC-135 Stratotanker, from the boom operator's perspective.

Subj: F-16 Air Refueling
Date: September 20, 1994
From: Bold Gold
File: F16CT.GIF (54082 bytes)
DL time: < 1 minute
Author: Steven Moraes
Needs: GIF viewer

Where

Clubs & Interests

Aviation Forum

Keyword

Aviation

Select

Software Libraries

Graphics

Download

F-16 Air Refueling

Tom Clancy Speaks

If you missed Tom Clancy on AOL's Center Stage, Military City Online captured his comments. The transcript is available for download. Find out what Tom Clancy really thinks about the downsizing of the military, nuclear disarmament, the baseball strike, Clipper Chip, threats to America and much more. It's an entertaining look at a most successful author, military supporter, and baseball team owner.

Subj: Tom Clancy on MCO
Date: October 17, 1994
From: MCOSPE
File: TCLANCY.TXT (28142 bytes)
DL time: < 1 minute
Needs: Text viewer

Where

Clubs & Interests

Military City Online

MCO Headquarters

Keyword

MCO HDQ

Select

Library

Text

Download

Tom Clancy on MCO

Where Are the Haitians and the Cubans?

With this picture you can take a look at the base that's been making news. It's an aerial photo of the U.S. Naval Base at Guantanamo Bay, Cuba, taken July 25, 1994. In the foreground are the Navy base buildings. On the peninsula in the background is the Haitian compound.

Subj: U.S. Naval Base, Guantanamo Bay, Cuba
Date: August 26, 1994
From: MCOGRA
File: Gitmo.gif (136439 bytes)

DL time: < 3 minutes
Author: Mario Villafuerte
Needs: Color or grayscale monitor, GIF viewer

Where

Clubs & Interests

Military City Online

MCO Headquarters

Keyword

MCO HDQ

Select

Library

Photos

Download

U.S. Naval Base, Guantanamo Bay, Cuba

Sailors and Tattoos

This is one of Jeff Bacon's Broadside cartoons for *Navy Times*. In this one, sailors line the rail of the ship as it comes into port. Two comment on the quiet beauty of the town. Then a third pipes up: "Anyone know where the tattoo parlor is?"

Subj: Bacon cartoon:Liberty port
Date: August 2, 1994
From: MCOSPE
File: BAC3-01A.GIF (93270 bytes)
DL time: < 2 minutes
Author: Jeff Bacon
Needs: GIF viewer

Where

Clubs & Interests

Military City Online

Keyword

MCO

Select

MCO Headquarters

Cartoons, Drawings & Graphics

Download

Bacon cartoon:Liberty port

Military & Vets Forum

Anyone with an interest in military and/or veterans affairs should take advantage of the Military and Vets Forum. This label includes all active duty personnel, reserves, National Guardsman, veterans, retirees, state defense forces, Civil Air Patrol, Naval Sea Cadets, and spouses. Civilians interested in military affairs can join this club, too.

In the club's libraries, you will find many programs, military graphics files, and transcripts.

The Military Trivia Games are great fun—with rewards. Post a joke on the "Humor, In and Out of Uniform" message board and you could win 30 minutes of AOL time in each week's humor contest.

Where

Clubs & Interests

Military & Vets Forum

Keyword

Military

Select

About the Military & Vets Club

NCOA Publications

The National Capital Office of the Non Commissioned Officers Association (NCOA) covers legislative updates, primarily on the "people" issues affecting active duty, reserve, and retired members. The weekly *NCOA News Briefs* and the monthly *NCOA Journal* excerpts are available for your review.

Subj: NCOA Journal
Date: October 24, 1994
From: NCOA USA
File: JOURNAL.DEC (34039 bytes)
DL time: < 1 minute
Author: NATCO

Where

Clubs & Interests

Military & Vets Forum

Keyword

Military

Select

Transcripts, Programs & Info Files

Download

NCOA Journal

NCOA Briefs week 10/24/94

So, You Wanna Learn to Fly

Guess what aviation buffs discuss? Things that fly! From the real thing to models to flight simulation software, you can get your zest for aviation off the ground in the Aviation Forum. The message boards cover general, commercial, and military aviation; airlines; careers; airshows; and hundreds of flight-hours more. Experienced pilots also dissect crashes and situations with other members. The September 1994 USAir crash near Pittsburgh is one of the folder topics.

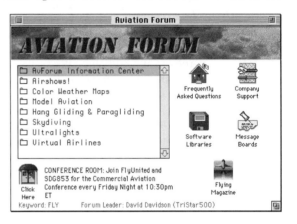

On the lighter side, each month brings a contest. The first to identify the aircraft in the GIF file wins one free hour of connect time. Read this file for participation information.

Where

Clubs & Interests

Aviation

Keyword

Aviation

Select

AvForum Information Center

Read/Save

Welcome to the Aviation Forum

Air Shows!

Air shows are absolutely spectacular but can be deadly. That doesn't stop them. There are over 400 air shows a year in North America. This file encompasses a listing of airshows and is updated as necessary. You can sort it to fit your needs.

Subj: Airshows! Database
Date: April 29, 1994
From: FKS
File: 94 ShowList Database (81408 bytes)
DL time: < 2 minutes
Author: FKS/Flyin Lady
Needs: Mac, FileMaker Pro or compatible database

Where

Clubs & Interests

Aviation

Keyword

Aviation

Select

Airshows!

Software Library

Download

Airshows! Database

Bozo Would Be Impressed

The Greatest Paper Airplanes 1.0 is a Windows program using fully interactive 3-D animation to fold extraordinary paper airplanes. The unique notebook features simple VCR style fold controls, color printing of decorated airplane designs, and animated tutorials on the history of flight and paper folding.

Subj: The Greatest Paper Airplanes
Date: July 12, 1994
From: KittyHawkS
File: GPA.ZIP (758457 bytes)
DL time: < 20 minutes
Author: KittyHawk Software
Needs: Windows 3.1, 2Mb RAM, 2Mb disk

Where
Clubs & Interests

Aviation

Keyword
Aviation

Select
Software Libraries

DOS/Windows Files

Download
The Greatest Paper Airplanes

FLYING ONLINE

Flying Online is the electronic version of *Flying* Magazine. *Flying* is written by pilots for pilots, or for those who want to become pilots. *Flying's* first issue appeared two months after Charles Lindbergh crossed the Atlantic.

The text of selected columns and features from the current issue appear during the middle of each month. In addition, selected articles from back issues are available and can be searched by keywords.

Where
Clubs & Interests

Aviation

Flying

Keyword
Flying

Aviation Sounds

This stack contains 16 aviation warning sounds. The names that are displayed fully capitalized are from an F-16. The rest are from a Boeing 757/767 Ground Proximity Warning System.

Subj: Aviation Sounds.STAK
Date: December 13, 1992
From: TriStar500
File: Aviation Sounds.sit (145449 bytes)
DL time: < 4 minutes
Needs: Mac, HyperCard 2.0 or greater, StuffIt

Where

Clubs & Interests

Aviation

Keyword

Aviation

Select

Software Libraries

Macintosh Files

Download

Aviation Sounds.STAK

Mac Navigator

This is a simple navigation log that contains all the necessary elements for quick and easy planning. It's simply an Excel stationery pad that's all set for you to enter your flight plan.

Subj: MacNavLog
Date: October 3, 1994
From: BioMann
File: Navigation Log Form (7169 bytes)
DL time: < 1 minute
Author: Michael R. Mann
Needs: Mac, Excel

Where

Clubs & Interests

Aviation

Keyword

Aviation

Select

Software Libraries

Macintosh Files

Download

MacNavLog

Used Aircraft Value Guide

Do you want an airplane for your birthday? Deciding between a Piper and a Cherokee can be tough. *The 1994 Guide to Used Aircraft* by Aerosoft Design can help you to make that decision. Over 150 aircraft and values for most model years are available.

Subj: Used Aircraft Value Guide
Date: October 11, 1994
From: BrianH9350
File: GUIDE.ZIP (154719 bytes)
DL time: < 4 minutes
Author: Aerosoft Design
Needs: Windows 3.x, vbrun 200.dll

Where

Clubs & Interests

Aviation

Keyword

Aviation

Select

Software Libraries

DOS/Windows Files

Download

Used Aircraft Value Guide

Used Aircraft Inspection Checklist

Will this baby fly? Before you buy, employ the expertise of The Used Aircraft Inspection Checklist to help you methodically evaluate an aircraft. The list is a four-page checklist covering the aircraft exterior, interior, landing gear, aircraft numbers, and avionics.

Subj: Used Acft Inspection Checklist
Date: November 24, 1993
From: ChuckM8
File: Acft Cndtn Chklst (12800 bytes)
DL time: < 1 minute
Author: Chuck Miller
Needs: Mac, MS Excel 5.1

Where

Clubs & Interests

Aviation

Keyword

Aviation

Select

Software Libraries

Macintosh Files

Download

Used Acft Inspection Checklist

How Do I Become a Pilot?

The requirements include the achievement of a certain age, passing a medical examination, and the ability to communicate in English.

But you really want the *details* right? Take a look at this fun FAQ for just the details you're looking for. It covers qualifications, training, costs, and Department of Transportation certification documents.

Where

Clubs & Interests

Aviation

Keyword

Aviation

Select

Frequently Asked Questions

Read/Save

10. How do I become a Pilot?

Aviators Little Instruction Book

The Aviators Little Instruction Book is a collection of thoughts, ideas, rules of thumb, and helpful suggestions that are great as a reminder to the experienced, as a primer to the novice, or just for a laugh or two. Think of this guide as the rules of the road for the air.

Subj: Aviators Little Instruction Book.
Date: August 29, 1994
From: Mtuning
File: E-book (7680 bytes)
DL time: < 1 minute
Author: Mtuning
Needs: Text reader, imagination, your input

Where
Clubs & Interests
Aviation

Keyword
Aviation

Select
Software Libraries
Text & Miscellaneous

Download
Aviators Little Instruction Book

Flight Simulators

The Flight Sim Resource Center is the source of hints, files, and information on all favorite flight simulators. Pilots can trade tips with other die-hard flight fans and participate in clubs with other flight simulator pilots.

The Flight Sim Resource Center has fabulous libraries, which include add-on files, as well as Microsoft Flight Simulator 4.0 (MSFS 4.0) utilities and enhancements. You'll find hundreds of V4.0 aircraft and scenery files in the MSFS 4.0 library.

Where (PC)
Computing

Keyword
Computing

Select
Computing Highlights
Flight Sim Resource Center

Where (Mac)
Computing

Keyword
Computing

Select
Resource Center
•Resources
Flight Sim Information

Island Scenes

You've passed over the Great Barrier Reef in search of a place to land, but where is the airstrip? Visions of *South Pacific*, Amelia Erhart, and uncharted islands come to mind with the Pacific Islands and Australia modules for Microsoft Flight Simulator 5.0. These two are representative of the dozens of Flight Simulator 5.0 files and enhancements that you can try out in the Aviation Forum libraries.

> *Subj:*   FS5 BGL: Pacific Islands
> *Date:*   August 20, 1994
> *From:*   Geoff017
> *File:*   PACIFIC.ZIP (87149 bytes)
> *DL time:* < 2 minutes
> *Author:*   various authors
> *Needs:*   PC, Flight Simulator 5.0 A

Where

Clubs & Interests

Aviation Forum

Keyword

Aviation

Select

Software Libraries

Virtual Airlines

Download

FS5 BGL: Pacific Islands

FS5 BGL: Australia

F/A-18 Hornet 1.1.1

Take the challenge as F/A-18 Hornet straps you in for the ride of your life. This demo takes place in Hawaii and supplies you with a cannon, two sidewinders, and a full tank of gas. Use your M61 Vulcan cannon or sidewinder and AMRAAM missiles for air-to-air defenses. Laser-guided bombs or HARM and Maverick missiles provide the most effective and destructive air-to-ground ordnance available to any fighting force. Tour Pearl Harbor, see the Arizona memorial, or take out an airliner! This is a *no time limit* demo for F/A-18 Hornet.

Please read the download instructions carefully as the demo file will only work with newer Macs running System 6.0.7 or better.

> *Subj:*   F/A-18 Hornet 1.1.1
> *Date:*   July 31, 1994
> *From:*   Komando3
> *File:*   F/A-18 Hornet 1.1 Demo.sea (1192639 bytes)
> *DL time:* < 32 minutes
> *Author:*   Graphic Simulations Corp.
> *Needs:*   Color Mac, System 6.07 or better, System 7 compatible

Where

Marketplace

Kim Komando's Komputer Klinic

Keyword

Komando

Select

Komando Libraries

Demonstration Versions (Mac)

Download

F/A-18 Hornet 1.1.1

Where to Find More Goodies

In *Free Stuff from America Online*, be sure to flip to the *Fun and Games* and the *Science and Space* sections for more goodies.

Online you can't beat the Flight Sim Center (Keyword: FlightSim), where you'll find much more than I was able to include here. Aviation fanatics will find pertinent articles in *Scientific American* (Keyword: SciAm). For even more Goodies, use *File Search* or the cross-platform Keywords *PC Software* and *Mac Software* and type: flight, flying, aviation, military, army, navy, and marine for dozens more terrific files.

FREE $TUFF

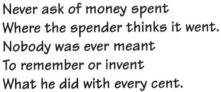

Never ask of money spent
Where the spender thinks it went.
Nobody was ever meant
To remember or invent
What he did with every cent.

Robert Frost

Personal Finance

Money and what you do with it. Now wouldn't that would be a fun chapter? I'll bet we could even get a rousing forum going on AOL. Money: Love it or leave it. To heir or not to heir...

Whether you grumble, joke, or exclaim over your paycheck, there never seems to be enough money. The key lies in maximizing what you have in the best possible way. Our friends at AOL know that money is a topic that's central to our lives, so they've put together an extensive personal finance area with dozens of reference sources, software libraries, message boards, and newsletters.

This section focuses primarily on your personal investments. I'll first explore the stock quotes, sample portfolios, and mutual funds analysis areas, which will help you define your investment strategies. In these locations, you'll find handy software—both shareware and freeware—that will aid in tracking your investments. You'll also find references and newsletters to keep you informed.

There's so much information available about personal finance. I don't have room to include it all. For instance, Real Estate Online (in the Personal Finance Department) has tons of free information and software designed to help you choose and purchase a home. Be sure to check out this site.

The Quotes & Portfolio System

With America Online's Quotes & Portfolio system, you can now stay abreast of the stocks, mutual funds, and money market mutual funds that interest you most. The Quotes & Portfolio system enables you to track prices and yields of stock funds listed on the NYSE, AMEX, and NASDAQ exchanges, maintain an updated portfolio, and more. You can even purchase stock through the Trade-Plus gateway.

Once you have added various stocks and funds to your portfolio, you can check on their progress by selecting Display Portfolio. You will see the total value of your portfolio, delayed 15 to 20 minutes. This is ideal for keeping track of your net gain/loss of each particular stock or fund. Currently, a portfolio can handle up to 100 stocks and funds.

From the Quotes & Portfolio menu you can also access the latest market reports. For up-to-date information on what's happening with the NYSE, AMEX, OTC, bonds, commodities, and more, select Market News.

AOL members can access the TradePlus discount brokerage to buy and sell stocks through the TradePlus Gateway.

Where

Personal Finance

Quotes & Portfolios

Keyword

Quotes

Use this area to look up, get quotes on, and create your own portfolio!

Morningstar

The Morningstar Online area offers performance, operations, and analytical information on 4,300 mutual funds. The information presented here is useful in choosing and monitoring your investments.

Morningstar is an independent company dedicated to the needs of its subscribers. They provide the data and analysis essential to making the best-informed investment decisions.

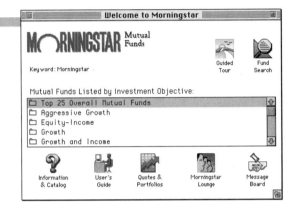

Where

Personal Finance

Morningstar

Keyword

Morningstar

Select

User's Guide

Search Funds by Investment Objective or Name

Fidelity Charts

So you want to really *see* how your investments are doing? Decision Point has assembled a bundle of 10 GIF files containing 35 Fidelity Select mutual fund charts plus Fidelity Contra, Low-Priced, Real Estate, Magellan, and Trend to provide you with a visual perspective of your investment dollars. Besides almost four years of price history (when available), it also displays two indica-

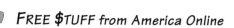

tors: the ROCS Oscillator (slow, black line) and V1 Oscillator (fast, green line). Each GIF file (page) contains four charts, and the charts are current as of the date shown in the subject line. These charts allow you to view ROCS behavior over a long period of time, especially during the 1990 Bear Market.

Subj: 40 Fidelity 4-Year Charts 8/22
Date: September 10, 1994
From: CarlS16Two
File: 4yr.sit (348138 bytes)
DL time: < 9 minutes
Needs: GIFConverter (Mac), GIF viewer and AOMac2PC (PC)

AOL software may unstuff this file automatically; otherwise, you can unstuff the file yourself using UnStuff (PC) or StuffIt Expander (Mac), both of which are available at Keyword: Aladdin.

Where

Personal Finance

Decision Point Timing/Charts

Keyword

DP

Select

Chart & Data Libraries

Mutual Funds

Download

40 Fidelity 4-Year Charts 8/22

E-Z Print Chart Book

The Decision Point Timing & Charts forum has introduced an exciting new product for investors, the *E-Z Print Chart Book*, which contains nearly 50 pages of charts and tabular statistics on 150 stocks, 160 mutual funds, and several market indexes and technical indicators.

The charts and stock tables featured are the same as the GIF files uploaded every week: 7 Index/Indicator Charts, 150 Stock Charts, 160 Mutual Fund Charts, Daily Stock Stats, and Daily Fund Stats.

Why is this exciting? Unlike by-mail chart books that are out-of-date by the time you get them, the *E-Z Print Chart Book* is current as of the Friday close and is available late Friday or early Saturday, so you get up-to-date information to peruse all weekend long.

Another exciting aspect of this product is its cost. Other than the connect time charges for the approximately 20 minutes it takes to download (at 9600 baud), there is no charge. Think of it, over 300 current charts every week for only the cost of the connect time to download!

As far as I know, this is a resource not equaled anywhere at any price, and it is free to America Online members.

Subj: EZ Print ChartBook(Excel Only)
From: CESwenlin
File: AllCharts.sit (704005 bytes)
DL time: < 19 minutes
Author: Decision Point
Needs: MS Excel 4.0 (Mac or PC) and a laser printer (or a printer with similar technology that has incremental reduction capability)

Where

Personal Finance

Decision Point Timing/Charts

Keyword

DP

Select

Chart & Data Libraries

Daily/Weekly

Download

EZ Print ChartBook(Excel Only)

Top Advisors' Corner

For the newsletter junkie in you: Here you will find periodic updates from some of the best known names in the stock market advisory business. The purpose of this feature is to provide you with continuing access to samplings of these advisory services so that you can benefit from the insights offered and evaluate them as a potential subscriber. There is, of course, no obligation to subscribe to any of these services, and the updates are provided compliments of the authors.

The Current Updates menu item contains all updates from all the advisors, listed in the order that they were received and with the most recent at the top. Previous issues for individual advisors can be found in separate folders located in the list box.

A subfeature of Top Advisors' Corner is *New Guru Review*. This space is available for regular contributions from new and aspiring market advisors who are interested in getting exposure, gaining a following, and establishing credibility in the stock market advisory field.

Following is a selected list of the Advisors and their writings:

- Daily Striking Price—Terry Bedford
- Dohmen Mutual Fund Hotline
- Dow Theory Letters—Richard Russell
- Richland Report—Kennedy Gammage
- Turnaround Letter—George Putnam
- Investment Quality Trends—Geraldine Weiss

Where

Personal Finance

Top Advisors' Corner

Keyword

Advisor

Select

Current Updates

or Advisor by name

Bulls and Bears Contest

Bulls and Bears is a stock market simulation game in which players buy and sell stocks and options, using real market prices in a race to accumulate the most wealth before the end of the game. When you sign up to play the game, you are given a $100,000 line of game credit to place your initial stock and option orders. You can then trade your stocks or options as frequently as you'd like until the game ends on the last day of the month.

This is only a game; the purchases you make are not real. When you enter your orders, the trade is executed immediately, using the closing price for the market on that day. Your portfolio will be automatically updated, and your cash balance will be adjusted also. Stock dividends, stock splits, broker's fees, and interest on the cash balance all affect your balance.

Over 20 hours of free time are awarded each month to the top five winners.

Where

Entertainment

Bull & Bears Game

Keyword

Entertainment

Select

Bull & Bears Game

Enter Bull & Bears/E*Trade

The Motley Fool

Stop by The Motley Fool to check out the current financial-prediction game that takes just a couple of minutes to play a week and gives you a shot at winning some serious free time online. Monthly winners earn their next month of America Online *free* (unlimited hours!). The six-month season's champion takes away a full *free six months online* (unlimited hours!) for being, quite simply, the biggest slugger in America when it comes to calling the markets.

In Today's Pitch, the mechanics of the game are simple. Each day brings a different "pitch," a single multiple-choice question upon which you are called to respond. If you pick the right one of five choices, you hit a homerun. If you pick one of the four incorrect choices, you strike out. All you need to do is click a button to play the game; they toss the pitches and keep the statistics. They'll also track your homerun totals both per month and for the overall season. The player with the most homeruns over a given period of time is that period's winner (or "Most Valuable Fool"). One answer per day, of course.

Reading and answering Today's Pitch takes about 30 seconds, so we're talking minimal time drain here. But what are the questions all about? Well, take a typical example—the very first Pitch of the Day:

Tomorrow, will the Dow Jones Industrial Average:

(a) rise more than 15 points?

(b) rise from 5 to 15 points?

(c) close somewhere between a 5-point loss and a 5-point gain?

(d) lose from 5 to 15 points?

(e) lose more than 15 points?

This pitch, like each one of Today's Pitches, calls upon the player to make a prediction about the future. Here, the time horizon is tomorrow, and the subject matter is, of course, investing. (You don't have to be an investor to play—just as you never *really* had to know the answer to a multiple-choice question on the SAT; you can simply guess.)

The sports change with the seasons, so when you stop in, who knows what will be playing?

Where

Personal Finance

Motley Fool

Keyword

Motley

Select

Foolish Games

Software

As you might expect, AOL provides an extensive clearinghouse of software for personal finance tasks. You'll find everything from stock market and other trading utilities to programs that help you balance your checkbook.

Quickening Quicken

A to Q is a HyperCard stack. Its purpose is to translate daily stock and mutual fund information retrieved from America Online's Stock Link into a text file that can be imported into Quicken 4.0. This simplifies a tedious step for Quicken users and allows them to easily translate AOL's data into numbers they can use. It's the best way to use AOL and Quicken for your portfolio.

Subj: AOL to Quicken
Date: August 22, 1993
From: EricMorgan
File: AtoQ.sit (2350 bytes)
DL time: < 1 minute
Author: Eric Lease Morgan
Needs: Mac, HyperCard, and Quicken 4.0

Where

The complete sequence of steps through Computing can be found on page 15. Of course, you can save time and money by using the Keyword shortcuts.

Keyword

File Search

Select

>Quicken

Download

AOL to Quicken

AOL $tock Quote Fetch 2.0

$tock Quote Fetch is a QuicKeys sequence that fully auto-mates the retrieval of daily stock quotes (for stocks you've pre-selected), from America Online. You can launch this sequence with a key stroke you select, or even better, you can set the program to run at a predetermined time, say 3 a.m. when you're asleep! The beauty of this sequence is just how fast it runs. According to the author, from connect to disconnect, $tock Quote Fetch has never taken more than a minute to gather the quotes of his three test stocks, and it usually takes under 45 seconds. A real online time saver.

Subj: AOL $tock Quote Fetch 2.0
Date: November 14, 1993
From: RonHovingh
File: Stock Quote Fetch 2.0 .sit (15306 bytes)
DL time: < 1 minute
Author: Brian Walker
Needs: Mac, System 7, QuicKeys 3.0; unStuff with AOL 2.x

Where

The complete sequence of steps through Computing can be found on page 15. Of course, you can save time and money by using the Keyword shortcuts.

Keyword

File Search

Select

>Quicken

Download

AOL $tock Quote Fetch 2.0

Fund Manager

Fund Manager is designed to help the individual investor monitor and analyze his or her investments with a wide variety of easy to use graphs and reports. One, four, or nine graphs may be viewed, side-by-side in the same window, or you may overlay multiple investments on the same graph for ease of comparison. Several types of graphs can be created including: price history, moving average, fund value, and portfolio value. The Windows program includes help functions and a return on investment feature. Registration is $20 for new users.

A Mac version is available, too; it's only a 3 minute download.

Subj: Fund Manager 6.2 (Win)
Date: September 7, 1994
From: AAIIPaul
File: FUNDMGRW.EXE (244903 bytes)
DL time: < 6 minutes
Needs: PC, Microsoft Windows

Where

Personal Finance

AAII Online

Keyword

AAII

Select

Software Library

AAII Software by Category

Portfolio Management

Download

Fund Manager 6.2 (Win)

Bonds Tracker

Bonds Tracker tracks up to 1,000 Series EE U.S. Savings Bonds. This program will allow you to input, delete, and arrange a bond portfolio. You will also find an option to provide a hard copy. Bonds Tracker allows the user to input new interest rates, or update the interest rates as they change when the U.S. Government publishes rates in May and November. The program rounds the calculated value of bonds by as much as ten cents. For this reason you should use the values this program generates only as an estimate of the actual value. Bonds Tracker will not accurately calculate values of bonds issued before 1983 (the value is underestimated).

Subj: EE Bonds Tracker 93.11
Date: June 6, 1994
From: AAIIPaul
File: EEBOND93.EXE (98620 bytes)
DL time: < 2 minutes
Author: Bob Fechtner
Needs: IBM PC or compatible

Where

Personal Finance

AAII Online

Keyword

AAII

Select

Software Library

AAII Software by Category

Financial Planning

Download

EE Bonds Tracker 93.11

EEBonds for the Mac

EEBonds is another in the continuing series of spreadsheets that calculates the value of Series EE U.S. Savings Bonds each year. This will not only help you keep track of your bonds but will also allow you to see what each bond earned between December 1992 and December 1993. This information is useful if you pay the tax on the bonds each year. The Read Me file tells you how to use the spreadsheet. Not shareware—this is a freebie.

Subj: EEBonds_93 XCEL
Date: January 20, 1994
From: Nail29
File: Bonds_93.sit (24648 bytes)
DL time: < 1 minute
Author: Rick Barrett
Needs: Mac, Excel 3.0 or 4.0

Where

Computing

Keyword

File Search

Select

Download

EEBonds_93 XCEL

Household Register 2.0

Do you have a definitive list of your valuables, such as your computer, mo-dem, printer, stereo, CD-player, refrigerator, and car? Household Register 2.0 by TurbosystemsCo is a possession inventory system that keeps track of your valuables by category, owner, and location. A warranty list that allows you to enter expiration dates and model and serial numbers is also provided. You can generate seven types of reports, including a total value report that shows the percent change between the original cost of items and their replacement prices. You will find this program extremely useful for insurance records. This is a self-extracting file.

Subj: Household Register v.2.0
Date: June 6, 1994
From: AAIIPaul
File: HOUSEREG.EXE (167681 bytes)
DL time: < 4 minutes
Needs: IBM PC or compatible

Where

Personal Finance

AAII Online

Keyword

AAII

Select

Software Library

AAII Software by Category

Financial Planning

Download

Household Register v.2.0

 If you're looking for a program that does something a little bit different from what I've included, try these file search keywords: Credit, Stock, Budget, Quicken, Money, and Bond. You'll find hundreds more!

Reference Sources

In the virtual community library, you'll find that AOL has all the answers to your tough reference questions.

American Association of Individual Investors

The American Association of Individual Investors (AAII) is an independent, non-profit organization that was formed in 1978 to assist individuals in becoming effective managers of their own investments.

Online, AAII is a reference center with scores of articles and downloadable files covering an extensive range of investment topics. Of particular interest are the Reference Shelf and the Investment Glossary.

Where

Personal Finance

AAII Online

Keyword

AAII

Select

Featured Articles

Software Library

Reference Library

Worth Online Portfolio

This online portfolio is a unique new stock-picking feature available exclusively to *Worth Online* users. It offers a daily look at how professional investment managers select stocks to buy and sell.

Launched on June 15, 1994, with $500,000, this model portfolio invests funds in stocks only, with no option trading or short selling. And though the manager is using virtual dollars and not the real thing, he does what any professional portfolio manager must do every day—he monitors the market, researches potential stock picks, and buys and sells stocks when opportunities arise.

By checking *Worth Online* each day, you can watch this portfolio's operation from the inside. Instead of seeing a simple summary of the action, you'll be privy to the manager's methods and opinions. And you'll watch first-hand how a portfolio manager responds to changing market conditions and breaking company developments. It's the best way to learn without losing money.

Where

Personal Finance

Worth Magazine

Keyword

Worth

Select

Online Portfolio

Worth Online's Top 50

Everything you ever wanted to know about personal finance, taxes, real estate, mutual funds, insurance, retirement, and investments in 50 questions and answers. With these quick downloads you'll get answers to the financial questions *Worth* readers ask the most.

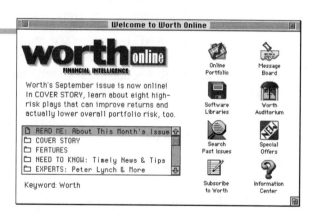

The READ ME file carries the list of questions. Download that first to save time, and on your next logon, download just the files you need. Each file takes less than 1 minute to download at 9600 baud.

Subj: READ ME: ABOUT SOLUTION SERIES
Date: November 22, 1993
From: AndrewS9
File: ****Read Me First (2589 bytes)

DL time: < 1 minute
Author: Worth
Needs: Text reader

Where

Personal Finance

Worth Magazine

Keyword

Worth

Select

Software Libraries

Worth Solutions Series

Download

READ ME: ABOUT SOLUTION SERIES

[or select from list]

Worth Online includes the feature stories and columns from each issue of *Worth Magazine*. Former Fidelity Magellan Fund Manager, Peter Lynch, shares his market views in a regular featured column.

It's Your Money

Finding it difficult to juggle the car and mortgage payments along with Orson's college tuition and Janie's othodontics? Well this forum is for you. You will find answers to your personal finance questions, including cash management and budgeting, insurance evaluation, education planning, investment analysis, portfolio allocation, retirement planning, estate planning, and debt and credit management. It is a non-commercial area designed to help individuals better educate themselves in the management of their personal financial affairs.

Here's a sounding board with sound advice!

Where

Personal Finance

Your Money

Keyword

Your Money

Select

Money, Debt & Credit

Education Planning

Insurance Planning

Investment Planning

Retirement Planning

Estate Planning

Tips, Tricks, & Scams

Where to Find More Goodies

I hope you've found a tip or a program that will make your money tracking a little bit easier.

With these prosperity-generating, money-multiplying tips, you may soon be ready to start a new business or to set up a trust for your heirs. If so, you'll want to turn to the *Business* and *The Law* sections.

Heigh ho, Heigh ho, it's off to work I go . . . .

FREE $TUFF

The science of today is the technology of tomorrow.

Edward Teller

Science and Space

FREE $TUFF from America Online

The sun, the moon, and the stars have fascinated people since ancient times. Together in this section, we'll cover the universe and the mysteries it contains. As you well know by now, fantastic discoveries can be made on AOL, and historic and significant discoveries in the areas pertaining to science and astronomy are no exception.

SCIENTIFIC AMERICAN

Scientific American gives readers access to science and enables them to share in scientific discoveries. In its online form, *Scientific American* contains all the articles and graphics from the current issue as well as back issues.

You can get an historical perspective from the 50 and 100 Years Ago Department, which provides excerpts from same-dated issues of *Scientific American*. The selections generally remind readers that everything—and nothing—has changed.

First Issue of SCIENTIFIC AMERICAN

The first issue of *Scientific American*, Volume 1, Number 1—August 28, 1845—is available online!

This file contains the complete text of the first issue, including articles on improved railroad cars, the steamship Great Britain, Morse's telegraph, electroplating, and India rubber, as well as a catalog of 1844 patents, interesting letters, news blurbs, advertisements, and more!

Subj: 1845 First Issue of SciAm
Date: September 1, 1994
From: JAMIG565
File: Vol1No1.TXT (96407 bytes)
DL time: < 2 minutes
Author: Scientific American
Needs: Text reader

Where
> Newsstand
>
> Scientific American

Keyword
> SciAm

Select
> Download Articles & Images
>
> Special Files

Download
> 1845 First Issue of SciAm

Earthquake!

This animated HyperCard stack shows the three main types of faults: normal, reverse, and lateral faults. Select the type of fault you are studying and the animated program will show you how Earth's forces affect the land formations.

Subj: Earth Science/Quake Faults SIT
Date: February 9, 1992
From: DoyleO
File: Faults.sit (101251 bytes)
DL time: < 2 minutes
Author: Doyle E. Oswald
Needs: HyperCard 2.x, StuffIt

Where
> The complete sequence of steps through Computing can be found on page 15. Of course, you can save time and money by using the Keyword shortcuts.

Keyword
> File Search

Select
> >earthquake

Download
> Earth Science/Quake Faults SIT

Northridge Quake Simulation

The Northridge earthquake was a nightmare to some and a fascinating scientific event to others. Here's a program that displays the events of this recent earthquake in California.

Subj: QUAKE: Earthquake Simulation
Date: May 15, 1994
From: SAC
File: QUAKE.ZIP (515983 bytes)
DL time: < 14 minutes
Author: Unknown
Needs: UnZIPing program, 386 or higher
Type: Shareware

Where

The complete sequence of steps through Computing can be found on page 15. Of course, you can save time and money by using the Keyword shortcuts.

Keyword

File Search

Select

> earthquake

Download

QUAKE: Earthquake Simulation

NETWORK EARTH

Network Earth Online is your link to Turner Broadcasting's *Network Earth*. The interactive arm of Network Earth Online encompasses transcripts from the *Network Earth* TV program, the League of Conservation, which keeps scorecards on U.S. representatives' and senators' voting records for conservation issues, and dynamic download libraries. You can also share your enviromental and earthly concerns with Network Earth's staff on the message boards.

GreenBBS

The GreenBBS is an international listing of environmental BBSs. Online environmentalists will find this to be an excellent source for contacts and information.

Subj: Environmental BBS Listing
Date: September 8, 1994
From: ShannonB94
File: GBBS0794.ARJ (19222 bytes)
DL time: < 1 minute
Author: Bob Chapman
Needs: Text reader

Where

Clubs & Interests

Environmental Forum

Network Earth

Keyword

Eforum

Select

Software Libraries

General Library #2

Download

Environmental BBS Listing

Nuclear Plant Status

This file is a sample of the Daily Event report issued by the Nuclear Regulatory Commission (NRC). It includes all events reported to the NRC for distribution on that date. The report details noted problems at nuclear plants, including operations and tests.

Subj: Plant status 9/9/94
Date: September 12, 1994
From: MikeNIRS
File: DER9994.TXT (20730 bytes)
DL time: < 1 minute
Author: US NRC
Needs: Text reader, monospace font

Where

Clubs & Interests

Environmental Forum

Network Earth

Keyword

Eforum

Select

Software Libraries

Nuclear Information & Resource Service

Download

Plant status [date]

San Onofre Nuclear Power Station

For a look at a power station, try the infamous San Onofre. Anyone who's driven Interstate 5, from Los Angeles to San Diego has passed this nuclear plant. The image file contains an impressionistic raytrace of Units 2 and 3 of the station.

Subj: GIF: San Onofre Power Station
Date: August 28, 1993
From: RAY TRACEY
File: SONOFRE.GIF (111995 bytes)
DL time: < 3 minutes
Author: John Berthoty
Needs: VGA, GIF Viewer
Type: Freely distributed

Where

The complete sequence of steps through Computing can be found on page 15. Of course, you can save time and money by using the Keyword shortcuts.

Keyword

PC: File Search
Mac: PC Software

Select

>nuclear

Download

GIF: San Onofre Power Station

Electricity and Nuclear Fission

This educational stack teaches the basic concepts about matter and electricity and also instructs on the principles of nuclear fission and the workings of nuclear power plants. The smooth animation will keep your attention through such topics as attraction and repulsion of charges, the structure of the atom, electrical currents, electromagnetism, and types of nuclear reactions. You will also get a chance to look inside a nuclear power plant.

Subj: Electricity And Nuclear Fission
Date: March 13, 1992
From: MarcioT
File: Electricity/Nuclear Fission.sea (160968 bytes)
DL time: < 4 minutes
Needs: Mac, HyperCard 2.1 or better

Where

Computing

Mac Software

Keyword

File Search

Select

>electricity

Download

Electricity And Nuclear Fission

Holographic Disk Development

The October 1994 issue of *Scientific American* included this GIF in the article entitled "Ready or Not: Holographic data storage goes to market—sort of" by W. Wayt Gibbs. This illustration shows how the holographic disk system under development by Tamarack Data Storage Devices works. The holographic disk records data as three-dimensional stacks of light patterns. Each "page" is created when a reference beam interferes with another beam that's reflected off a computer-controlled liquid crystal.

Subj:　　10/94 Holographic disk.GIF
Date:　　September 30, 1994
From:　　Wayt
File:　　1094SB1.GIF (46762 bytes)
DL time: < 1 minute
Author:　Laurie Grace
Needs:　GIF viewer

Where

Newsstand

Scientific American

Keyword

SciAm

Select

Download Articles & Images

Images Files

Download

10/94 Holographic disk.GIF

What's the Weather?

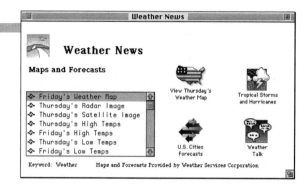

With AOL's online weather center you can get the picture of the weather in your area and across the USA in color weather maps! A new file of the nation's precipitation and temperatures is released each day. In addition, tropical weather and hurricane maps are available when warranted. The precipitation, jet stream, and tropical outlook maps are released between 10 and 11 a.m. EST each day, and the temperature bands for the next day are available in the evening.

Where

Travel

Weather

Keyword

Weather

Select

Color Weather Maps

Color Weather Maps (yes again!)

Download

US SATELLITE PIC [date] 9AM

US RADAR PIC [date] 9AM

US SATELLITE PIC [date] 4AM...

US RADAR PIC [date] 4AM

US MAX TEMPS [day/date] 4AM...

US MIN TEMPS [day/date] 4AM...

US WEATHER [day/date] 2PM ...

2- DAY JETSTREAM OUTLOOK [date]

Hurricane Andrew

Follow Hurricane Andrew's historic path to Southeastern Florida where the infamous storm of the same name devastated that area and the Gulf region in August 1992.

Subj: 1992- Track for Andrew
Date: June 4, 1994
From: WSC PaulC
File: ANDREW.GIF (10055 bytes)
DL time: < 1 minute
Needs: GIF viewer

Where

Travel

Weather

Keyword

Weather

Select

Color Weather Maps

Color Weather Maps (yes, again!)

Download

1992- Track for Andrew

Hurricane Andrew Landfall

Hurricane Andrew crossed Florida and picked up steam when it hit the gulf. This color satellite photo shows Hurricane Andrew as the eye crossed the Louisiana shoreline. The shot was taken at 0500 Zulu time, August 26.

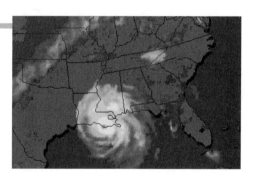

Subj: Hurricane Andrew
Landfall.GIF
Date: August 29, 1992
From: Antlers
File: Andrew Landfall.GIF (14761 bytes)
DL time: < 1 minute
Needs: GIF Viewer

Where

The complete sequence of steps through Computing can be found on page 15. Of course, you can save time and money by using the Keyword shortcuts.

Keyword

Mac: File Search

PC: Mac Software

Select

>Hurricane Andrew

Download

Hurricane Andrew Landfall.GIF

NOAA Weather Radio Stations

Goin' fishing? Don't go out on the water without checking the weather! This is a listing of approximately 380 NOAA Weather Radio Stations located in the 50 states, District of Columbia, Puerto Rico, and U.S. Virgin Islands. The listing includes the location of each transmitter by city and the broadcast frequency.

Subj: NOAA: Weather Radio Stations
Date: July 25, 1994
From: WalterO500
File: NOAAWRN.ZIP (4346 bytes)
DL time: < 1 minute
Author: Walter O'Connell
Needs: An UnZIPing program, text reader
Type: Freely distributed

Where

The complete sequence of steps through Computing can be found on page 15. Of course, you can save time and money by using the Keyword shortcuts.

Keyword

PC: File Search

Mac: PC Software

Select

>weather

Download

NOAA: Weather Radio Stations

WindChill 1.0

WindChill 1.0 is a freeware HyperCard stack that calculates the wind chill factor when the temperature and wind speed are entered. Wind speed can be set for miles, nautical miles, or kilometers per hour. Both English (F°) and metric (C°) temperature units are supported. The animated graphics will help spice up those cold days . . . brrr.

Subj: WindChill 1.0
Date: December 14, 1993
From: Victor9444
File: WindChill 1.0.sit (11700 bytes)
DL time: < 1 minute
Needs: Mac, HyperCard 2.0 or greater, StuffIt Expander or AOL 2.0

Where

The complete sequence of steps through Computing can be found on page 15. Of course, you can save time and money by using the Keyword shortcuts.

Keyword

File Search

Select

>wind chill

Download

WindChill 1.0

DL Hurricane Lists

Helga or Hilda—what's the name of the next hurricane? This self extracting application written in QuickBASIC lists the assigned names of hurricanes or storms for the period of 1993 to 1998. A separate list of names is provided for each year's hurricane season. The lists are provided by the National Hurricane Center in Coral Gables.

Subj: Hurricane Name Lists sea
Date: June 4, 1994
From: GregM24198
File: HurcNaming.APP.sea (62326 bytes)
DL time: < 1 minute.
Needs: Mac SE or better, System 6.08 or higher

Where

The complete sequence of steps through Computing can be found on page 15. Of course, you can save time and money by using the Keyword shortcuts.

Keyword

File Search

Select

>hurricane

Download

Hurricane Name Lists sea

The Hitchhiker's Guide to the Internet

"The Hitchhiker's Guide to the Internet" consists of pointers to other places and hints that are not normally documented. The guide assumes that the reader is familiar with the workings of a non-connected simple IP network. It then aims to help the user (armed with a simple network and versed in the "oral tradition" of the Internet) to connect to the Internet with little danger to either network.

Subj: TEXT: Hitchhikers Guide/Internet
Date: November 13, 1991
From: PC MMaggi
File: GUIDE.TXT (61018 bytes)
DL time: < 1 minute
Needs: Text reader
Type: Freely distributed

Where

The complete sequence of steps through Computing can be found on page 15. Of course, you can save time and money by using the Keyword shortcuts.

Keyword

PC: File Search

Mac: PC Software

Select

>Internet

Download

TEXT: Hitchhikers Guide/Internet

Johns Hopkins BBS

This text file provides a full description of the Johns Hopkins University Bulletin Board System (JHUBBS) and contains an application form for membership. JHUBBS provides conferences on politics, economics, science, medicine, and computing. JHUBBS also provides online university information and a souvenir store.

Subj: Info on Johns Hopkins BBS (TEXT)
Date: February 17, 1992
From: AFL Cheryl
File: JHUBBS Info (Text) (3874 bytes)
DL time: < 1 minute
Needs: AOL or text reader

Where

The complete sequence of steps through Computing can be found on page 15. Of course, you can save time and money by using the Keyword shortcuts.

Keyword

Mac: File Search

PC: Mac Software

Select

>Johns Hopkins BBS

Download

Info on Johns Hopkins BBS (TEXT)

Science Public Domain Catalog

Look here for a catalog of science, math, and engineering public domain software and shareware for Mac and MS-DOS computers. The topics include all things scientific: chemistry, physics, math, biology, biochemistry, astronomy, meteorology, engineering, and electronics. The program sources include commercial information services, such as America Online, CompuServe, and GEnie, as well as several Internet archives.

Subj: Science public domain catalog
Date: August 14, 1991
From: TomOhaver
File: PD_Science.sea (182896 bytes)
Author: Tom O'Haver
DL time: < 5 minutes
Needs: Text reader

Where

The complete sequence of steps through Computing can be found on page 15. Of course, you can save time and money by using the Keyword shortcuts.

Keyword

Mac: File Search

PC: Mac Software

Select

>science catalog

Download

Science public domain catalog

Astronomy Forum

The Astronomy Forum is the first place to check if you're looking for anything to do with the sun, the moon, and the stars. NASA photos, Hubble Telescope GIFs, and satellite images of the earth can all be found in this forum.

Holy Jupiter and Comets!

This booklet offers background material on Jupiter, comets, and how scientists study and take advantage of the impact events, including information on the glorious ending of the Shoemaker-Levy 9 comet as it crashed into our solar system's largest planet.

Subj: Comet Collision Booklet
Date: June 29, 1994
From: Mr Astro
File: SL9BOOK.sit (34724 bytes)
DL time: < 1 minute
Author: Ray L. Newburn, Jr., JPL
Needs: Text reader, unStuffIt

Where

Clubs & Interests

Astronomy Forum

Keyword

Astronomy

Select

Astro's Archives

SPECIAL: Comet Crash

Download

Comet Collision Booklet

E-mail to Space

Well, almost. With this list you can send E-mail to hundreds of observatories and astronomical facilities. This list contains the E-mail addresses, fax, phone, telex, and World Wide Web addresses for hundreds of observatories and astronomical facilities around the world. These same directions will also provide you with the postal addresses of the observatories.

Subj: Observatory Listings
Date: May 23, 1994
From: Mr Astro
File: OBSLIST.TXT.sit (35423 bytes)
DL time: < 1 minute
Needs: Text reader, unstuffing utility

Where

Clubs & Interests

Astronomy Forum

Keyword

Astronomy

Select

Astro's Archives

General Files

Download

Observatory Listings

Observatory Addresses

Jupiter from Hubble

Gorgeous reds and yellows color this 24-bit compressed image of Jupiter from the Hubble Space Telescope.

Subj: Jupiter from Hubble TIFF
Date: November 28, 1993
From: AFR 1
File: Jupiter w/Hubble.sit (262242 bytes)
DL time: < 7 minutes
Needs: 24-bit color display, TIFF reading software

Where

The complete sequence of steps through Computing can be found on page 15. Of course, you can save time and money by using the Keyword shortcuts.

Keyword

Mac: File Search

PC: Mac Software

Select

>NASA Telescope

Download

Jupiter from Hubble TIFF

THE PLANETARY SYSTEM

The Planetary System is an ExInEd Electronic PictureBook. This sensational collection from the golden era of space exploration contains 100 informative images of our solar system, including all the planets, their planetary rings and satellites, and the asteroids and comets. The images have been selected both for their variety and how well they illustrate the wide range of physical and geological features present in the solar system. This is a very large download, so make sure you have the time and space. Teachers will find this a valuable classroom aid.

Subj: The Planetary System
Date: October 25, 1994
From: ChristianL
File: The Planetary System Installer (5577501 bytes)
DL time: < 152 minutes
Needs: Color capable Mac, HyperCard 2.1, 2500K+ RAM allocated to HyperCard

Where

The complete sequence of steps through Computing can be found on page 15. Of course, you can save time and money by using the Keyword shortcuts.

Keyword

File Search

Select

>planetary system

Download

The Planetary System

SkyView

SkyView is a neat little planetarium program that shows a view of the whole sky at a given time and date for your location. It shows stars down to magnitude 6, solar system objects, and has several display options.

Subj: SkyView Planetarium for Windows
Date: April 15, 1994
From: JBUCHANAN
File: SKYVIEW.ZIP (258228 bytes)
DL time: < 7 minutes
Needs: PC, Windows 3.1
Type: Freeware

Where

Clubs & Interests

Astronomy Forum

Keyword

Astronomy

Select

Astro's Archives

Astro Computing PC

Download

SkyView Planetarium for Windows

MoonPhaser 1.0.1

Will there be a full moon on Halloween? You can use MoonPhaser to find out. This is an easy to use program that draws the phase of the moon for any day between 1984 and 2006. The user can specify any date within that period, quickly jump to today's moon, or locate the next full moon and new moon. In this updated version, the program now gets the Mac's latitude from the Map Control Panel, and "flips" the moon for friends "down under."

Subj: MoonPhaser 1.0.1
Date: June 6, 1992
From: Mr Astro
File: MoonPhaser.sit (18137 bytes)
DL time: < 1 minute
Author: Dave Kalin
Needs: StuffIt 1.5.1 or higher

Where

Clubs & Interests

Astronomy Forum

Keyword

Astronomy

Select

Astro's Archives

Astro Computing Macintosh

Download

MoonPhaser 1.0.1

Views of Earth

Back on Earth, we'll take a closer look at our planet and some new ways to check the time.

Mount Rainier

This is a radar image of Mount Rainier in Washington state. The volcano last erupted about 150 years ago and numerous large floods and debris flows have originated on its slopes during the past century. Today, the volcano is heavily mantled with glaciers and snowfields. More than 100,000 people live on young volcanic mudflows that are less than 10,000 years old. Consequently, these residents are within the range of future, devastating mudslides. This image was acquired by the Spaceborne Imaging Radar-C and X-band Synthetic Aperture Radar (SIR-C/X-SAR) aboard the space shuttle Endeavor on its 20th orbit on October 1, 1994. The area shown in the image is approximately 59 kilometers by 60 kilometers (36.5 miles by 37 miles).

Subj: Mt Rainier, WA - Sat. View *GIF
Date: October 9, 1994
From: OMNI Muse
File: SC-RAINI.GIF (275715 bytes)
DL time: < 7 minutes
Author: SIR-C/X-SAR
Needs: GIF viewer
Type: Public domain

Where
Newsstand
Omni Magazine Online

Keyword
Omni

Select
File Libraries
OMNIpurpose Library

Download
Mt Rainier, WA - Sat. View *GIF

Christopher Columbus . . . Where Are You?

Christopher Columbus could have used this handy program when he was seeking investment bankers to back his voyage. This is a public domain program that generates different views of the globe as if from space. You cannot print the images, but you can save them to disk and then import them into another program.

Subj: Earthplot
Date: May 26, 1992
From: Michel1767
File: Earthplot 3.0.sit (59590 bytes)
DL time: < 1 minute
Author: Black Swamp Software
Needs: Mac, UnStuffIt

Where

The complete sequence of steps through Computing can be found on page 15. Of course, you can save time and money by using the Keyword shortcuts.

Keyword

File Search

Select

>earthplot

Download

Earthplot

SolarClock 2.0

If you've ever been to the enchanting Nature Company stores, you may have noticed a fascinating clock that shows which part of the earth is in daylight and which area is covered by darkness. Now you can have a very similar world map on your computer. SolarClock 2.0 is an application that displays the current Day/Night on a map of the Earth, using the system clock, your location, and the current season.

Subj: SolarClock 2.0 (self-extract)
Date: July 20, 1991
From: RonaldT5
File: SolarClock 2.0.sea (73164 bytes)
DL time: < 2 minutes
Author: Ron Tjoelker
Needs: Any Mac, System 7

Where

Clubs & Interests

Astronomy Forum

Keyword

Astronomy

Select

Astro's Archives

Astro Computing Macintosh

Download

SolarClock 2.0 (self-extract)

Sunrise, Sunset

Do you know how many hours of daylight and darkness you'll experience in Scotland next week? With this easy to use HyperCard program, you'll be able to find the sunrise and sunset times anywhere on Earth.

Subj: SunRise SunSet Times 1.1
Date: March 23, 1992
From: SwamiG
File: SunR/S.sit (10986 bytes)
DL time: < 1 minute
Author: SwamiG
Needs: HyperCard 2.0, StuffIt

Where

The complete sequence of steps through Computing can be found on page 15. Of course, you can save time and money by using the Keyword shortcuts.

Keyword

File Search

Select

>sunrise time

Download

SunRise SunSet Times 1.1

Where to Find More Goodies

Turn to *Around the House* for an earthquake preparedness guide. The AOL areas covered in *Military and Aviation* are likely to carry more of the GIFs you are seeking. And, the *Education* section features science topics as well.

When science makes news, you'll find it in Time Online (Keyword: Time). The Chicago Tribune's Graphics Libraries (Keyword: Chicago) contain an impressive treasure of Hubble Telescope memorabilia, as well as GIFs of space shuttle launches and landings. In the libraries of the Mercury Center (Keyword: Mercury), you'll find photos of planets and earthquakes, as well as sound bites from the Apollo missions. And speaking of soundbites, the archives at ABC Radio (Keyword: ABC) have sound clips from the Challenger disaster.

If you are working on a research project, try the Reference Desk (Keyword: Reference), Scientific American (Keyword: SciAm), and the Smithsonian Online (Keyword: Smithsonian).

FREE $TUFF

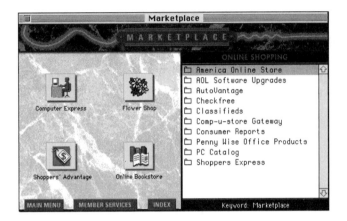

In *God* we trust; all others
must pay cash.

Anonymous

Shopping

Marketplace is America Online's shopping Mecca. It is here that you'll find everything from an America Online sweatshirt (like mine) to a new car (not like mine).

So, what's free when it comes to shopping? I'll direct you to catalogs that are free as well as to two \$1 memberships that can lead you to great savings.

You'll also find special, online discounts for AOL members. And at the conclusion of this section, I'll share some tips on where to find more shopping goodies.

CONSUMER REPORTS

Consumer Reports is published by Consumers Union (CU). CU is an independent, nonprofit testing and information organization serving only consumers. Since 1936, CU's mission has been to test products, inform the public of their findings, and protect consumers.

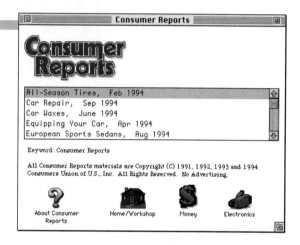

Consumer Reports provides America Online with product and service reviews, ratings, and advice. Summaries of tests and evaluations are specially prepared for the America Online service by the staff of *Consumer Reports*.

On America Online, *Consumer Reports'* viewers will discover a wealth of good advice:

- The Automobiles Collection includes reports on road tests of specific vehicles, as well as a listing of new-car profiles, new-car ratings, and automobile recall information.
- The Electronics Collection provides information and recommendations on radio, television, video and stereo equipment, services, and supplies.
- The Home/Workshop Collection includes reports on a wide range of products and services for home and workshop use.
- The Money Collection offers advice on personal finance issues.

The reports on products and services available on the America Online service are based on articles published in *Consumer Reports* magazine.

Where

Marketplace

Consumer Reports

Keyword

Consumer

Trade in your Miata for a Minivan

Whether you're looking for a big family van or a little sports car, you can get car ratings, reliability scores, and recall notices from *Consumer Reports*. Air bags, ABS brakes, crumple zones, seating comfort, and engine size statistics will help you make your decision to get the best deal.

Where

Marketplace

Consumer Reports

Keyword

Consumer Reports

Read/Save:

The 1994 Cars: Ratings,

The 1994 Cars: Profiles

The 1994 Cars: Reliability

How To Buy a Used Car

AutoVantage Online

If you are buying or selling a car, or are interested in getting the best parts and service for your car at the lowest possible price, then you'll appreciate what AutoVantage Online has to offer: new-car summaries, new-car deals, used-car pricing, used-car summaries, and pre-negotiated national service discounts. Although it's not free, a trial three-month membership can be yours for a buck when you register for a full membership. At the end of the trial period, and annually, your membership will be automatically renewed for a full year at $49 (still not a bad deal). Your membership satisfaction is always guaranteed or you may request a full refund of your annual membership fee simply by calling 1-800-843-7777.

Where

Marketplace

AutoVantage

Keyword

Auto

Select

How to Join AutoVantage Online

CheckFree Mac or DOS

No one likes to pay bills, but you could make the process easier by paying bills electronically. Thanks to CheckFree's easy-to-use software, you'll never have to mail another check. Just enter the payment information into your computer, and the software automatically records transactions, adjusts your balance, and transmits payments via modem to the CheckFree Processing Center. You can try CheckFree without obligation for 90 days.

Subj: CheckFree for MS-DOS Demo
Date: September 16, 1992
From: DLaBorde
File: CFDEMO.ZIP (76904 bytes)
DL time: < 2 minutes
Needs: 512K RAM

Where

Marketplace

CheckFree

Keyword

CheckFree

Select

Download our demos!

Download

CheckFree for MS-DOS Demo

CheckFree for Mac Demo

Penny Wise Office Products

Penny Wise Office Products is your key to the most inexpensive brand-name office supplies around.

Ordering from Penny Wise is simple. Just place your order for at least $25.00, and wait for UPS to deliver your purchase to your door—free anywhere in the continental United States. You'll get your Penny Wise order anywhere in the country within two to three working days.

Penny Wise Office Products will also take $10 off your first order of $25 or more. All you need to do is request the free catalog and you'll receive this gift certificate.

Where

Marketplace

Penny Wise Office Products

Keyword

Penny

Select

Send for FREE Penny Wise Catalog

Shopper's Advantage

Shoppers Advantage Online allows all America Online subscribers to shop for more than 250,000 name brand products at 10 to 50 percent off the manufacturers' suggested retail prices. However, membership to this service can provide you with even more savings:

- Lower, members-only prices
- Automatic 2-year warranty
- 3 month trial membership for $1
- Money back guarantee on the annual membership fee

A sampling of the product categories includes:

- TV and Video Equipment
- Portable, Car & Home Stereos
- Phones & Home Office Equipment
- Tools & Housewares
- Sports, Exercise & Outdoor Gear
- Cameras
- Domestics, Bed/Bath
- Home Furnishings
- Luggage

- Computers & Peripherals
- Toys & Games
- Jewelry, Watches, China, Crystal & Silver

The price list carries member and nonmember prices, so if you're planning to shop, you can use that information to help you make your membership decision.

Where

Marketplace

Shoppers Advantage

Keyword

Shoppers Advantage

Select

How to Join Shoppers Advantage

Flower Shop

They're not free, but they could save your relationship! You can order flowers while you're tooling around online. So, while your significant other thinks you're just a computer-playing dweeb, order some roses and redeem yourself.

The Flower Stop is run by Long Distance Roses, the flower delivery service that offers a unique way to send premium roses at an affordable price. Fresh cut daily from their own greenhouses in Colorado, Long Distance Roses are carefully packed in wet foam and shipped in a special styrofoam box. Other selections include a single rose in a crystal vase and orchids from Hawaii.

And, don't worry—all flowers are delivered by Federal Express Priority 1 virtually anywhere in the U.S. Your satisfaction is 100 percent guaranteed.

Where

Marketplace

Flower Shop

Keyword

Flower Shop

Select

Long Stem Roses

Single Rose

Delivery/Price Information

Shopping Scenes

If you miss the hustle and bustle of the mall or a crowded street, fret no longer. These three photos are sure to charm and calm the frustrated (online) shopper within.

Escalator, Shopping Mall, Suburban America

This escalator from a shopping mall in Maryland summons the pleasant, some would say antiseptic, symmetry found in new shopping-mall designs. My shopping experience leads me to believe that this was taken in Towson, Maryland, one of Baltimore's northern suburbs.

Subj: Escalator, Shopping Mall, MD
Date: May 14, 1994
From: CarlPix474
File: NA000325.GIF (88064 bytes)
DL time: < 2 minutes
Author: Carl & Ann Purcell
Needs: GIF viewer or Adobe Photoshop

Where
Travel

Pictures of the World

Keyword
Pictures

Select
File Search

>shopping

Download
Escalator, Shopping Mall, MD

Union Station, Washington, D.C.

This landmark train station is also a shopping center. Union Station is a popular shopping center in downtown D.C., and should definitely be added to your itinerary when you next visit D.C.

Subj: Interior, Union Station, Wash. D.C.
Date: May 14, 1994
From: CarlPix474
File: NA000152.GIF (77312 bytes)

DL time: < 2 minutes
Author: Carl & Ann Purcell
Needs: GIF viewer or Adobe Photoshop

Where

Travel

Pictures of the World

Keyword

Pictures

Select

File Search

>shopping

Download

Interior, Union Station, Wash. D.C.

Shanghai Shopping

If you're looking for something a bit more exotic (silk perhaps?), why not try a trip to Shanghai? This crowded street shows shoppers on a chilly day on Nanning Road in Shanghai, China.

Subj: Crowded street, Shanghai, China
Date: May 14, 1994
From: CarlPix474
File: AS000022.GIF (95232 bytes)
DL time: < 2 minutes
Author: Carl & Ann Purcell
Needs: GIF viewer or Adobe Photoshop

Where

Travel

Pictures of the World

Keyword

Pictures

Select

File Search

>shopping

Download

Crowded street, Shanghai, China

Consumer Complaint

Solicit Your Consumer Complaint (SYCC) is a database package that comes with the name, address, contact representative, and phone of all of the Better Business Bureaus and federal and state agencies across the United States. It also lists almost 700 consumer product companies. With this program, you'll be able to write scathing letters to just about anyone who deserves a piece of your mind. It's easy to use and provides you with many options to make this type of correspondence even more enjoyable.

The complete program requires a three-file download.

Subj: SYCC: Consumer Complaint DB (1/3)
Date: April 1, 1993
From: Nick WT
File: SYCC1.ZIP (167639 bytes)
DL time: < 4 minutes
Author: T-Lan Systems
Needs: 640K RAM, hard drive with 2.5 Mb free, UnZIPing program,
             parts 2 and 3
Type: Shareware

Where

The complete sequence of steps through Computing can be found on page 15. Of course, you can save time and money by using the Keyword shortcuts.

Keyword

File Search

Select

>Consumer

Download

SYCC: Consumer Complaint DB (1/3)

SYCC: Consumer Complaint DB (2/3)

SYCC: Consumer Complaint DB (3/3)

THE CONSUMER CONNEXION

The Consumer ConneXion is a newsletter that investigates scams and ripoffs and exposes them to the public. It includes scads of information about small businesses, including sources for funding and methods of incorporating your business. There are some fun letters from readers who have seen "Get Rich Quick" ads and want to know the real story. Protect yourself from scam artists, read *The Consumer ConneXion*.

Subj: PAGEMKR5: Newsletter - Consumer ConneXion
Date: June 18, 1994
From: DK4CASH
File: JULY94.PM5 (128896 bytes)
DL time: < 3 minutes
Author: Daks Keenan
Needs: Windows 3.x or Mac, PageMaker 5.0
Type: Freely distributed

Where

The complete sequence of steps through Computing can be found on page 15. Of course, you can save time and money by using the Keyword shortcuts.

Keyword

PC: File Search
Mac: PC Software

Select

>consumer

Download

PAGEMKR5: Newsletter - Consumer ConneXion

Consumer's Guide Demo

Looking for more free stuff? This is a demo version of Consumer's Guide to Free and Dramatically Discounted Products and Services. The uploader states that there are over $10,000 worth of free items and unbelievable values available through the registered version of the catalog. (The only active portion of the demo is the software portion.) The full, registered version is $19.95.

Subj: FREEDEMO: Products/Services Catalog Demo
Date: May 29, 1994
From: PCA Op
File: FREEDEMO.ZIP (139748 bytes)
DL time: < 3 minutes
Author: Weick Products
Needs: 640k RAM, mouse optional, UnZIPing program
Type: Shareware demo

Where

The complete sequence of steps through Computing can be found on page 15. Of course, you can save time and money by using the Keyword shortcuts.

Keyword

File Search

Select

>consumer

Download

FREEDEMO: Products/Services Catalog Demo

Catalog Sources

Now you can get a catalog for almost anything! This file is a listing of over 500 sources to call or write for catalogs in 32 different categories. You can register this program and get it on CD-ROM (a bit more expensive), which includes lots more information like Free Stuff, Government Free Stuff, World Travel Info, EPA Software, Consumer Information, and more.

Subj:	CATALOG: V1.0 Catalogs & Where to Find Them
Date:	August 29, 1994
From:	PCC DanP
File:	CATALOGS.ZIP (90562 bytes)
DL time:	< 2 minutes
Author:	Advantage Plus
Needs:	UnZIPing program
Type:	Shareware $10-$29 (CD)

Where

The complete sequence of steps through Computing can be found on page 15. Of course, you can save time and money by using the Keyword shortcuts.

Keyword

File Search

Select

>consumer

Download

CATALOG: V1.0 Catalogs & Where to Find Them

Window Shopper

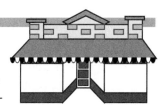

Window Shopper is designed to eliminate the frustration of multi-store shopping, saving you time and money. Window Shopper allows you to comparison shop among up to five stores and automatically selects the lowest price, saving you the time you would have spent running around comparing prices.

Subj: WSHOPPER: V1.5 Shopping Planner
Date: January 1, 1994
From: NormMorgan
File: WSHOP15.ZIP (461464 bytes)
DL time: < 12 minutes
Author: Norman Morgan
Needs: UnZIPing program, VBRUN300.DLL (included), Win 3.x
Type: Shareware $20

Where

The complete sequence of steps through Computing can be found on page 15. Of course, you can save time and money by using the Keyword shortcuts.

Keyword

File Search

Select

>shopping

Download

WSHOPPER: V1.5 Shopping Planner

The Internet Mall

Shopping on the information highway has never been so easy. When you are feeling overwhelmed by the abundance of goodies, grab a cup of warm cocoa, sit in your reclining desk chair and review The Internet Mall. This file contains a monthly list of commercial services available through the Internet, including books, magazines, music and video, personal items, games, florists, software, CD-ROMs, and more. You'll have fun with the shopping discoveries you'll find with this guide.

Subj: The Internet Mall
Date: March 26, 1994
From: Foxy
File: The Internet Mall (13811 bytes)
DL time: < 1 minute
Needs: Text reader

Where

The complete sequence of steps through Computing can be found on page 15. Of course, you can save time and money by using the Keyword shortcuts.

Keyword

Mac: File Search

PC: Mac Software

Select

[x] Communications

>shopping

Download

The Internet Mall

Downtown Anywhere

Downtown Anywhere Inc. has announced its World Wide Web-based online environment known as "Downtown Anywhere™." Arranged like a thriving metropolis, Downtown Anywhere's museums, libraries, and newsstands provide free and friendly access to global Internet resources, while its Main Street allows visitors to browse goods and innovative services that can be purchased with a few keystrokes. Downtown Anywhere boasts the first real-time, consumer-oriented credit card processing system on the Internet, and its innovative Personal Payment system eliminates the need for transmitting sensitive credit card numbers over the Internet.

Subj: Downtown Anywhere
Date: July 28, 1994
From: AFC Ellen
File: Downtown anywhere (5599 bytes)
DL time: < 1 minute
Needs: Text reader

Where

The complete sequence of steps through Computing can be found on page 15. Of course, you can save time and money by using the Keyword shortcuts.

Keyword

Mac: File Search

PC: Mac Software

Select

>shopping communications

Download

Downtown Anywhere

Where to Find More Goodies

Take a good look through the Marketplace (Keyword: Marketplace) and you'll be astounded at the merchandise purchasing opportunities online.

You'll also find more information on PC Catalog (Keyword: PC Catalog) and Kim Komando's Komputer Klinic (Keyword: Komando) in the *Computers* section of this book. I've provided detailed information about the Online Bookstore (Keyword: Books) in the *Books, Magazines, and Literature* section, and, covered in the same section, you'll find some great information on Stacey's Bookstores.

Virtually all of the online magazines have a special subscription offer—just check in each magazine's area. You may even find T-shirts, hats, and other accessories.

True America Online fans will want a T-shirt, sweatshirt, or mug from the America Online Store (Keyword: Marketplace), but I think everyone should have a bumper sticker like the one you'll find in the Mercury Center (Keyword: Mercury).

Chicago Online (Keyword: Chicago) expands its offerings with Chicago sports gear. And you'll find items with the ABC logo in ABC Sports (Keyword: ABC).

Airline tickets, priced to meet the latest airfare war, are yours in EAAsy Sabre in the Travel department (Keyword: Travel).

FREE $TUFF

It ain't over until it's over.

Yogi Berra

Sports and Recreation

Whether you're a spectator or an avid competitor in the world of sports, you're bound to find something of interest in this section. I'll guide you to a few hot areas where you can find the latest sports news and grab photos and icons. Further on we'll encounter outdoor recreation.

The Grandstand

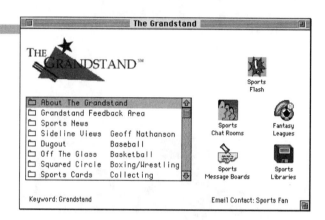

The Grandstand was founded in August 1985 as a place for sports fans to talk, write, and at times, yell about the latest happenings on and off the field, court, rink, ring, and track.

For the latest sports news, select the SportsLink icon and you'll be transported to America Online's fine sports service. The Grandstand Sports Software headquarters is the #1 location for team logos, sports-based computer games, GIFs, and icons.

Where

Entertainment

The Grandstand

Keyword

Grandstand

Select

Sport Software

1st Round Picks Library

Download

[your favorites]

Grandstand Sports Trivia

Think you're a sports nut? And you know everything there is to know about just about every sport going, eh? Well, how about trying to pit your sports knowledge against a room full of sports lovers and see who really knows more?

Check the schedule for nightly contests. Two hours of free online time are awarded at each trivia show. For the full details, check the Special Events message board.

Where

Entertainment

The Grandstand

Sports Message Boards

Keyword

Sports Boards

Select

Special Events

Giants Logo

Where would you like to see the San Francisco Giants logo? On your computer screen? (Perhaps some of you would like to see it somewhere else?) This file is a 640 x 380 GIF image of the San Francisco Giants' new logo.

Subj: (GIF) Giants logo
Date: August 7, 1994
From: SteveCroke
File: GIANTS.GIF (18980 bytes)
DL time: < 1 minute
Author: SteveCroke
Needs: GIF viewer
Type: Freely distributed

Where

Entertainment

The Grandstand

Keyword

Grandstand

Select

Sports Libraries

Baseball

Download

(GIF) Giants logo

Nancy Kerrigan

Here's a terrific shot of Nancy Kerrigan, wearing the famous Vera Wang costume from the '94 Winter Olympics in Lillehammer. The picture was taken during her long (free) program. Isn't that Tonya Harding plotting in the background?

Subj: (GIF) Nancy Kerrigan 2
Date: October 8, 1994
From: DinoRaptor
File: KERRIG5A.GIF (341938 bytes)
DL time: < 9 minutes
Needs: GIF viewer, 256-color display

Where

Entertainment

Grandstand

Keyword

Grandstand

Select

Sports Libraries

Winter Sports

Download

(GIF) Nancy Kerrigan 2

The Grandstand Fantasy Baseball League

The Grandstand Fantasy Baseball League (GFBL) is modeled after "Rotisserie League Baseball" as delineated in the book of the same name by Glen Waggoner (Bantam Books). As the owner, you will get to draft 23 players from the available talent in the American League and National League (depending on which league you join). The player's actual MLB performance will be used in computing the standings of his GFBL team.

You will find standings, stats, newsletters, and other league information in the accompanying message board and library sections of this area. To join the GFBL, read the GFBL sign-up file.

Where

Entertainment

The Grandstand

Fantasy Leagues

Keyword

Fantasy Leagues

Select

Fantasy/Simulation [sport]

Grandstand Gazette

Fantasy fever, trivia updates, and sports commentary are wrapped into this fun newsletter. *The Grandstand Gazette* is published monthly by One Two Many Productions.

Subj: (ANY) GrandstandGazette 10/94
Date: October 1, 1994
From: Sabata
File: GSG-9410.TXT (27197 bytes)
DL time: < 1 minute
Author: Sabata
Needs: UnZIPing program, text reader

Where

Entertainment

Grandstand

Keyword

Grandstand

Select

Sports Libraries

New Files/Free Uploading

Download

(ANY) GrandstandGazette [date]

ABC Sports

When ABC designed the Sports area, they didn't miss the kickoff. Within ABC Online, ABC Sports features the SportsTicker Sports News Roundup on the Sports board, the latest scores on the Scoreboard, Sports Trivia and Polls, and the always-current programming schedule found within

Inside ABC Sports. GIFs, WAVs and video clips are just seconds away.

Where

Entertainment

ABC Online

ABC Sports

Keyword

ABC Sports

Joe Montana

Joe Montana throws his arms up in the air in a classic Montana touchdown pose after throwing the game winner to Willie Davis in a battle against Denver.

Subj: Montana Arms in Air (photo)
Date: October 26, 1994
From: ABCPhoto1
File: MONTANA.jpg (109319 bytes)
DL time: < 3 minutes
Needs: JPEG viewer

Where

Entertainment

ABC Online

ABC Sports

Keyword

ABC Sports

Select

Pixs & Clips

1994 Season Pixs & Clips

Download

Montana Arms in Air (photo)

Indy 500

Wave the checkered flag! This photo was taken at the start of the 1994 Indy 500. In 1995, ABC's *Wide World of Sports* will cover the race for the 10th consecutive year.

Subj: Indy 500 (photo)
Date: October 5, 1994

From: ABCPhoto1
File: ABCWWS4.jpg (99329 bytes)
DL time: < 2 minutes
Needs: JPEG viewer

Where

Entertainment

ABC Online

ABC Sports

Keyword

ABC Sports

Select

Pixs & Clips

Wide World of Sports

Download

Indy 500 (photo)

Chicago Online

The Chicago Tribune's download libraries contain a superb treasury of information and images for sports fans. In addition to the numerous GIFs of athletes, you'll find the rosters and schedules for dozens of teams. It's the most complete "database" I've found online. They are constantly updating this database, so check it at the beginning of each sport's season.

Where

Newsstand

Chicago Tribune Online

Keyword

Chicago

Select

Download Libraries

Download

[Pro & College Schedules, Rosters and Draft Picks]

His Name Is Air

To air is definitely not human, but don't tell that to Michael. Here's a GIF of Michael Jordan doing what he does best!

Subj: Michael Jordan (#2) - Color GIF
Date: October 27, 1994
From: COL David
File: JORDANB.GIF (165309 bytes)
DL time: < 4 minutes
Needs: MAC or PC, GIF viewer

Where

Newsstand

Chicago Tribune

Keyword

Chicago

Select

Download Libraries

Tribune Sports Graphics Reference Library

Download

Michael Jordan (#2) - Color GIF

Mercury Sports

You can count on Mercury Sports for this morning's sports scores as well as today's statistics. Under the Baseball icon there are articles and information about the San Francisco Giants, the Oakland A's, and other baseball teams nationwide. Click on the Football icon for the 49ers and Bay Area college teams, including San Jose State, Stanford, and U.C. Berkeley.

Click on the Basketball icon for the scoop on the Golden State Warriors, other NBA teams, and college basketball. For Sharks fans, there's the Hockey icon.

For the latest sports stats and reports, click on America Online Sports.

Where

Newsstand

San Jose Mercury News

Keyword

Mercury

Select

In the News

Today's Paper

Sports

[article]

Notre Dame's Golden Dome

Love 'em or hate 'em, there's no college team that draws more attention than Notre Dame. Now all fans can have a view of the Golden Dome. Go Irish!

Subj: Notre Dame Golden Dome PNTG
Date: August 3, 1993
From: Tj1
File: NDDome.sit (5824 bytes)
DL time: < 1 minute
Needs: Program that can read PNTG files

Where

The complete sequence of steps through Computing can be found on page 15. Of course, you can save time and money by using the Keyword shortcuts.

Keyword

Mac: File Search

PC: Mac Computing

Select

>Notre Dame

Download

Notre Dame Golden Dome PNTG

Winning ClipArt

The Sports ClipArt stack is brought to you by SchoolHouse Mac. This stack is one of SchoolHouse Mac's fifteen collections of public domain graphics. This sampler contains 19 of the 200+ images included in the complete package.

Subj: Sports ClipArt Sampler sea
Date: June 22, 1994
From: Charlie938
File: Sports ClipArt Sampler.sea (61485 bytes)
DL time: < 1 minute
Needs: Mac, HyperCard 2.x

Where

The complete sequence of steps through Computing can be found on page 15.

Of course, you can save time and money by using the Keyword shortcuts.

Keyword

File Search

Select

>Charlie938 sports

Download

Sports ClipArt Sampler sea

Wayne Gretzeky's Hockey

This is a demo version of Wayne Gretzeky's Hockey. You get to play five minutes of the third quarter. It is fun and you can use any team in the NHL. The fight scenes are killer too!

Subj: Wayne Gretzeky's Hockey Demo
Date: April 19, 1992
From: PeePingToM
File: Waynes Hockey (985355 bytes)
DL time: < 27 minutes
Needs: Mac, System 7 compatible, StuffIt 1.5.1

Where

The complete sequence of steps through Computing can be found on page 15. Of course, you can save time and money by using the Keyword shortcuts.

Keyword

File Search

Select

>hockey

Download

Wayne Gretzeky's Hockey Demo

Bicycling

In Bicycling Online, you'll find selected articles from each month's current issue of *Bicycling Magazine*. *Bicycling* is the world's number one road and mountain bike magazine. The online articles

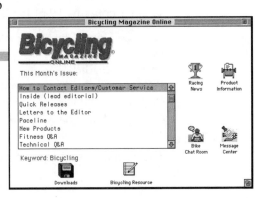

"arrive" at the same time the paper magazine ships to subscribers. Whether you're a road or dirt rider, you'll enjoy *Bicycling*.

Where

Newsstand

Bicycling Magazine

Keyword

Bicycling

Motorola Team Time Trial

This is the gem of the recent batch of Tour de France uploads. This horizontal image shows the entire Motorola team in the '94 Tour's Stage 3 team time trial. The riders are echeloned to the right, coming directly at the photographer. It's dramatic, because you can see the pain and strain on the riders' faces—a superb image. A color Tour De France route map is available at the same location.

Subj: Motorola Team Time Trial
Date: July 19, 1994
From: Bic Mag
File: MOTORTT.GIF (248644 bytes)
DL time: < 6 minutes
Author: Frederic Mons
Needs: PC or Mac, GIF viewer

Where

Clubs & Interests

Bicycling Magazine

Keyword

Bicycling

Select

Downloads

Bicycling Images

Download

Motorola Team Time Trial

Cyclist's Logbook

Do you remember last week's riding schedule? Did you train for distance or speed, hills or flat road? Now you can keep track of your training with the Cyclist's Logbook. Log your daily rides by distance, route, bicycle type, physiology, weather, and more. You can use the diary screen to record your ride and conditions. This program also generates weekly reports, and a gear ratio calculator is included.

Subj: Cyclist's Logbook (Mac)
Date: March 29, 1994
From: Jfabian
File: Cyclists Logbook (111104 bytes)
DL time: < 3 minutes
Needs: Mac, FileMaker Pro 2.0

Where
Clubs & Interests
Bicycling Magazine

Keyword
Bicycling

Select
Downloads
Cycling Shareware & Images

Download
Cyclist's Logbook (Mac)

BikeNet

BikeNet is the online place to find out all you would like to know about the art, sport, and science of bicycling. Several biking associations can be found together in this area—you'll have just about every biking resource except a bike. The BikeNet's libraries allow you to upload and download entire newsletters, maps, bicycle graphics, software, and even the full text of the Intermodal Surface Transportation Efficiency/Enhancement Act (ISTEA), an important law affecting bicycles that is usually distributed as a thick binder.

Where
Clubs & Interests
BikeNet — The Bicycle Network

Keyword
BikeNet

Bikes Fly Free!

Traveling cyclists no longer need to worry about the expense of flying their bikes. Members of the League of American Bicyclists (L.A.B.) are now entitled to receive free bike passes on TWA, America West, USAir, Continental, and Northwest Airlines when they purchase their ticket through the Sports National Reservation Center. Annual membership costs only $25 for an individual—quite a break on the $90 you would pay to transport your bike on a cross-country, round-trip ticket. Follow these directions to membership information.

Where

Clubs & Interests

BikeNet — The Bicycle Network

Keyword

BikeNet

Select

League of American Bicyclists

Read/Save

Bikes Fly Free

The National Bike Registry

The National Bike Registry (NBR) was started in 1984 by bicycle enthusiasts in Sacramento, California to help police identify the legal owner of a recovered bicycle. In essence, NBR is the link between cyclists who lose their bikes and police who recover them. NBR's Certificate of Registration is also legal proof of ownership. Registration is as low as $5.00 per year for one bike and the special AOL rate for lifetime registration is only $20.

Where

Clubs & Interests

BikeNet — The Bicycle Network

Keyword

BikeNet

Select

Publications

Search the BikeNet Collections

>national bike registry

Download

National Bike Registry

BACKPACKER Magazine

Backpacker's readers can access editorial content from the magazine of self-propelled wilderness travel. Hikers and backcountry travelers look to Backpacker for the information they need before each outdoor adventure and reviews of all the latest gear. Through the Trailhead Register, hikers can find a companion for the trails.

Where

Clubs & Interests

Backpacker

Keyword

Backpacker

Select

Trailhead Register

Read/Save

Find a Hiking Companion

Backpacker Trivia

With the correct answers you could win a Backpacker Technical T-shirt. An average of 100 online hikers and outdoor enthusiasts have participated in Backpacker's contests, answering such questions as "What is the name of the North American Big Horn sheep?" or "What are the four classic peaks in New Hampshire's Presidential Range?" Hint: You'll find the answers to the trivia questions in each month's issue.

Where

Clubs & Interests

Backpacker

Keyword

Backpacker

Select

Contests & Promos

Read/Save

This Month's Backpacker Contest

Official Backpacker Entry Form

Planning Your Next Adventure

TRAIL, a backpacking trip planning program, helps you to plan extended back-packing trips in Washington State's Olympic National Park. With TRAIL you can graphically plot your trip, and then plan each day based on elevation gain/loss and accumulated mileage. After defining your trip, you can print detailed and summarized trip statistics. As your mother would say, "Just don't get lost."

Subj: TRAIL: V1.0 Backpack Trip Planner
Date: August 24, 1994
From: PC Robin
File: TRAIL.ZIP (101488 bytes)
DL time: < 2 minutes
Needs: PC, 640K RAM, DOS 3.1 or higher, UnZIPing program
Type: Shareware

Where

The complete sequence of steps through Computing can be found on page 15. Of course, you can save time and money by using the Keyword shortcuts.

Keyword

File Search

Select

>recreation

Download

TRAIL: V1.0 Backpack Trip Planner

Where to Find More Goodies

If you're looking for crafts, rather than hobbies, turn to *Around the House* for some great ideas.

Online, it's easy to find the packed departments filled with sports news and images. The first place to check for current news is at Today's News (Keyword: News). You'll find a great sports link there. Don't stop short—you'll find more of what you're looking for at NBC Online (Keyword: NBC) with sports schedules and special events.

If your home is your hobby, as it is for many, you'll want to wander over to the Homeowners Forum (Keyword: Homeowner).

And if you just don't know where else to look, stop at the main download libraries and use the Keywords: File Search, Mac Software, and PC Software. You never know what you'll find there.

FREE $TUFF

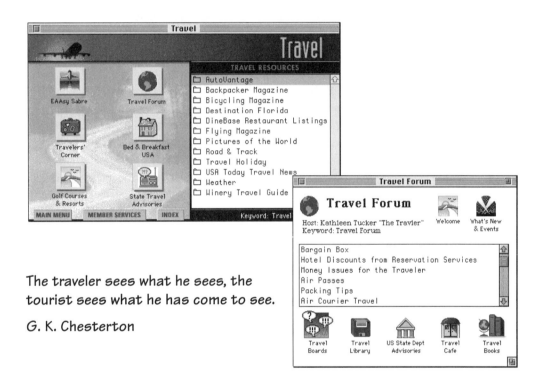

The traveler sees what he sees, the
tourist sees what he has come to see.

G. K. Chesterton

Travel

The Travel Freebies on AOL are some of the best around. For trip pre-planning and last-minute advice, be sure to check AOL's Travel Forum. The downloads will save you the cost of many travel books and your fellow travelers on AOL can provide "Been there–done that" concise information on the message boards.

In these pages you'll find that I've selected several regions, rather than provided worldwide coverage. This way you'll see both the depth and breadth of the travel information on America Online.

Florida, New York, Chicago, and Massachusetts are the main features.

Bargain Box Air Fare Deals

You should check out the Bargain Box in the Travel section every time you sign on. We all know that the airlines are constantly making new offers and adding new deals. The Bargain Box is a compilation of all known offers at any point in time. Air fare wars, Peanut Fares, 2-for-1s, Half Price Companion Coupons, Kids Fly Free, and contests for free tickets and accommodations are posted all the time.

Highlights of the current offerings include:

- Half price companion tickets on USAir with American Express
- Kids fly free to London on Virgin Atlantic
- Chart House restaurants contest for two around the world tickets
- Automatic upgrades
- American Express Platinum buy 1 get 1 free on international flights
- Friends fly free fares

Where

Travel

Travel Forum

Keyword

Travel Forum

Read/Save

Bargain Box

Bed & Breakfast U.S.A.

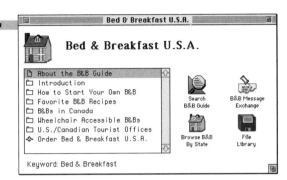

Bed & Breakfast U.S.A. is a product of a membership organization whose credo is "Comfort, cleanliness, cordiality, and fairness of cost."

Bed & Breakfast U.S.A. online covers bed and breakfast accommodations priced under $85 for double occupancy and far less than that for single occupancy and shared bath accommodations. All must serve breakfast to be included. For those who do not mind paying a higher rate, the reservation services listed in Bed & Breakfast U.S.A. will be able to help you take the hassle out of reserving your own room.

Where

Travel

Bed & Breakfast USA

Keyword

Bed & Breakfast

Select

Browse by State

>state

or Search B&B Guide

Read/Save

[selected B&B]

Travel Books—Discounted!

Plan on heading into the Pyrenees, but don't know which way to go? It's always nice to find out which buses will get you to the start of your adventure—and at what cost. All travel books reviewed and recommended in the Travel Forum may be ordered through AOL's Online Bookstore at 10 to 20 percent off the list price.

While not "free," this discount extends a great value to travel book buyers.

Where

Travel

Travel Forum

Keyword

Travel Forum

Select

Travel Books

[Search, select, and order!]

Cruise Values

The Cruise message board is the spot to check for ongoing postings of cruise bargains. Cruise travelers, consolidators, brokers, and travel agents often post the best available values. The time you spend in this forum will be well worth this month's membership fee!

You'll recognize the cruise lines—they include Royal Caribbean, The Big Red Boat, Windstar, Norwegian Cruise Line, Holland America, and Carnival.

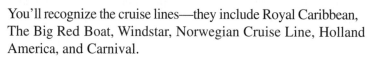

Where

Travel

Travel Forum

Keyword

Travel Forum

Select

Travel Boards

The Cruise Traveler

Read/Save

Cruise Discounts

Don't Go Hungry

Goldwyn's DineBase provides AOL users with a reference list of the nation's best restaurants. Version 1.0 contains the 1,200 top award-winning restaurants in every nook and cranny of the United States. All the restaurants on the list are recommended by one or more of the following prestigious reviews: AAA Dining Award, DiRoNA, Mobil Frequent Traveler's Guide to Major Cities, Restaurant Hospitality Wine List Awards, Wine Spectator's Great Restaurant Wine Lists, and Zagat Restaurant Surveys. Very useful for hungry travelers!

Where

Travel

Keyword

Travel

Select

DineBase Restaurant Listings

Search DineBase

>restaurant or city

Read/Save

[restaurant/city]

Travel Newsletters

Travel newsletter freebies and subscriptions abound in the Travel Newsletters message board. Many of these newsletters have uploaded sample issues to the Travel Library. The newsletters cover discount travel, family travel, Florida, nautical travel, and gay/lesbian travel. You never know what you'll find!

Where

Travel

Travel Forum

Keyword

Travel Forum

Select

Travel Boards

General Travel Tips

Read/Save

Travel Newsletters

TRAVELWISE NEWS

Europe on $5.00 a day? Well probably not anymore, but there is some sound advice for the penny-pinching traveler. *TravelWise News, An Insider's Guide to Discount Travel*, lists discounts primarily publicized through travel agents. This file includes a sample downloadable issue of *TravelWise News*, and this issue features special offers from hotels and ski resorts.

Subj: TravelWise News
Date: May 9, 1994

From: NRCOOCH
File: TVLWISE.DOC (3038 bytes)
DL time: < 1 minute
Author: Nancy Rocks
Needs: Text reader

Where

Travel

Travel Forum

Keyword

Travel Forum

Select

Travel Library

Download

TravelWise News

The Big Easy

The 1994 Guide to New Orleans provides a comprehensive, up-to-date guide to the sights, music, food, hotels and neighborhoods of New Orleans. I'm already dreamin' about those beignets, muffalettas, po-boys, and gumbo. The *New Orleans Guide* thoroughly uncovers the sights, sounds, and tastes of New Orleans. Written by a travel writer who lived in New Orleans for many years.

Subj: New Orleans Guide 1994
Date: June 24, 1994
File: New Orleans Guide AOL (36919 bytes)
DL time: <1 minute
Author: Lan Sluder
Needs: Any word processor

Where

Travel

Travel Forum

Keyword

Travel Forum

Select

Travel Library

Download

New Orleans Guide 1994

TRAVEL HOLIDAY ONLINE

Getaways are more fun with *Travel Holiday Online*—you have direct access to superb vacations at a sensible price. America's most value-conscious travel magazine, *Travel Holiday* presents ten issues yearly with pertinent articles on fascinating destinations, political briefings, phone numbers, hotel bargains, and strategies for saving money.

You can also search *Travel Holiday*'s archives for past reports on a destination and communicate with travelers in the Travelers' Message Center. The eye-witness sources include a remarkably diverse range of observant writers, from Arthur Frommer to Saul Bellow, as well as other readers who are happy to share their recent travel experiences.

In April 1994, *Travel Holiday* was honored with a gold award for the Best Travel Magazine in North America by the Society of American Travel Writers.

Where

Travel

Keyword

Travel Holiday

Free Travel Brochures

Ever wanted to see London, Paris, Rome, and Salzburg in five days? Maybe you can with the Europe Travel Planner! In addition to the magazine excerpts, *Travel Holiday Online* also features free brochures on great travel destinations. These free brochures change with each issue, but you're sure to find the current offerings with these easy directions. If you don't find brochures listed on the main screen (the current issue) be sure to check the archived issues.

Where

Travel Holiday

Keyword

Travel Holiday

Select

This Month's Issue or Past Issues

Search Past Issues

>Brochure

Read/Save

Free Brochure: Europe Planner

Free Brochure: Northeast US Guides

Free Brochures: California's Marina del Rey

Travel Holiday Free Subscription

With the new Global Games contest you can test your geography knowledge and win a one-year subscription. Today's travelers can hop on a plane and be halfway around the world in the same day, without having to give much thought to which direction they are traveling, or how many miles they cover. Many are unaware of geographical relationships, and are surprised to find that Reno is west of Los Angeles or that part of Ontario lies due south of Detroit.

Where

Travel Holiday

KeywordTravel Holiday

Select

This Month's Issue

Read/Save

New! Global Games...Win a Sub

PASSPORT NEWSLETTER

Now you can download a sample issue of the *Passport Newsletter*, written for the knowledgeable and discriminating traveler. The newsletter covers a range of national and international destinations and thoroughly prepares the traveler with details of accommodations and restaurants.

Subj: Passport Newsletter
Date: May 19, 1994
File: PASSPORT.TXT (60131 bytes)
DL time: < 1 minute
Author: Remy Publishing Co
Needs: Text reader

Where

Travel

Travel Forum

Keyword

Travel Forum

Select

Travel Library

Download

Passport Newsletter

ITALIAN TRAVELER NEWSLETTER

This is a sample of the *Italian Traveler Newsletter*, published by AOL member ItalTrav. It is a great newsletter full of current information and tips on travel to Italy. You'll read an incredibly thorough presentation on the goings-on in Italy, including currency news, cost of living stats, art and cultural exhibits, restaurant reviews, train ticket pricing, legal tips, and on and on! If you've even "just thinking" about planning a trip, download this comprehensive file and you'll soon be dialing your travel agent or signing back on AOL to use EAAsy Sabre.

Subj: Italian Traveler Newsletter
Date: May 9, 1994
From: TheTravler
File: ITLTRV.TXT.sit (79625 bytes)
DL time: < 2 minutes
Author: Howard Isaacs, ItalTrav
Needs: AOL, StuffIt Expander or unStuffIt utility, text reader

Where

Travel

Travel Forum

Keyword

Travel Forum

Select

Travel Library

Download

Italian Traveler Newsletter

All Aboard!

Businesses are jumping onto the AOL train with increasingly frequency. Even the rail business itself is jumping on board. Take a look at what Amtrak has to offer.

Riding the Rails

Hobo or not, there's nothing quite like riding the rails. Whether for business or pleasure, you just might find yourself in need of the Amtrak schedule for the Northeast Corridor Line. This file contains a complete listing of all Amtrak trains running on the Northeast Corridor between Washington D.C. and Boston. The timetable shows north and southbound trains.

Subj: Amtrak NE Timetable [date]
Date: May 25, 1994
File: AMTRAKNE.TXT (71430 bytes)
DL time: < 2 minutes
Author: William C. Davis
Needs: Computer, spreadsheet or text reader

Where

Travel
Travel Forum

Keyword

Travel Forum

Select

Travel Library

Download

Amtrak NE Timetable [date]

Amtrak Passenger Train

Have you ever traveled by train? Does the smell of diesel (or sometimes coal) bring tears to your eyes? If you're a rail aficionado, you'll want to see this EPS image, which was originally part of an Amtrak ad.

Subj: Amtrak Passenger Train EPSF
Date: May 1, 1992
From: BBUD BSS
File: amtrak.sit (67764 bytes)
DL time: < 1 minute
Author: Bruce Shanker
Needs: Illustrator or other program that accepts EPS images

Where

Macintosh Graphics Forum

Keyword

MGR

Select

Software Libraries

Software Search

>Amtrak

Download

Amtrak Passenger Train EPSF

Do-It-Yourself Travel

Most people like to control their own destiny, especially where travel is concerned. America Online provides several great resources that you can use to make your own travel plans, including booking airline flights, hotels, and rental cars.

Bypass Your Travel Agent

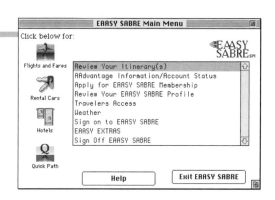

Sometimes you just don't want to deal with a travel agent or you might find that she or he never returns your calls. Other nights you can't sleep, and you still don't have tickets for Omaha, but you don't want to make happy chatter with the representative at the other end of the airline's 800 number. EAAsy Sabre comes to the rescue and you may never return to your old travelin' ways.

Where

Travel

Keyword

Travel

Select

EAAsy Sabre

Air Travel Consumer Report

The highlights for on-time airline performance are reported in the Air Travel Consumer Report. Each month's report is 60 days behind since the U.S. Department of Transportation needs that lag time to compile the statistics. Thus, the December 1994 report will be for October 1994, and so forth.

The report covers on-time arrivals and departures, mishandled baggage reports, consumer complaints, and passengers involuntarily denied boarding.

If you absolutely, positively have to be there on time (sorry, FedEx!), check this list.

Where

Travel

Travel Forum

Keyword

Travel Forum

Select

Air Travel Consumer Report

You Can Make It There

New York City is a popular travel destination for people from around the world. And the reasons for the Big Apple's popularity are easy to identify. There's just so much to do and see there! Don't let the sheer enormity of New York's day and night life overwhelm you. Use America Online to navigate your way through a great business trip or vacation to the city and the rest of the Empire State.

On Broadway

New York and Broadway: they're like bagels and lox, Astaire and Rogers, Paris and romance. A special version of the New York Times Online, @Times, is a treasure for travelers coming to New York to see the lights and dazzle of Broadway. The Broadway Theater Directory lists theaters and phone numbers for the historic theaters. Synopses of current shows, along with theater addresses and phone numbers, can be obtained from the same screen.

Where

New York Times Online

@Times

Keyword

Times Arts

Select

Theater

Miss Saigon

Who needs Siskel and Ebert? *The New York Times* review of *Miss Saigon* is just one of the many Broadway show reviews in the @Times archives. Start with this and you'll find the others!

Where

New York Times Online

@Times

Keyword

Times Arts

Select

Theater

Reviews & Current Theater

Broadway

Read/Save

Miss Saigon

New York Wine Country Brochures

Guess what? New York is the nation's second-largest producer of grapes and wine after California. According to the New York Wine & Grape Foundation, the state's 1,500 vineyards cover 38,000 acres and produce an average annual grape crop of 170,000 tons estimated to be worth $30 to 40 million. About 50 percent of the crop is used for grape juice, 45 percent for wine, and 5 percent for table consumption.

You'll want to read this file for the details on how to receive the following wine-based information:

- *Uncork New York!* This is a four-color pictorial map with a comprehensive listing of the state's wineries by region, showing the approximate location of 73 wineries, with addresses, phone numbers, and tour hours.

- *Wine Country Calendar.* This handy brochure lists special events from May 1 to Christmas. The listings are by region, date, and winery, and include phone numbers to call for additional information.

- *Finger Lakes Travel Guide.* The Finger Lakes Association publishes a magazine size guide book to this delightful destination. In addition to listing the local wineries, it contains history and geography, restaurant info, hotel info, maps, and other attractions.

Where
> Travel

Keyword
> Travel

Select
> Winery Travel Guide

Read/Save
> NY Wine Country Brochures

Walt's World

Disneyland and Disney World are two of the most popular vacation destinations in the world. And with that kind of popularity, you can bet that both of these Magic Kindoms will have crowds, crowds, crowds. Avoid the hassles that go hand-in-hand with wall-to-wall people: With America Online, you'll find several resources to help you plan for a relaxing, trouble-free Disney vacation for you and the kids.

Disney World Frequent Questions

What are the hours? Will the kids be tall enough this year to ride Space Mountain? Are there still E-Ticket rides? What are the best times to go? What's under construction? If you're heading to Disney World, you need answers to these questions!

Here you'll find a listing of frequently asked questions concerning Walt Disney World and the answers you need. This version includes the park hours for the summer, along with the parade and special events times and places. You will find this regularly updated file to be very useful if you are planning a trip to Disney World.

Subj: Disney World Frequent Questions
Date: June 6, 1994
File: WDW FAQ June (49028 bytes)
DL time: < 1 minute
Author: Tom Tanida
Needs: Text reader

Where
> Travel
>
> Travel Forum

Keyword

Travel Forum

Select

Travel Library

Download

Disney World Frequent Questions

Disney World: A Very Unofficial Guide

Here's a great source of information on all aspects of Walt Disney World. An absolute must for anyone planning a trip to Disney World. In this free guide to Walt Disney World, you will find the history of the Disney empire, when to travel, where to stay, packages, passes, transportation, and directions—in short, everything except a map! The Spoilers and Insider's Tips are outstanding! Future updates will no longer be free, because the author is preparing a book. You can still get the last version, updated in May 1994.

Subj: Disney World Very Unofficial Guide
Date: May 9, 1994
From: EdwardV2
File: LAST Very Unofficial Guide.txt (245153 bytes)
DL time: < 1 minute
Author: Todd McCartney
Needs: Text reader

Where

Travel

Travel Forum

Keyword

Travel Forum

Select

Travel Library

Download

Disney World Very Unofficial Guide

Which Way to the Magic Kingdom?

Plan your attack at Disney World—don't miss a single ride or event. This file includes a map of the Orlando Disney Properties, including the resorts, campgrounds, and Magic Kingdom.

Subj: Disney Properties Map - PC or Mac Version
Date: June 2, 1994
From: DFKim
File: disney.sit (338442 bytes)
DL time: < 9 minutes
Author: Steve Thornton
Needs: Mac, UnStuffIt, GIF viewer

Where

Travel

Destination Florida

Keyword

Florida

Select

Attractions

Attractions Software Library

Download

Disney Properties Map - Mac Version

Disney Properties Map - PC Version

Sun and Fun in Florida

There's a lot more to Florida than Disney World. With beautiful weather year 'round and some of the best beaches in the world, a Florida vacation is pretty much a gauranteed family pleaser. Take a look at some of the many Florida travel aids provided on America Online.

Florida Finder

The Destination Florida section is part travel guide and part travel agent. You can check on the weather, NASA launches, fishing information, find accommodations, consult maps, and plan your trip. This area is ever improving; eventually, you'll be able to book hotel rooms, buy airline tickets, and order Florida souvenirs through Destination Florida. Visit often for a chance to win a trip to Florida!

Where

Travel

Destination Florida

Keyword

Florida

Read/Save

Places to Stay

Attractions

Space News

Weather

Search Destination Florida

Jacksonville Regional Map

Your travel agent didn't have a map of Jacksonville and your trip begins to-morrow? You don't have to spend your vacation driving through the "they-all-look-the-same" streets in downtown Jacksonville.Get online and check the map section for the maps you need and you'll have them in minutes!

Subj: Jacksonville Regional Map - Fixed
Date: June 13, 1994
From: DFKim
File: JAX.GIF (319019 bytes)
DL time: < 2 minutes
Source: Florida Department of Transportation
Needs: Mac or PC, GIF viewer

Where

Travel

Destination Florida

Keyword

Florida

Select

Downloadable Maps and Library

Download

Jacksonville Regional Map - Fixed

Something for Everyone—Sports

Do members of your family spend their vacation molded to the chair in front of the TV watching every sport? As you coordinate your family's vacation, you're likely to find out that you have one of these fans lurking in the closet. Sports fans will want to know just what major events will be taking place while they're in Florida, so make sure to check Destination Florida to appease their sense of fair play.

Where

Travel

Destination Florida

Keyword

Florida

Select

Sports

Calendar of Sports Events

Read/Save

Major Sporting Events - [month]

That Toddlin' Town

Chicago is one of the true cultural meccas of the U.S. You won't want to overlook any of the outstanding attractions available here. So, before you plan your next trip to the windy city, make sure you check out these America Online sites.

Chicago #1 Attractions

Some of us might go to Chicago just for the pizza, but there are others who travel for the sites. The Chicago Convention and Tourism Bureau, Inc. has compiled this useful list of attractions including Buckingham Fountain, Capone's Chicago, Chicago Board of Trade, Daley's Civic Center, John Hancock Center, and Sears Tower. Frankly, I'd rather have the pizza!

Where

Newsstand

Chicago Online

Keyword

Chicago

Select

Visitor's Guide

Visitor's Highlights

Read/Save

Chicago: Attractions

'Round & About the Loop

A Directory of Local Museums

A Guide to Weekend Hotel Packages

Chicago Map

There's only 30 minutes left until the taping of Oprah. Too bad you're from Telluride and can't drive your way out of a paper bag. Never fear. This Chicago Area Map shows major roads, cities, and counties in the region. Maybe you'll make it on time after all.

Subj: Chicago Area Map - 6 County (PICT)
Date: July 25, 1994
From: COL David
File: METRO Roads (Chgoland TV).pic (47560 bytes)
DL time: < 1 minute
Author: ChicagoLand TV News
Needs: PICT viewer

Where

Newsstand

Chicago Online

Keyword

Chicago

Select

Download Libraries

Transportation and Timetables Library

Download

Chicago Area Map - 6 County (PICT)

Chicago Museum Directory

Take in the DNA to Dinosaurs Exhibit at The Field Museum or view the Omnimax Film, *Antarctica*, at the Museum of Science and Industry. The Chicago Tribune's Museum Directory is presented in Chicago Online. Provided by the Chicago Convention and Tourism Bureau, Inc., this directory is a comprehensive listing of exhibits, and museum information. It's a good starting point for any museum lover planning a trip to Chicago. It's also a useful list for those who are on business trips and have time to kill between meetings. (It's been known to happen, really!)

Where

Newsstand

Chicago Online

Keyword

Chicago

Select

Visitor's Guide

Visitor's Highlights

Read/Save

Chicago: Museums

Branson Welcomes You

Branson, Missouri now welcomes over 5 million travelers a year, and has become one of the nation's largest tourist destinations. Branson has become the new Nashville, filled with country and other music shows—and great shopping. A frequent Branson visitor has compiled stacks of information on Branson shows and attractions, phone numbers, and personal observations!

Subj: Branson MO Travel Information
Date: July 20, 1994
From: DC 1051
File: B-TOWN (10873 bytes)
DL time: < 1 minute
Author: DC1051 Doug Cannon
Needs: Text reader

Where

Travel

Travel Forum

Keyword

Travel Forum

Select

Travel Library

Download

Branson MO Travel Information

Massachusetts On Your Mind

You want history? We got history. Or at least Massachusetts does. And America Online includes some excellent resources to help you and your family enjoy the historic and just plain fun sites in the U.S.'s most difficult-to-spell state.

Massachusetts Getaway Guide

The all new Massachusetts Getaway Guide is now available free from the Massachusetts Office of Travel and Tourism. The 96-page, four-season guide features attractions, accommodations, maps, handicapped accessible locations, family activities, and an outdoor section.

Where

Capital Connection

Massachusetts Forum

Keyword

Mass

Select

Travel & Tourism

Read/Save

Massachusetts Getaway Guide

Massachusetts Public Golf Courses

Why not try teeing off this season on one of the many golf courses featured in the premiere edition of *Bay State Fairways*, a guide to public golf courses and an absolute must for golf enthusiasts traveling to Massachusetts. The 80-page color guide lists more than 200 public and semi-public golf courses within the state.

The courses are listed alphabetically within each region, and the list also includes the size of each course, par, green fees for weekdays and weekends, name of pro, shop and restaurant facilities, and availability of pull and power carts. This handy guide features a color map, regional photos, and directions to each golf course. The guide is divided into ten geographical regions and begins with a brief history outlining each area. To request your free copy, use these directions.

Where

Capital Connection

Massachusetts Forum

Keyword

Mass

Select

Travel & Tourism

Read/Save

Guide to Public Golf Courses

Where to Find More Goodies

To enjoy the cuisine of another region or foreign land, turn to this book's *Cooking* section. And the *Books, Magazines, and Literature* section can guide you to more bookstores.

If you're planning a trip to our nation's capital, skim the *Government* section for Smithsonian information.

On AOL, locate the Pictures of the World Forum (Keyword: Pictures) and stop by National Geographic (NGS).

The Travel Message boards in both Travelers' Corner (Keyword: Travel) and the Travel Forum (Keyword: Travel forum) contain thousands of tips—but you may have to spend a few minutes searching for your preferred destination.

Last, but not least, *The New York Times Online* (Keyword: @times), the *Chicago Tribune* (Keyword: Chicago) and the *San Jose Mercury News* (Keyword: Mercury) can be counted on to have travel news and articles.

List of Keywords

Using the Keyword Dialog Box

America Online PC users press Ctrl+K or select Keyword from the Go To Menu. When the Keyword Window appears, type the name of the keyword from the list below. Then, choose GO.

America Online Macintosh users press ⌘+K or select Keyword from the Go To Menu. When the Keyword Window appears, type the name of the keyword from the list below. Then, choose GO.

Legend:

MAINKEYWORD	Area/Forum name (OTHER KEYWORDS)

GENERAL KEYWORDS

BESTOFAOL	Best of America Online showcase
CLOCK	Time of day and length of time online
DISCOVER	Discover AOL area
GUIDEPAGER	Page a Guide
HOLIDAY	AOL Holiday Central
HOT	What's Hot This Month showcase
MAILGATEWAY	Mail Gateway
MEMBERS	Member Directory
NAME(S)	Add, change or delete screen names
NEW	New Features & Services showcase
PAPERMAIL	Fax/Paper Mail (USMAIL, FAX)
PARENTALCONTROL	Parental Controls
PHOTOFOCUS	Graphics and Photo Focus area
PRESS	AOL Press Release Library
POSTOFFICE	Post Office (MAIL, EMAIL)
PRODIGY	Prodigy Refugees Forum
SERVICES	Directory of Services
SHORTHAND(S)	Online Shorthands
TOUR	AOL Highlights Tour
VIEWER	Viewer Resource Center

TODAY'S NEWS

NEWS	Today's News department
BUSINESS	Business News area
DTSPORTS	DataTimes Sports Reports
HAITI	Haiti Crisis[NewsPlus area; may disappear without warning]
MARKETNEWS	Market News area
NEWSBYTES	Newsbytes
NEWSPAPER(S)	Local Newspapers
NEWSPLUS	NewsPlus area
NEWSSEARCH	Search News Articles
SIMPSON	O.J. Simpson area [NewsPlus area; may disappear without warning]
SKI	Ski Reports [seasonal]
SPORTSNEWS	Sport News area
TROPICALSTORM	Tropical Storm and Hurricane Info (HURRICANE)
USNEWS	U.S. & World News
WEATHER	Weather

PERSONAL FINANCE

FINANCE	Personal Finance department
AAII	AAII Online
ADVISOR	Top Advisors' Corner
BULLSANDBEARS	Bulls and Bears Game
BUSINESSSTRATEGIES	Business Strategies
CAPITAL	Capital Connection
CBD	Commerce Business Daily
CHICAGO	Chicago Online
COMPANY	Hoovers' Handbook of Company Profiles
CONSUMER(S)	Consumer Reports
DP	Decision Point Forum
FOOL	The Motley Fool
HOME	Homeowner's Forum
HOOVER(S)	Hoover's Business Resources
ICF	International Corporate Forum
INVESTORS	Investors Network
MCBUSINESS	Mercury Center Business & Technology area
MORNINGSTAR	Morningstar Mutual Funds
MSBC	Microsoft Small Business Center
NBR	The Nightly Business Report
PFSOFTWARE	Personal Finance Software Center
PORTFOLIO	Your Stock Portfolio
REALESTATE	Real Estate Online
SOS	Wall Street SOS Forum
STOCK(S)	Stock Market Timing & Charts area
TAX	Tax Forum
TELESCAN	Telescan Users Group Forum
WORTH	Worth Magazine
YOURMONEY	Your Money area

CLUBS & INTERESTS

CLUBS	Clubs & Interests department
AARP	American Association of Retired People
ASTRONOMY	Astronomy Club
AVIATION	Aviation Club
BABYBOOMERS	Baby Boomers area
BACKPACKER	Backpacker Magazine
BICYCLING	Bicycling Magazine
BIKENET	The Bicycle Network
BUSINESSSTRATEGIES	Business Strategies
CAPITAL	Capital Connection
CHRIST	Christianity Online
CHICAGO	Chicago Online
COOKBOOK	Celebrity Cookbook

COOKING	Cooking Club
DEAD	Grateful Dead Forum
DIALOGUE	American Dialogue
DIS	DisABILITIES Forum
DISCOVERY	The Discovery Channel
DOLBY	Dolby Audio/Video Forum
EFORUM	Environmental Forum
EMERGENCY	Emergency Response Club
EXCHANGE	The Exchange
FLYING	Flying Magazine
GADGETGURU	Gadget Guru Electronics Forum
GENEALOGY	Genealogy Club
GLCF	Gay & Lesbian Community Forum
GOLFIS	Golf Courses & Resort Information
GRANDSTAND	The Grandstand
HAM	Ham Radio Club
HATRACK	Hatrack River Town Meeting
HEALTH	Better Health & Medical Forum
HOME	Homeowner's Forum
IMH	Issues in Mental Health
LEGAL	Legal SIG
LONGEVITY	Longevity Magazine Online
MCO	Military City Online
MERCURY	Mercury Center
NAMI	National Alliance of Mentally Ill
NATURE	The Nature Conservancy
NETWORKEARTH	Network Earth
NGLTF	Nation Gay & Lesbian Task Force
NMSS	National Multiple Sclerosis Society
NSS	National Space Society
OGF	Online Gaming Forums
OMNI	OMNI Magazine Online
PET(S)	Pet Care Club
PHOTO	Kodak Photobraphy Forum
REALESTATE	Real Estate Online
RELIGION	Ethics and Religion Forum
ROADANDTRACK	Road & Track
ROCK	Rocklink
SCUBA	Scuba Club
SENIOR	SeniorNet
SF	Science Fiction Forum
SPORTS	Sport News area
SRO	Saturday Review Online
STUDENT	Student Access Online
TICKET	Ticketmaster
TIMES	The New York Times Online
TREK	Star Trek Club
TRIVIA	Trivia Club
UCPA	United Cerebral Palsy Association, Inc.
VETS	Military and Vets Club
WINE	Wine & Dine Online
WOMANS DAY	Woman's Day
WRITERS	Writer's Club

COMPUTING

COMPUTING	Computing Department
CONFERENCE	Weekly calendar of forum activity
CRC	Computing Resource Center
FILESEARCH	Search database of files
HALLOFFAME	Downloading Hall of Fame
MAC	Mac Computing & Software department
MACSOFTWARE	Mac Software Center
PCSOFTWARE	PC Software Center
SOFTWARE	Software Center
TITF	Today/Tonight in the Forums

VIEWER	Viewer Resource Center

Mutual Interest Forums:

HELPDESK	Beginners' Forum (BEGINNERS)
BBS	BBS Corner
FSRC	Flight Sim Resource Center
MULTIMEDIA	The Multimedia Exchange
NEWTON	Newton Resource Center
PDA	Personal Digital Assistant's Forum
REDGATE	Redgate/IIN Online
ROTUNDA	Rotunda Forum Auditorium
UGF	User Group Forum
VR	Virtual Reality Resource Center

PC Forums:

DOS	DOS Forum
OS2	OS/2 Forum
PAP	Applications Forum
PDV	Development Forum
PGM	Games Forum (PCGAMES)
PGR	Graphics Forum
PHW	Hardware Forum
PMM	Multimedia Forum
PMU	Music and Sound Forum
PTC	Telecom/Networking Forum
WIN	Windows Forum (WINDOWS)

Macintosh Forums:

MAC	Mac Computing & Software Department
MBS	Business Forum
MCM	Communications Forum
MDP	Desktop Publishing/WP Forum
MDV	Development Forum
MED	Education
MGM	Games & Entertainment
MGR	Graphic Arts & CAD Forum
MHC	HyperCard Forum
MHW	Hardware
MMM	Multimedia Forum
MMS	Music & Sound Forum
MOS	Operating Systems Forum
MUT	Utilities Forum

Other Areas of Interest in Computing & Software:

CROSSMAN	Craig Crossman's Computer America
CYBERLAW	CyberLaw, Cyberlex
DES	DeskMate
DOS6	MS-DOS 6.0 Resource Center
IBM	IBM Forum
INCIDER	inCider
KOMANDO	Kim Komando Komputer Tutor
MAC500	Mac Shareware 500
MACTIVITY	Mactivity '94 Forum
MACWORLD	MacWorld Magazine
MACWORLDEXPO	MacWorld Expo Center
MAGICLINK	Sony Magic Link area (SONY)
PCEXPO	Redgate Online > PC Expo
PCTODAY	PC Novice/PC Today (PCNOVICE)
PCWORLD	PCWorld Online
PERFORMA	Apple Club Performa
POWERBOOK	PowerBook Resource Center
POWERMAC	Power Mac Resource Center (POWERPC)
PRODIGY	Prodigy Refugees' Forum

PU	Programmer University
TANDY	Tandy Headquarters
TUNEUP	Tune Up Your PC
WIN500	Windows Shareware 500
WINNEWS	Windows News area
WPMAG	WordPerfect Magazine

Special Interest Groups:

3D	3D Resource Center
3DSIG	3D Interest Group
ADSIG	Advertising Special Interest Group
AECSIG	Architects, Engineers and Construction
SIG	
APPLESCRIPT	AppleScript SIG
AUTOCAD	Cad Resource Center
BCS	Boston Computer Society
BMUG	Berkeley Macintosh Users Group
BOARDWATCH	Boardwatch Magazine
BRAINSTORM	Brainstorm Products
CHARTER	Charter Schools Forum
CMC	Creative Musician's Coalition
COMPOSER(S)	Composer's Coffeehouse
COREL	CorelDRAW Resource Center
DATABASE	Database Support SIG
DTP	Desktop Publishing Resource Center
EFF	Electronic Frontier Foundation
EPUB	EPub Resource Center
GROUPWARE	GroupWare SIG
GSMAG	GS+ Magazine
IA	Instant Artist Resource Center
IPA	Advanced Color Imaging
LEGAL	Legal SIG
MACHACK	MacHack area
MADA	MacApp Developers Association
MCAFEE	McAfee Associates
NAQP	National Association of Quick Printers
NOMADIC	Nomadic Computing Discussion SIG
PHOTOSHOP	Photoshop SIG
PLACES	P.L.A.C.E.S. Interest Group
VISUAL BASIC	Visual Basic Support
VIDEOSIG	Video SIG
VIRUS	Virus Information Center SIG
WIRELESS	Wireless Communication

Industry Connection:

IC	Industry Connection
AATRIX	Aatrix Software, Inc.
ABBATEVIDEO	Abbate Video
ACCOLADE	Accolade, Inc.
ACER	Acer America Corporation
ACTIVISION	Activision
ADS	auto*des*sys, Inc.
ADVANCED	Advanced Software, Inc.
AFFINITY	Affinity Microsystems
ALADDIN	Aladdin Systems, Inc.
ALDUS	Aldus Corporation
ALPHATECH	Alpha Software Corporation
ALTSYS	Altsys Corporation
ALYSIS	Alysis Software
AMBROSIA	Ambrosia Software
ANIMATEDSOFTWARE	Animated Software
ANOTHERCO	Another Company
APDA	Apple Professional Developer's Ass.

APOGEE	Apogee Software
ARES	Ares Microdevelopment, Inc.
ARGOSY	Argosy
ARIEL	Ariel Publishing
ARTEMIS	Artemis Software
ARTIFICE	Artifice, Inc.
ASI	Articulate Systems
ASYMETRIX	Asymetrix Corporation
ATTICUS	Atticus Software
AVID	Avid DTV Group
AVOCAT	Avocat Systems
BASELINE	Baseline Publishing
BASEVIEW	Baseview Products, Inc.
BERKELEY	Berkeley Systems
BEST	Best Products
BETHESDA	Bethesda Softworks
BEYOND	Beyond, Inc.
BITJUGGLERS	Bit Jugglers
BOWERS	Bowers Development
BRODERBUND	Broderbund
BUNGIE	Bungie Software
BUSINESSSENSE	Business Sense
BYTE	ByteWorks
BYTEBYBYTE	Byte By Byte Corporation
CAERE	Caere Corporation
CALLISTO	Callisto Corporation
CARDINAL	Cardinal Technologies, Inc.
CASABLANCA	Casa Blanca
CASADY	Casady & Greene
CESOFTWARE	CE Software
CLARIS	Claris
CODA	Coda Music Tech
COMPAQ	Compaq
CONNECTIX	Connectix
COOPER	JLCooper Electronics
COSA	Company of Science and Art
COSTAR	CoStar
CPI	Computer Peripherals, Inc.
CPS	Central Point Software
DACEASY	DacEasy, Inc.
DANCINGRABBIT	Dancing Rabbit Creations
DATAPAK	DataPak Software
DATAWATCH	Datawatch (VIREX)
DAVIDSON	Davidson & Associates
DAYNA	Dayna Communications
DAYSTAR	DayStar Digital
DELL	Dell Computer Corporation
DELRINA	Delrina Corporation
DELTAPOINT	Delta Point
DELTATAO	Delta Tao
DENEBA	Deneba Software
DFX	Digital F/X
DIAMOND	Diamond Computer Systems
DIGISOFT	DYA/Digisoft Innovations
DIGITAL	Digital Vision
DIGITALECLIPSE	Digital Eclipse
DIGITALTECH	Digital Technologies
DIRECT	Direct Software
DISNEYSOFTWARE	DisneyBuena Vista Software
DREAMWORLD	Dreamworld
DUBLCLICK	Dubl-Click Software
DYNAWARE	Dynaware USA
DYNO	Portfolio Systems, Inc.
EBBS	EBBS
ECON	Econ Technologies

ECS	Electronic Courseware
EDMARK	Edmark Technologies (KIDDESK)
ELECTRIC	Electric Image
EMIGRE	Emigre Fonts
EXPERT	Expert Software, Inc.
FARALLON	Farallon
FIFTH	Fifth Generation
FOCUS	Focus Enhancements
FONTBANK	FontBank
FRACTAL	Fractal Design
FRANKLIN	Franklin Quest
FULLWRITE	FullWrite
FUTURELABS	Future Labs, Inc.
GAMETEK	Gametek
GATEWAY	Gateway 2000, Inc
GCC	GCC Technologies
GENERALMAGIC	General Magic
GEO	GeoWorks
GIFCONVERTER	GIF Converter
GLOBAL	Global Village Communication
GRAPHICSIMULATIONS	Graphic Simulations
GRAPHISOFT	Graphisoft
GRAVIS	Advanced Gravis
GRYPHON	Gryphon Software
GSS	Global Software Support
HDC	hDC Corporation
HELIOS	Helios USA
HSC	HSC Software
IBVA	IBVA Technologies
INFOCOM	Infocom
INLINE	Inline Design
INSIGNIA	Insignia Solutions
INTEL	Intel Corporation (PENTIUM)
INTELLIMATION	Intellimation
INTERCON	InterCon Systems Corporation
INTERPLAY	Interplay
IOMEGA	Iomega Corporation
ISIS	ISIS International
ISLANDGRAPHICS	Island Graphics Corporation
IYM	IYM Software Review
JPEGVIEW	JPEGView
KENSINGTON	Kensington Microware, Ltd.
KENTMARSH	Kent*Marsh
KIWI	Kiwi Software, Inc.
KNOWLEDGEBASE	Microsoft Knowledge Base
KOALA	Koala/MacVision
LANGUAGESYS	SYS Language Systems
LAPIS	Lapis Technologies
LAWRENCE	Lawrence Productions
LEADER	Leader Technologies
LEADINGEDGE	Leading Edge
LETRASET	Letraset
LINKS	Access Software
LINKSWARE	LinksWare, Inc.
LUCAS	LucasArts Games
MACBIBLE	The Macintosh Bible/Peachpit Forum
MACROMEDIA	MacroMedia, Inc.
MAINSTAY	Mainstay
MALLARD	Mallard Software
MANHATTANGRAPHICS	Manhattan Graphics
MARKET	Market Master
MARKETFIELD	Marketfield Software
MARTINSEN	Martinsen's Software
MAXIS	Maxis
MECC	MECC
MERIDIAN	Meridian Data

METROWERKS	Metrowerks
METZ	Metz
MGX	Micrografx, Inc.
MICRODYNAMICS	Micro Dynamics, Ltd.
MICROFRONTIER	MicroFrontier, Ltd.
MICROJ	Micro J Systems, Inc
MICROMAT	MicroMat Computer Systems
MICROPROSE	MicroProse
MICROSEEDS	Microseeds Publishing, Inc.
MICROSOFT	Microsoft Resource Center
MIRROR	Mirror Technologies
MORAFFWARE	MoraffWare
MSA	Management Science Associates
MSFORUM	Microsoft Product Support
MSTATION	Bentley Systems, Inc.
MUSTANG	Mustang Software
NEC	NEC Technologies
NEOLOGIC	NeoLogic
NEWWORLD	New World Computing
NIKON	Nikon Electronic Imaging
NILES	Niles and Associates
NOHANDS	No Hands Software
NOVELL	Novell Desktop Systems
NOW	Now Software
OBJECTFACTORY	Object Factory
OLDUVAI	Olduvai Software, Inc.
ON	ON Technology
ONYX	Onyx Technology
OPCODE	Opcode Systems, Inc.
OPTIMAGE	OptImage Interactive Services
OPTIMAS	OPTIMAS Corporation
ORIGIN	Origin Systems
OTTER	Otter Solution
PACEMARK	PaceMark Technologies, Inc.
PACKER	Packer Software
PALM	Palm Computing
PAPYRUS	Papyrus
PASSPORT	Passport Designs
PCCATALOG	PC Catalog
PCPC	Personal Computer Peripherals
PEACHTREE	Peachtree Software
PIXAR	Pixar
PIXEL	Pixel Resources
PLAYMATION	Playmation
POWERUP	Power Up Software
PPI	Practical Peripherals, Inc.
PRAIRIESOFT	PrairieSoft, Inc.
PROGRAPH	Prograph International, Inc.
PROVUE	ProVUE Development
PSION	Psion
QUALITAS	Qualitas
QUARK	Quark, Inc.
RADIUS	Radius, Inc.
RASTEROPS	RasterOps
RAY	Ray Dream
REACTOR	Reactor
RESNOVA	ResNova Software
ROCKLAND	Rockland Software
ROGERWAGNER	Roger Wagner Publishing
SALIENT	Salient Software
SERIUS	Serius
SHAREWARESOLUTIONS	Shareware Solutions
SHIVA	Shiva Corporation
SIERRA	Sierra On-Line
SOFTARC	SoftArc
SOFTDISK	Softdisk Superstore [PC platform only]

SOPHCIR	Sophisticated Circuits
SPECTRUM	Spectrum HoloByte
SPECULAR	Specular International
SSI	Strategic Simulations
SSSI	SSSi
STAC	STAC Electronics
STF	STF Technologies
STRATA	Strata, Inc.
SUPERMAC	SuperMac
SURVIVOR	Survivor Software
SWC	Software Creations
SYMANTEC	Symantec (NORTON)
SYNEX	Synex
TACTIC	Tactic Software
TACTIC	Tactic Software Corporation
TECHWORKS	Technology Works
TEKNOSYS	Teknosys Works
THREESIXTY	Three-Sixty Software
THRUSTMASTER	Thrustmaster
THUNDERWARE	Thunderware
TI	Texas Instruments
TIA	True Image Audio
TIGERDIRECT	TIGERDirect, Inc.
TIMESLIPS	Timeslips Corporation
TIMEWORKS	Timeworks
TMAKER	T/Maker
TOOLWORKS	Software Toolworks
TSENG	Tseng
TWI	Time Warner Interactive
UA	Unlimited Adventures
USERLAND	Userland
VDISC	Videodiscovery
VERTISOFT	Vertisoft
VIACOM	Viacom New Media
VIDI	VIDI
VIEWPOINT	Viewpoint DataLabs
VIRTUS	Virtus Walkthrough
VISIONARY	Visionary Software
VOYAGER	The Voyager Company
VOYETRA	Voyetra Technologies
VRLI	Virtual Reality Labs, Inc.
WEIGAND	Weigand Report
WESTWOOD	Westwood Studios
WORDPERFECT	WordPerfect Support Center
WORKING	Working Software
WWW	Wilson Windowware
XAOS	Xoas Tools
XCEED	Xceed Technology
ZEDCOR	Zedcor, Inc.

TRAVEL

TRAVEL	Travel department
B&B	Bed & Breakfast U.S.A.
BACKPACKER	Backpacker Magazine
BICYCLING	Bicycling Magazine
FLORIDA	Destination Florida
FLYING	Flying Magazine
GOLFIS	Golf Courses & Resort Information
PICTURES	Pictures of the World
ROAD	Road & Track
SKI	Ski Reports [seasonal]
SABRE	EAAsy Sabre
TRAVELADVISORIES	US State Department Travel Advisories
TRAVELERSCORNER	Traveler's Corner
TRAVELFORUM	Travel Forum
TRAVELHOLIDAY	Travel Holiday Magazine
TROPICALSTORM	Tropical Storm and Hurricane Info (HURRICANE)
WEATHER	Weather

MARKETPLACE

MARKETPLACE	Marketplace department
AOLSTORE	AOL Products Center
AUTO	AutoVantage
BOOKSTORE	Online Bookstore
CHECKFREE	CheckFree
CLASSIFIED(S)	Classifieds Online
COMPUSTORE	Comp-u-store Gateway
COMPUTEREXPRESS	Computer Express
CONSUMER(S)	Consumer Reports
FLOWERSHOP	Flower Shop
KOMANDO	Kim Komando's Komputer Clinic
OFFICE	Penny Wise Office Products Store
PCCATALOG	PC Catalog
SHOPPERSEXPRESS	Shoppers' Express
TICKET	TicketMaster

PEOPLE CONNECTION

PEOPLE	People Connection Department
ADVICE	Advice & Tips
CARTOONS	Cartoon collection
CENTERSTAGE	Center Stage
COMPUTOON	CompuToon area
DILBERT	Dilbert Cartoon area
GALLERY	Portrait Gallery
GUIDEPAGER	Page a Guide
KEEFE	Mike Keefe Cartoons
LAPUB	LaPub
OLT	OnLine Tonight
PARLOR	Games Parlor
PCSTUDIO	PC Studio
QUE	The Quantum Que and Graffiti message boards
ROMANCE	Romance Connection message boards
TEEN(S)	Teen Scene message boards
TRIVIA	Trivia Club

NEWSSTAND

NEWSSTAND	Newsstand department
ODEON	Center Stage
ABCNEWS	ABC News on Demand
ATLANTIC	The Atlantic Monthly Online
BACKPACKER	Backpacker Magazine
BICYCLING	Bicycling Magazine
BOAT	Boating Online
CAMPUSLIFE	Campus Life
CARANDDRIVER	Car and Driver
CHRIST	Christianity Online
CHRISTIANCOMPUTING	Christian Computing
CHRISTIANHISTORY	Christian History
CHICAGO	Chicago Online
COLUMNISTS	Columnists & Features Online
COMPUTE	Compute
CONSUMER(S)	Consumer Reports
COWLES	Cowles/SIMBA Media Information Network
CT	Christianity Today

CYCLE	Cycle World Online
DCCOMICS	DC Comics Online
DISNEYMAG	Disney Adventures Magazine
FAMILYPC	FamilyPC Onlinr
FLYING	Flying Magazine
HOME DESIGN	Home Magazine
HOMEOFFICE	Home Office Computing
HOMEPC	HomePC Magazine
LEADERSHIP	Leadership Journal
LONGEVITY	Longevity Online
MACHOME	MacHome Journal
MACTECH	MacTech Magazine
MACWORLD	MacWorld Magazine
MARRIAGEPARTNERSHIP	Marriage Partnership
MERCURY	Mercury Center
MMW	Multimedia World Online [PC users only]
MOBILE	Mobile Office Online
NGS	National Geographic Online
OMNI	OMNI Magazine Online
PCTODAY	PC Novice/PC Today (PCNOVICE)
PCWORLD	PCWorld Online
PHOTOS	Popular Photography
ROAD	Road & Track
SMITHSONIAN	Smithsonian Online
SRO	Saturday Review Online
STEREO	Stereo Review Online magazine
TCW	Today's Christian Woman
TIME	Time Magazine Online
TIMES	@times/The New York Times Online
TNR	The New Republic Magazine
TRIBUNE	Chicago Tribune
WINMAG	Windows Magazine
WIRED	Wired Magazine
WOMANS DAY	Woman's Day
WORTH	Worth Magazine
WWIR	Washington Week In Review
YOURCHURCH	Your Church

ENTERTAINMENT

ENTERTAINMENT	Entertainment department
ABC	ABC Online
ABM	Adventures by Mail
ADD	AD&D Neverwinter Nights
ATLANTIC	The Atlantic Monthly Online
BOOKS	Book Bestsellers area
BULLSANDBEARS	Bulls and Bears Game
CARTOONNETWORK	Cartoon Network
CARTOONS	Cartoon collection
CASINO	RabbitJack's Casino
COMPUTOON	CompuToon area
COURTTV	Court TV
CRITICS	Critic's Choice
CSPAN	C-SPAN
DEAD	Grateful Dead Forum
DILBERT	Dilbert Cartoon area
DISNEY	Disney Adventures Magazine
ENERGYEXPRESS	Energy Express
EXTRA	EXTRA: Television's Entertainment Show
FFGF	Free-Form Gaming Forum
FOG	Fellowship of Online Gamers/RPGA Network
GAMEBASE	Game Base
GAMEDESIGN	Game Designers Forum
GAMES DOWNLOAD	Free online game downloading
GAMEWIZ	Dr. Gamewiz: Game Master Extraodinaire
GCS	Gaming Company Support

GERALDO	The Geraldo Show
GIX	Gaming Information Exchange
GRANDSTAND	The Grandstand
HOLLYWOOD	Hollywood Online
HOROSCOPE(S)	Horoscopes
IMPROV	The Improv Forum
KEEFE	Mike Keefe Cartoons
KIDSNET	KIDSNET Forum
LAPUB	LaPub
LASTCALL	Last Call Talk Show
MASTERWORD	MasterWord
MCLAUGHLIN	The McLaughlin Group
MOVIES	Movies menu
MTV	MTV Online
NBC	NBC Online
NICKATNIGHT	Nick at Nite
OGF	Online Gaming Forums
OMNI	OMNI Magazine Online
PBM	Play-By-Mail & Strategy Gaming Forum
RICKILAKE	The Ricki Lake Show
ROCK	Rocklink
RPG	Role-Playing Forum
SCIFICHANNEL	The Sci-Fi Channel
SOLIII	Sol III Play-by-Email Game
TELEVISION	Soap Opera Summaries
TRIVIA	Trivia Club
TV	Television
TVGOSSIP	TV Gossip
TMS	TMS TV Source
VIDEOGAMES	Video Games area (NINTENDO, SEGA)
WARNER	Warner/Reprise Records Online

EDUCATION

EDUCATION	Education department
ACHIEVEMENTTV	Achievement TV
ACOT	Apple Classrooms of Tomorrow
ACT	Kaplan Online/SAT, ACT, College (SAT)
ADOPTION	Adoption Forum
AFT	American Federation of Teachers
AFTERWARDS	Afterwards Coffeehouse
ASCD	Assoc. for Supervisor & Curriculum Development
BOOKNOTES	Barrons Booknotes
BULLMOOSE	Bull Moose Tavern
BUSINESSSCHOOL	Kaplan Online/GMAT, Business School (GMAT)
CAREER	Career Center
CB	College Board
CHARTER	Charter Schools Forum
CHICO	California State University
CNN	CNN Newsroom Online
COMPUTERTERMS	Dictionary of Computer Terms
CONTACTS	Employer Contacts
COSN	Consortium for School Networking
CSPAN	C-SPAN Online
DIPLOMATS	Diplomats in the Classroom
DISCOVERY	The Discovery Channel
DISNEYMAG	Disney Adventures Magazine
ENCYCLOPEDIA	Encyclopedia (COMPTONS)
ERIC	AskERIC
ESH	Electronic Schoolhouse
EUN	Electronic University Network
EXAMPREP	Exam Prep Center
GIFTED	Giftedness Forum
GRADUATESCHOOL	Kaplan Online/GRE, Graduate School (GRE)

HBSPUB	Harvard Business School Publishing
HELPWANTED	Search Help Wanted—USA
HOMEWORK	Academic Assistance Center
ICS	International Correspondence Schools
IES	Interactive Education Services
IMPACTII	IMPACT II: The Teachers Network
INTERNATIONAL	International House
JOBS	Job Listings Database
KAPLAN	Kaplan Online
KIDSNET	KIDSNET
LABNET	TERC LabNetwork
LAWSCHOOL	Kaplan Online/LSAT, Law School (LSAT)
LOC	Library of Congress Online
MEDICALSCHOOL	Kaplan Online/MCAT, Medical School (MCAT)
MONTESSORI	Montessori Schools
MULTIMEDIA	The Multimedia Exchange
NAPC	Employment Agency Database
NCTE	Nat'l Council of Teachers of English
NEAPUBLIC	National Education Association
NGS	National Geographic Online
NMAA	National Museum of American Art
NMAH	National Museum of American History
NPR	National Public Radio Outreach
NSDC	National Staff Development Council
NURSING	Kaplan Online/NCLEX, Nursing School (NCLEX)
PIN	Parents' Information Network (PARENT)
PREVENTION	Substance Abuse Forum
PRINCIPALS	National Principals Center
READ	Adult Literacy Forum
REFERENCE	Reference Desk department
REGISTER	IES Registration Center
SCHOLASTIC	Scholastic Network/Scholastic Forum
SCOUTS	Scouting Forum
SMITHSONIAN	Smithsonian Online (SI)
SRO	Saturday Review Online
STUDENT	Student Access Online
STUDY	Study Skills Service
TALENT	Talent Bank
TEACHERPAGER	Teacher Pager
TEACHERU	Teachers' University
TIN	Teachers' Information Network
TLC	The Learning Channel
TNEWS	Teachers' Newsstand
TNPC	The National Parenting Center
TOMORROW	Tomorrow's Morning
TRAINING	Career Development Training
TTALK	Teachers' Forum
USF	University of San Francisco

REFERENCE DESK

REFERENCE	Reference Desk department
COMPUTERTERMS	Dictionary of Computer Terms
ENCYCLOPEDIA	Encyclopedia (COMPTONS)
ERIC	AskERIC
FILESEARCH	Search database of files
GOPHER	Internet Gopher & WAIS
MEMBERS	Member Directory
NEWSSEARCH	Search News Articles
REFERENCEHELP	Reference Desk Help area
SERVICES	Directory of Services
TEACHERPAGER	Teacher Pager

INTERNET CONNECTION

INTERNET	Internet Connection department
COSN	Consortium for School Networking
EFF	Electronic Frontier Foundation
FTP	Internet FTP
GOPHER	Internet Gopher & WAIS
MAILGATEWAY	Mail Gateway
MAILINGLISTS	Internet Mailing Lists
MCM	Mac Communications Forum
NEWSGROUPS	Internet Usenet Newsgroup area
PTC	PC Telecom/Networking Forum VERIFY
WIRED	Wired Magazine

SPORTS

SPORTS	Sports department
ABCSPORTS	ABC Sports
DTSPORTS	DataTimes Sports Reports
GOLFIS	Golf Courses & Resort Information
GRANDSTAND	The Grandstand
SPORTSNEWS	Sports News area

KIDS ONLY

KOOL	Kids Only department (KIDSONLY)
CARTOONNETWORK	Cartoon Network
DCCOMICS	DC Comics Online Preview
DISNEYMAG	Disney Adventures Magazine
ENCYCLOPEDIA	Encyclopedia (COMPTONS)
HATRACK	Hatrack River Town Meeting
KIDSNET	KIDSNET Forum (EDTV)
NGS	National Geographic Online
SCHOLASTIC	Scholastic Network/Scholastic Forum
TEACHERPAGER	Teacher Pager
TIME	Time Magazine Online
TMS	TMS TV Source
TOMORROW	Tomorrow's Morning
WEATHER	Weather

MEMBER SERVICES

HELP	Member Services (SUPPORT)
9600	9600 Baud Access Center
ACCESS	Local access numbers
BILLING	Account and Billing
CANCEL	Cancel account
CREDIT	Credit for connect problems
CSLIVE	Tech Help Live
FRIEND	Sign on a friend to AOL
LETTER	A Letter From Steve Case
MARKETINGPREFS	Marketing Preferences
MODEMHELP	Modem Help area (PC users only)
MHM	Members Helping Members message board
NEWAOL	New AOL Information area
PASSWORD	Change your password
PROFILE	Edit your member profile
SUGGESTION(S)	Suggestion boxes
TOS	Terms of Service
UPGRADE	Upgrade to the latest version of AOL

Miscellaneous

MCINTIRE	University of Virginia Alumni/McIntire School of Commerce
PRODIGY	Prodigy Refugees' Forum
WOODSTOCK	Woodstock Online

A Final Note on Keywords

There are hundreds more keywords than you'll find listed here. In all, there are almost 2,000 keywords, and many online areas have multiple keywords. In refining this list, I've selected the *easiest to remember* keywords to speed your mission on AOL.

Updated Keyword List

AOL member "Jennifer" has compiled two comprehensive Keyword lists. One is sorted alphabetically by keyword, and the other, like the one above, is sorted by AOL department. The Ultimate Keyword Lists can be found in the Macintosh Software Libraries.

PC Directions

Keyword

Mac Software

Select

File Search - Over 60,000 files
Search ALL Files
>ultimate keyword

Download

Ultimate Keyword List by Dept
Ultimate Keyword List A-Z

Mac Directions

Keyword

File Search

Select

>ultimate keyword

Download

Ultimate Keyword List by Dept
Ultimate Keyword List A-Z

Index